PROJECT APPRAISAL AND MACROECONOMIC POLICY

Project Appraisal and Macroeconomic Policy

TSJALLE VAN DER BURG
Rotterdam School of Management,
Erasmus University, Rotterdam,
The Netherlands

Kluwer Academic Publishers
Dordrecht / Boston / London

Library of Congress Cataloging-in-Publication Data

Burg, Tjalle van der.
Project appraisal and macroeconomic policy / by Tsjalle van der Burg.
p. cm.
Includes bibliographical references.
ISBN-13: 978-94-010-6503-0 (hardcover : alk. paper)
1. Economic policy--Econometric models. 2. Equilibrium (Economics)--Mathematical models. I. Title.
HD87.B87 1996 95-40137

ISBN-13: 978-94-010-6503-0 e-ISBN-13: 978-94-009-0033-2
DOI: 10.1007/978-94-009-0033-2

Published by Kluwer Academic Publishers,
P.O. Box 17, 3300 AA Dordrecht, The Netherlands.

Kluwer Academic Publishers incorporates
the publishing programmes of
D. Reidel, Martinus Nijhoff, Dr W. Junk and MTP Press.

Sold and distributed in the U.S.A. and Canada
by Kluwer Academic Publishers,
101 Philip Drive, Norwell, MA 02061, U.S.A.

In all other countries, sold and distributed
by Kluwer Academic Publishers Group,
P.O. Box 322, 3300 AH Dordrecht, The Netherlands.

Printed on acid-free paper

Softcover reprint of the hardcover 1st edition 1996

Table of contents

Foreword

Environmental economics addresses the issues that arise on the boundaries between economic systems and natural systems, such as pollution and natural resource depletion and degradation. Like any other branch of applied economics, it has drawn its tools and techniques from the wide range already available in economics generally, selecting, adapting and extending these to meet its own particular requirements in its own particular context. Here, as elsewhere in economics, public policy analysis requires quantitative assessments of the economic impact of different policy choices. Perhaps the most distinctive contribution of environmental economics has been the development of techniques for the economic valuation of environmental goods and services in the absence of markets for such goods and services, or in the presence of markets that are at best imperfect or incomplete. Nevertheless policy analysis still relies on one or another of three broad groups of methods used in economics generally. One is project appraisal, which at the micro level provides an evaluation of the costs and benefits of investment options to inform the choice among them, while at the macro level policy analysis rests either on computable general equilibrium (CGE) models or on economy-wide macroeconometric models.

All models are simplifications, designed to focus attention on the important features of the problem at hand, and neglecting other features that might for a different problem assume greater importance. Project appraisal typically takes the macro environment as given, and focuses on individual projects in a partial equilibrium setting. In contrast, when aggregate macroeconometric models are used to assess the consequences of an increase in public expenditure, no attention is typically paid to the nature of the projects that might be funded by the incremental expenditure. CGE models provide greater sectoral detail, having focused in early applications on trade and public finance questions. With a foundation in Walrasian general equilibrium theory, they are essentially comparative static models, in which policy exercises rest on a comparison of a 'base' solution and a 'new policy' solution, each comprising a set of relative prices that support flow equilibria in all product and factor markets. The nature of the adjustment process that might lead from one equilibrium to another is not addressed. On the other hand, dynamic adjustment in disequilibrium situations has been a focus of attention in macroeconometric models, and issues of inflation, unemployment, and balance-of-payments disequilibrium are high on the agenda.

Each approach in this stereotype form has obvious limitations, and the practical methods have been adapted to overcome them. Project appraisal in a partial equilibrium context, in which the markets for the project's inputs and outputs are analyzed in isolation, gives misleading guidance if other markets are affected in important ways. Shadow prices that take account of general equilibrium interactions might then be generated by a CGE model. Such models in turn might require modification or extension if their neoclassical assumptions are at variance with the behavioural or institutional rigidities found in many economies. However, *ad hoc* changes designed to increase the realism of the model may be difficult to interpret in the received theoretical framework; on the other hand a theoretically pure model is unlikely to yield reliable policy guidance in a situation where its assumptions are not satisfied. There is always tension between theoretical purity and empirical accuracy, and macroeconometric models have tended to emphasize the latter, having been concerned to provide a good statistical description of the actual economy, market imperfections, non-optimizing behaviour, and all. In this case recent developments are in the opposite direction to that of the CGE developments noted above, namely towards a greater theoretical coherency, particularly in respect of the model's steady-state or long-run implications, as economic theories heavily based on equilibrium concepts are more relevant to these than to the process of short-run adjustment. Environmental policy studies typically require a longer horizon than the macroeconomic policy analysis of everyday political debate, hence such modifications make macroeconometric models more useful to the environmental economist.

Exciting developments in quantitative methods occur on the interface between existing methods, when complementary strengths overcome individual weaknesses. At the macro level an input–output model might be incorporated into a macroeconometric model to provide missing sectoral detail, or a macroeconometric model might be used to provide the macroeconomic closure of a CGE model. The interface between microeconomics and macroeconomics, with which this book is concerned, is a more difficult one. Although the use of a CGE model to generate shadow prices for use in project appraisal, as mentioned above, provides an example, the author argues that the theoretical characteristics of the CGE approach are at variance with the practical aims of project appraisal. Instead, he seeks to integrate project appraisal and macroeconomic policy analysis by using macroeconometric models for the evaluation of small projects in a situation of disequilibrium. The method is applied to a wind energy project, and it is estimated that such projects and a number of similar projects have positive macroeconomic effects. I was honoured to serve as an external examiner of the dissertation on which this book is based and, coming to this work from a background in macroeconometric modelling, I found many challenging and provocative ideas. As a contribution to the discussion of the macroeconomic effects of environmental policy and to the development of quantitative methods more generally the book now deserves a wide readership.

Kenneth F. Wallis
ESRC Macroeconomic Modelling Bureau
University of Warwick

Acknowledgements

This book is a revised version of my dissertation, which I wrote when I was working at the Faculty of Economics in Groningen. In writing the dissertation and the book I have received aid and encouragement from a number of people. I would like to express my thanks to the following people in particular:

Professor A. Nentjes for his supervision, his many stimulating comments, and his patience in dealing with my intuition. Professor J.A. Kregel for his useful comments and his confidence in the project in its early stages, which made it possible to get started. Professor J. Muysken and Professor K.F. Wallis for giving me some critical and helpful comments in the last stage of the research.

Bernard ter Haar has done the calculations with the Freia-model, and wrote the main part of the computer program for calculating the effects of the wind energy project. I have been lucky in having an assistant with very high scientific standards.

I would further like to express my thanks to Diana Galjaard-Vrijenhoek and Thérèsa Hekman-Huizinga for typing parts of the manuscript.

Without the good library of the Faculty of Economics in Groningen it would have been rather difficult to do research, and I am grateful to Mr. H.A. Woensdregt and his colleagues for their friendly way of helping me.

Finally, I would like to thank Caroline Cost Budde, Ellen Koen, and Maaike van der Rijst for improving my English grammar.

CHAPTER 1

Introduction

> It is curious how common sense, wriggling for an escape from absurd conclusions, has been apt to reach a preference for wholly 'wasteful' forms of loan expenditure rather than for partly wasteful forms, which, because they are not wholly wasteful, tend to be judged on strict 'business principles'. (J.M. Keynes)

In the present western world there is a lack of consistency between project appraisal and macroeconomic policy. Project appraisal takes, of course, the specific characteristics of projects into account. In most cases, it is based on the assumption of full employment. In a few cases, it takes account of the existence of unemployment. However, as will be explained later in this study, in these cases it is nearly always based on a partial analysis, or at least on an analysis which is not consistent with the macroeconomic analyses used for decisions about macroeconomic policy.

Macroeconomic policy refers to policy decisions on aggregate variables (total demand, the money stock, the exchange rate). In many cases it is based on an integral analysis of the economy that takes account of the existence of unemployment. A restriction of such an analysis is that specific factors at a lower level of aggregation tend to be neglected. For instance, many studies about the macroeconomic effects of Keynesian policies concerning increases in government expenditures are based on the implicit assumption that there is only one type of government expenditure.

A number of economists have combined macroeconomic analysis with analyses at a more disaggregated level in order to investigate the effects of specific portfolios of government projects, or of other mesoeconomic policies. Some of these analyses will be discussed in this study. At this point it can be said that despite these analyses there is still a lack of integration between project appraisal and macroeconomic policy.

This study is concerned with situations of unemployment. It is based on the idea that, if unemployment exists, full employment cannot always be (quickly) reached by using conventional macroeconomic policies, or by supply-side policies aiming to improve the free functioning of markets, or by a combination of both.

Given this starting point, the lack of integration between project appraisal and macroeconomic policy could lead to a non-optimal total policy. The selection of individual public projects is generally not based on the criterion that they should have characteristics that are associated with positive macroeconomic effects. The possibility that different portfolios of projects have different macroeconomic effects is not taken into account. This possibility, however, could be important. For instance, suppose that one of the criteria for selecting individual projects is that a project should use specific types of labour that are relatively abundant. The resulting portfolio may then have a limited effect on inflation. It may also have effects on other macroeconomic variables which are more positive than those of a portfolio based on the conventional rules.

Two points should be emphasized. First, if the government budget is given, then the possibility that different portfolios of public projects have different macroeconomic effects would indicate that, in selecting individual projects, in one way or another this difference should be taken into account. Second, one could question the prevailing rule that the budget should already be determined before project appraisal starts. When the portfolio of government expenditures has average characteristics, the effects of an increase in total expenditure will be less positive than when individual projects are selected in such a way that the total portfolio has non-average characteristics which lead to relatively positive macroeconomic effects. Therefore, the conclusions with regard to the optimal total amount of expenditure might also be dependent upon the question which portfolio of projects constitutes government expenditure. This implies that macroeconomic analysis should be influenced by project appraisal.

This study deals with two problems. The first problem is a methodological one: it is how to analyse and evaluate individual, small as well as large projects in situations of unemployment in such a way that the following conditions are fulfilled. First, specific factors are taken into account. Second, the evaluation of a project is based on an integral analysis. Third, it is possible to use the outcomes of the appraisals of individual projects to compose portfolios of projects that have optimal macroeconomic effects. This implies that project appraisal is consistent with macroeconomic analysis. The second problem is the question which projects and portfolios of projects have positive effects in certain situations of unemployment. This problem, however, will only be investigated with regard to a limited number of projects and portfolios and a limited number of situations of unemployment.

The structure of this study is as follows. Chapter 2 deals with the macroeconomic effects of certain portfolios of projects in certain situations of unemployment. First, it is argued in a predominantly qualitative way that, in situations of unemployment such as have existed since the end of the seventies to the present day in countries like the Netherlands, portfolios of projects that lead to savings on fuels and other raw materials have positive macroeconomic effects. This holds good even if the projects are not wholly profitable from the private point of view. This conclusion is not based on an analysis of the effects on the environment, since they are not the focus of this study. Second, it is argued that the results of analyses with econometric macro-models of such portfolios in the Netherlands, which have been made by other researchers, support this argument (although in some cases this contradicts the conclusions of these other researchers themselves). One of the deficiencies of these analyses, however, is that they do not pay explicit attention to the profitability of the portfolio from the private point of view. They do not answer the question to what extent a portfolio can be unprofitable from the private point of view without having negative macroeconomic effects. Third, it is argued in a qualitative way that portfolios of projects which use types of labour that are relatively abundant might have positive macroeconomic effects. It will be shown that, if a natural rate of unemployment exists, it might be decreased by a Keynesian policy which takes project-specific characteristics into account.

Chapter 3 gives a critical analysis of existing methods of project appraisal in situations of unemployment. An important point of criticism concerns the lack of consistency between project appraisal and macroeconomic policy. This point of criticism does not apply to a certain method that consists of the analysis of large projects or portfolios of projects by means of an econometric macro-model. However, this method has other deficiencies: the fact that it has not been applied to small projects will be discussed in particular.

In Chapter 4 a method for the appraisal of both small and large projects is developed which is based on the use of an econometric macro-model, and which takes account of project-specific characteristics. The method for the calculation of the effects of individual projects will be described. It will be explained how the evaluation of these effects can be based on neo-Paretian welfare theory. One of the advantages of the method is that it can be used to select the individual elements of a portfolio in such a way that the portfolio as a whole has optimal effects.

Chapters 5 and 6 deal with the application of the method. Chapter 5 discusses the characteristics of the econometric macro-model that is used. This is the Freia-model of the Dutch Central Planning Bureau, which describes the economy of the Netherlands. In Chapter 5 attention is paid to the outcomes of the calculations made with the Freia-model, insofar as these outcomes can be used for the analysis of any project in the Netherlands. In Chapter 6 the method developed in Chapter 4 is applied to a Dutch wind energy project. It is shown that even if the private profitability of the project is negative, it can still have positive macroeconomic effects. Thus, the results of Chapter 6 support the argument of Chapter 2.

The method used in Chapter 6 is a primal method: the effects of a project as a whole are first calculated, and then evaluated on the basis of one or more criteria. Chapter 7 shows that the method can be changed into a dual method by the following procedure: first, the effects of each type of input or output are calculated separately. Second, these effects are evaluated on the basis of one or more criteria, and third, on this basis each input and output is given a shadow price. All projects are then evaluated on the basis of these shadow prices. It will be demonstrated how shadow prices can be derived with the help of the Freia-model.

From Chapters 2 to 7 the study is based on a national point of view. In Chapter 8 some international aspects will be discussed. One of the conclusions is the following: if, in reaction to the oil crises of the seventies, the western world had pursued a policy aiming at a reduction of the imports of oil on a large scale the debt problem would have been less serious. Chapter 9 gives a summary of the study.

CHAPTER 2

The macroeconomic effects of specific portfolios of projects

2.1. Introduction

The analyses used to help formulate macroeconomic policies and to determine the optimal level of government expenditure are generally based on the assumption that the portfolio of government projects has characteristics which are more or less equal to the average characteristics of all projects; broad distinctions, such as that between government investment and government consumption, are the only ones sometimes taken into account. The question whether or not the macroeconomic effects of a portfolio of government projects will be more positive if the individual projects are selected on the basis of criteria which are important from a macroeconomic point of view, is generally left unanswered.

In Section 2.2 it will be argued that a portfolio of projects which lead to savings on fuels and other raw materials has relatively positive effects in a situation of unemployment such as the one experienced by many western countries since the end of the seventies. Section 2.3 will show that a portfolio of projects in which relatively abundant types of labour are used might have relatively positive effects on inflation. Section 2.4 will give some conclusions. One of them is that macroeconomic policy and project appraisal should be regarded in an integrated way, with macroeconomic policy being partly dependent upon project appraisal.

2.2. The macroeconomic effects of projects which lead to savings on fuels and other raw materials[1]

2.2.1. *The essence of the analysis*

Many economists are of the opinion that environmental policies, if carried out by one country in isolation, have negative economic effects – at least if the environment is not taken into account. The aim of this section is to demonstrate that with regard to a policy of saving on fuels and other raw materials this opinion is incorrect in the context of a certain situation of unemployment. The effects of this policy on the environment will be neglected if not stated differently. For practical reasons, in this chapter the word 'fuels' is used as an abbreviation for 'fuels and other raw materials'.

It should be noted at this point that the analysis given below resembles an earlier analysis of the Cambridge Economics Policy Group (CEPG) to a certain extent. The CEPG argued that control of the imports of certain goods, among which oil, through tariffs or quotas, would be favourable for the national (British) economy in the situation of unemployment that existed at the end of the seventies (Godley and May, 1977; Cripps, 1978; Cripps and Godley, 1978). This implied among other things that the promotion of fuel-saving by means of tariffs or quotas was favourable for the economy. Below it will be argued that the promotion of fuel-saving by means of subsidies has positive effects in a similar situation of unemployment. The arguments of the CEPG will be discussed in Chapter 8, together with the subject of the difference between tariffs and quotas on the one hand and subsidies on the other hand. In relation to this, the arguments of the CEPG will not be discussed explicitly in this section.

It will be assumed throughout Section 2.2 that in the country pursuing a fuel-saving policy a specific situation of unemployment exists. This situation has the following characteristics: despite some counterbalancing effects (which will be discussed in detail in Section 2.2.1), a long-term increase in demand for exports caused by an increase in world trade leads to an increase in production, employment and consumption both in the short and in the long run.

Another characteristic is that a long-term increase in government consumption has the following effects. Initially, the government deficit increases with the increase in government expenditure. Also, the policy leads to a long-term increase in demand in the form of an increase in government expenditure. This long-term increase in demand viewed apart (that is, without taking the initial increase in the government deficit into account) leads, despite the existence of some counterbalancing effects, to a long-term increase in production, employment and private consumption. Consequently, tax revenues increase and unemployment benefits decrease, so that the government deficit decreases. This decrease, however, is smaller than the initial increase: on balance the government deficit increases. Because part of the spending induces additional imports, the balance on current account deteriorates. The increase in the government deficit and the deterioration of the balance on current account lead to an increase in the interest rate. This causes a decrease in investment and an increase in prices, and in connection with this a decrease in production, employment and private consumption in the long run. This causes a further increase in the government deficit, and so on. Given these negative effects, and given the counterbalancing effects of the increase in demand viewed apart, a long-term increase in government consumption has negative consequences for production, employment, private consumption, the balance on current account and the government deficit in the long run.

The reason why an increase in exports has more positive effects than an increase in government consumption is that exports are financed abroad, while goverment consumption is financed by the government. If one neglects the fact that it has to be financed, an increase in government consumption has essentially the same effects as an increase in exports (apart from the effect on the balance on current account). More generally speaking, any long-term increase in demand viewed apart (that is, without taking the fact that it has to be financed into account) has similar effects to an increase in exports.

It will be clear that the situation of unemployment described above does not (exclusively) concern classical unemployment, but (to a large extent at least) Keynesian unemployment.[2] At the same time this situation is such that the effects of a Keynesian policy of increasing government consumption are negative on balance. According to many mainstream economists the situation of unemployment described above has been experienced by the Netherlands and many other western countries since the end of the seventies (with regard to the Netherlands see, e.g., CPB, 1983).

The effects of a fuel-saving policy in a situation of unemployment such as the one described above are discussed below in a qualitative manner. It is assumed that the savings on fuels concern imported fuels. An alternative assumption will be discussed in Section 2.2.4. In the first instance the argument is based on the following starting points: first, the policy concerns private projects which are not profitable from the private point of view. Second, the government gives subsidies in order to stimulate energy-saving investments. Third, investments and subsidies are financed by capital market loans.

Given these starting points, energy-saving projects have the following effects: first, demand increases as a result of the expenditures on the projects. Given the situation of unemployment as described above, this increase in demand viewed apart leads to an increase in production, employment, consumption and imports, and to a decrease in the government deficit.

Second, imports of fuels decrease. Thus, there are two opposite effects on the balance on current account: imports increase as a result of the increase in demand, and they decrease as a result of the energy-saving.

Third, the provision of subsidies leads, in itself, to an increase in the government deficit. As was explained above the spending effects of the projects have the opposite effect. Therefore, it is still an open question whether on balance this deficit increases or decreases. However, the effects of the fuel-saving policy on the government deficit are more positive than those of a Keynesian policy of increasing government consumption. The reason is that only part of the investments in fuel-saving projects are financed by the government (by means of subsidies), while expenditures on government consumption are fully financed by the government.

A simple illustration may give the reader some insight into the question whether the positive effects on the government deficit and on the balance on current account mentioned above will outweigh the negative effects on these variables mentioned above. Suppose that all costs and benefits of the projects occur in one year, and that all macroeconomic effects occur in the same year. Suppose that the costs of the projects amount to 1 billion guilders. Suppose also that the spending effects of the payments of these costs lead to a reduction in the government deficit amounting to 40% of the costs, and to an increase in imports amounting to 55% of the costs. This includes all multiplier effects. The benefits of the project consist of savings on imported fuels only.[3] Suppose that the projects need a 35% subsidy to be implemented.

This implies that the revenues in terms of energy saved are at least 65% of the costs of the project. Consequently imports will decrease with at least 65% of the costs. Given these figures, the implementation of the projects together with the payment of the subsidies will ultimately lead to a decrease in the government deficit with 5% of the costs of the projects, and to an improvement in the balance on current account with at least 10% of the costs. It is emphasized that the figures given above are not based on serious empirical research; the reader should judge for him or herself to what extent they are plausible. However, given the situation of unemployment described above, any reader must admit that for projects needing a very low subsidy (5% or even smaller) in order to be profitable from the private point of view, the positive effects of the expenditures on the project will outweigh the payments for subsidies.

The fourth effect of fuel-saving projects is the following: because the private sector will only invest in the projects if they are profitable (including subsidies), the effects on production costs in the private sector and on energy-intensive industries are not negative; they may even be positive because the subsidies create new investment opportunities.[4]

Fifth, the project has effects on the capital market. The investments in the projects, which are financed by the private sector and by the government (which subsidizes these investments), lead to an increase in demand on the capital market. This is counterbalanced to some extent by the positive effects on the government deficit which result from the multiplier process initiated by the investments. In so far as one only takes account of the two effects mentioned above, one can say the following: on balance the projects lead to an increase in demand on the capital market, and therefore to an increase in the interest rate. This has further negative macroeconomic effects. These effects are similar to the effects of a Keynesian policy concerning consumption expenditures.

The benefits of the projects lead to a decrease in demand of the private investors on the capital market. Because with the subsidies the projects are profitable for the private investors, in the long run the increase in demand of private investors on the capital market caused by the investments in the projects will be made undone, and on balance total demand of the private sector will even decrease. This long-term effect does not occur when a Keynesian policy concerning consumption expenditures is pursued. Therefore, over the period of operation of the projects as a whole the effects on the interest rate are much more positive than those of a policy of increasing government consumption.

Nevertheless, on the basis of the analysis given thus far it can be concluded that in the short run there is an increase in the interest rate, which has further negative macroeconomic effects, among other things on the government deficit. (Note that this effect has not been taken into account in the illustration given above.) In Section 2.2.3 the capital market will be discussed in more detail, and it will be shown that the conclusion given above is not completely correct in all circumstances.

Summarizing, on the one hand an energy-saving policy may be said to induce a spending impulse in the domestic economy, which leads to increases in production, employment and consumption. On the other hand the effects of this policy on the government deficit, the balance on current account and the capital market are more positive than those of a policy of increasing government consumption. Thus, in the situation of unemployment described above, this policy has the advantages of a Keynesian policy concerning government consumption, whereas it largely, if not completely, lacks some of its main disadvantages.

Until now, the argument has been concerned with private fuel-saving projects. However, essentially the same argument can be made with regard to public fuel-saving projects.

It was assumed above that the government stimulates the projects by means of subsidies that are financed by capital market loans. Of course it is also possible to finance the subsidies by means of increased tax rates. This would, in the short run at least, be more favourable for the government deficit, but on the other hand it would stimulate inflation and increase production costs, which would have negative effects on exports, economic growth, and the government deficit. It is not impossible that on balance the effects of this method of financing the subsidy are more positive than those of financing the subsidy by means of capital market loans. There are also other instruments than subsidies to stimulate fuel-saving projects, such as levies. These will not be discussed here. It is not impossible that the effects of one of these other instruments are more positive than those of subsidies. The above implies that the macroeconomic effects of a well-designed fuel-saving policy may be even more positive than indicated above.

Let us now consider the question whether there are many other projects that have equally positive effects as the ones discussed above. Let us first discuss public projects that produce public consumption goods (e.g. public gardens). These projects do not have financial returns, while the government has to pay their costs. Therefore, the macroeconomic effects of these projects will be less positive than those of fuel-saving projects.

Projects that produce for the domestic market may also be stimulated by the government. (An example is the contruction of a sports stadium which leads to sales of tickets to local citizens.) The benefits of these projects consist of the revenues of selling the outputs on the domestic market. This implies that part of the budget of domestic households (or firms) available for the purchase of goods is used to buy these outputs. Consequently, these households will have less money available to buy other goods. This will probably lead to a decrease in the sales of other domestic firms, and therefore to a decrease in domestic production. Such a decrease in production does not occur when fuel-saving projects are implemented. The benefits of the latter projects entail a decrease in imports of fuels instead of a decrease in alternative expenditures on domestic goods. It can be concluded that the macroeconomic effects of projects producing for the domestic market are less positive than those of fuel-saving projects.

Apart from projects that lead to savings on fuels, there are many other projects that lead to import substitution. There are also projects that lead to an artificial increase in exports. On the basis of the analysis so far, it might be concluded that these other projects have effects which are as positive as those of fuel-saving projects.

However, in the analysis the following points have so far been neglected. First, fuel-saving projects have positive effects on the environment; many other projects have not. Second, in many cases a policy that stimulates these other projects is a beggar-thy-neighbour policy, which can only succeed if other countries do not retaliate. However, the stimulation of fuel-saving projects is not a beggar-thy-neighbour policy in many cases, even if the effects of this policy on the environment are neglected. This point will be discussed in Chapter 8.

It is not unlikely that certain public projects aiming to improve the economic infrastructure (such as projects in the field of education, or projects concerning the physical infrastructure) also have positive macroeconomic effects. This point will not be discussed in detail in this study. Suffice it to say that these projects and fuel-saving projects are not mutually exclusive in a situation of unemployment. This is related to the fact that, as explained above, fuel-saving projects need not be financed by expenditure cuts elsewhere.

2.2.2. Counterbalancing effects related to an increase in spending

The situation of unemployment described above is such that the increase in spending caused by the fuel-saving projects viewed apart (that is, without taking the fact that it has to be financed into account) leads to an increase in domestic production and employment. However, some counterbalancing effects could occur.

The main counterbalancing effects are related to problems on the labour market. Despite the existence of unemployment in general, two problems could occur. First, the increase in domestic production caused by the projects could involve the employment of some labourers who are drawn from other occupations. In relation to this, alternative production could decrease. This problem will be particularly serious if there are shortages on specific labour markets. Second, the decrease in unemployment caused by the projects could lead to an increase in the wage level, and therefore in the price level too. This could also lead to a certain decrease in production, for example because exports are negatively affected by increases in prices.[5]

Another counterbalancing effect is related to the fact that private enterprises may face shortages of capital goods. In that case an increase in production caused by the projects may (also) lead to a decrease in alternative production or to an increase in the price level. However, this is a temporary problem, because it can be solved by an increase in investment.[6] Furthermore, it can be regarded as part of a general problem that relates to any type of production; which is that entrepreneurs cannot exactly predict the level of future demand, and that because of this they may be confronted with capacity constraints when demand is higher than expected. Now, there is no reason to expect that, in case a policy of stimulating fuel-saving projects is carried out during a period of many years, the difference between entrepreneurs' expectations of demand and actual demand will be higher than in case such a policy is not pursued. Therefore, when one evaluates the expected effects of a fuel-saving policy, the capacity constraints of entrepreneurs can be neglected.

Finally, the following should be emphasized once again. The specific situation of unemployment to which this chapter refers is such that the counterbalancing effects do not completely outweigh the original increase in production and employment caused by an increase in demand viewed apart. According to many economists this situation has existed in many western countries since the end of the seventies.

2.2.3. Effects on financial markets

Investments in fuel-saving projects have effects on the domestic capital market and on the market for the domestic currency. These effects are the subject of this section, the structure of which is as follows. First, the effects of the projects on the domestic capital market and the interest rate will be analysed, without paying attention to the balance of payments. Second, the effects on the balance of payments and on the exchange rate of the domestic currency will be discussed. In relation to this, the effects of the projects on the interest rate will be reconsidered. In the first instance the analysis in this section will deal with the effects of the projects on the interest rate, and not with the further effects of the changes in the interest rate. These further effects will be discussed at the end of this section.

The investments in the projects, which are subsidized by the government, lead to an increase in demand on the capital market of private investors and of the government. This increase in demand is equal to the investments.[7] The spending effects of the investments will lead to a reduction in the government deficit and to an increase in private savings. The former will lead to a decrease in demand on the capital market, and the latter to an increase in supply. This will counterbalance the effects on the capital market of the original increase in demand. However, even when the multiplier process caused by the increase in investments has completely worn off, this counterbalance will not be complete. The main reason is that part of the money used for the investments will flow via imports to foreign countries.[8] The multiplier process has worn off when all the money has flown to private savings, the government deficit and imports. Generally, this will not take much time. In relation to this, the short run is defined in this section as the period during which the multiplier process initiated by the investments is in operation. Thus, it can be concluded that in the short run the interest rate will rise as a result of the investments in the projects.

As long as the multiplier process has not completely worn off, the demand for money related to the transaction motive will also be at a higher level. However, this point can be neglected, because increases in demand for money caused by increases in transactions are generally neutralized by the monetary authorities.

The benefits of the projects appear during their whole lifetime. The related financial revenues for private investors will be used to repay the debts made to finance the investments in the projects. Given that with subsidies the projects are profitable from the private point of view, all debts will ultimately be repaid, so that the original increase in demand of the private sector on the capital market will be undone. Moreover, once all debts have been repaid there will be some money left for the private investors (because the projects are profitable for them). Part of this money will be supplied on the capital market. Another part will be used directly for investments. This implies that the relevant investments need not be financed on the capital market, so that the demand on the capital market will decrease. It can be concluded that the net demand of private investors on the capital market will decrease in the long run.

It is repeated that for the time being the analysis deals with the effects of the projects on the interest rate only, and not with the further effects of changes in the interest rate. This considered, the investments in the projects have two effects on the government deficit. On the one hand the deficit increases in the short run as a result of the payment of subsidies. On the other hand it decreases in the short run as a result of the multiplier-process caused by the investments. In Section 2.2.1 it was argued that in the short run the second effect is at least as large as the first one – at least, if the projects are not too unprofitable and the subsidies not too high. This implies that in the short and in the long run the demand of the government on the capital market will not increase, or it will only increase to a small extent, depending on the extent to which the projects are unprofitable.

As a result of the multiplier-process private savings have increased in the short run, which implies that the wealth of households and firms has increased. This implies that in the short and in the long run supply on the capital market will be at a higher level. Given all the effects on demand and supply on the capital market mentioned above, in the long run the interest rate will fall – if the projects are not too unprofitable.

Let us now leave the capital market for a moment, and let us pay attention to the effects on the balance of payments. The further effects of changes in the interest rate caused by the projects are still neglected for the moment. This considered, a policy of saving on fuels has two effects on the trade balance. First, imports will rise as a result of the multiplier process initiated by the spendings on the projects. Second, imports of fuels will decrease. The first effect will occur in the short run only. The second effect occurs during the whole lifetime of the projects. In relation to this, the net effect on the trade balance will be negative in the short run and positive after that. The improvements in the trade balance caused by the fuel savings can be expressed in terms of the present value in the year of the investments, using the international interest rate. This present value will be more or less equal to the present value of the benefits of the projects.[9] In a similar way, the changes in imports resulting from the expenditures on the cost side of the projects can also be expressed in terms of a present value. The present value of these changes in imports is much lower than the present value of the costs of the projects (because in the multiplier process part of the increase in spendings caused by the costs of the projects flows to the government and to private savings). The above implies that the present value of all changes in the trade balance caused by the project will be positive – if the projects are not too unprofitable. Therefore, the balance on current account will improve in the long run, and net foreign assets will increase.

If international investors behave rationally, they will, even in the short run, take account of the effects of the policy in the long run. This implies that the exchange rate will not change much; it will slightly rise if the fuel-saving projects are not too unprofitable, and this rise will occur in the short run too. The rise in the exchange rate in the short run is caused by an inflow of capital that is larger than the increase in imports caused by the multiplier process initiated by the investments. Now, in discussing the capital market effects, it was stated that the main reason for the increase in net demand on the capital market in the short run was that part of the spendings caused by the investments leaked away to imports. This considered, it can be said that the inflow of capital leads to an increase in supply on the domestic capital market, which is larger than the increase in net demand caused by the investments. In other words, when one takes account of the reaction of international investors, and when it is assumed that these investors are rational, the conclusion which was drawn earlier, that in the short run the interest rate will rise, turns out to be wrong. It can also be noted that the small rise of the exchange rate mentioned above will probably lead to a small decrease in inflation, and, initially at least, to a decrease in exports, production and employment.

If international investors are not rational, and if, in the short run, they do not take account of the decrease in imports in the long run, the rate of exchange of the domestic currency will fall in the short run, and it will rise in the long run. The fall of the exchange rate will have effects which are the opposite of the effects of the rise in the exchange rate mentioned above.

It can also be assumed, however, that the government pursues a monetary policy such that the rate of exchange remains constant. For the Netherlands this is a realistic assumption, and the remainder of this chapter will be based on it.

In case international investors are rational, a somewhat less restrictive monetary policy can be pursued in the short and in the long run in order to keep the exchange rate constant. On balance the fuel-saving policy then leads to a small decrease in the interest rate. In case international investors are irrational, the government will have to pursue a more restrictive monetary policy in the short run, and a less restrictive monetary policy in the long run. In that case the interest rate will rise in the short run, and it will fall in the long run.

Up to now the further effects of changes in the interest rate caused by the project have been neglected. Clearly, a decrease in the interest rate has positive effects on the economy. This implies that when international investors behave rationally the macroeconomic effects of the fuel-saving projects are even more positive than indicated in Section 2.2.1. In the situation in which investors are irrational, however, the short run increase in the interest rate will lead to a decrease in investment and production, and to an increase in the government deficit. This increase in the government deficit will increase demand on the capital market, so that it is possible that even in the long run the interest rate will rise as a result of the projects. These negative effects were already referred to in the preliminary analysis of the capital market in Section 2.2.1, which can now be said to be implicitly based on the assumption that international investors are irrational.

Thus, given the characteristics of the situation of unemployment described in this chapter, there are two reasons why fuel-saving projects which are not profitable from the private point of view may not have positive macroeconomic effects. The first reason is that the extent to which the projects are unprofitable is too large. The second reason is that investors may not be rational, and that in relation to this the projects will lead to an increase in the interest rate in the short run, having further negative effects on the economy. This implies that in quantitative analyses of fuel-saving policies the interest rate is an important variable.

2.2.4. Savings on non-imported fuels

So far it was assumed that the fuel savings concern imported fuels. If they concern fuels from domestic sources the argument changes, as will be illustrated with an example. If the Dutch government stimulates natural gas conservation projects, this will (generally) cause a decrease in sales of Dutch natural gas and in government revenues from natural gas sales. The government deficit will increase, which will have other negative consequences. Besides, employment and profits in the natural gas industry will decrease. Thus, one could argue that the effects of Dutch natural gas-saving projects are less positive than those of projects saving on imported fuels (Bovenberg *et al.*, 1991).

However, this argument is too short-sighted. The decrease in natural gas sales leads to an increase in the natural gas reserves. (To be precise, the natural gas reserves do not increase, but they are depleted more slowly. This point however is neglected.) The question is how to evaluate this increase. There are three possibilities to react on it. First, one can immediately counterbalance any increase in natural gas reserves caused by the energy-saving policy by an equal increase in the domestic use of natural gas for other purposes. This implies that government revenues from natural gas sales, and employment and profits in the natural gas industry, increase again while imports of oil and coal are reduced. Stimulating the domestic use of natural gas involves certain costs, for instance the costs of subsidies. These costs however will be smaller than the benefits of selling the natural gas. (One can see this when one realizes that, if the government 'subsidized' the use of natural gas by selling it for a low price, other fuels would almost completely be replaced by natural gas if the natural gas price was low enough, whereas at the same time there would still be benefits from selling the natural gas.) It can be concluded that, in the situation described above, the macroeconomic effects of natural gas conservation projects will probably be somewhat less positive than those of projects that save on imported fuels. However, they are more positive than indicated by an analysis in which the increase in the natural gas reserves is neglected.

The second alternative is to counterbalance any decrease in natural gas sales caused by the energy-saving policy immediately by an equal increase in natural gas exports. (The Dutch government has set limits to the use of natural gas, because it wants to retain self-sufficiency for a long period of time. For this reason, the existing contracts for natural gas exports concern a total amount that is lower than it might have been.) In many respects this alternative has the same effects as the one discussed in the previous paragraph. Both alternatives imply that in the final analysis the total sales of Dutch natural gas remain constant. Both lead to a decline in net energy imports. The second alternative leads to an increase in natural gas exports, while the first one leads to a decrease in imports of other fuels. However, this difference is of no consequence for the domestic economy. A difference which argues in favour of the first alternative is that the price of natural gas sold on the domestic market is generally higher than the price of exported natural gas. A difference which argues in favour of the second alternative is that the first alternative involves costs related to the government measures needed to increase the domestic use of natural gas. Therefore, on the basis of a qualitative analysis alone it is difficult to say which of the two alternatives has the more positive effects.

As an aside, it can be noted that an increase in the domestic use of natural gas at the cost of oil and coal is positive for the environment. An increase in natural gas exports may lead to decrease in the use of coal and oil abroad, so that it may also be beneficial for the environment.

The third alternative is to do nothing with the increase in the natural gas reserves for a certain period (e.g. 30 years). The increase in the natural gas reserves implies that government wealth increases, but in comparison with the first two alternatives government revenues from natural gas sales decrease, and the balance on current account deteriorates. The decrease in government revenues leads to an increase in the government debt, and to an increase in interest payments which further increases the government debt. If the energy market were characterized by an intertemporal Pareto-optimum, the increase in government debt caused by the factors mentioned above would be equal to the increase in government wealth related to the increase in the natural gas reserves.[10] Of course, generally a Pareto-optimum does not exist. However, it is difficult to predict whether the yearly increases in gas prices will be higher or lower than the real interest rate. To estimate the increase in the value of the gas reserves, it is reasonable to assume that a Pareto-optimum does exist.

An increase in government debt which is accompanied by a deterioration in the balance on current account leads to an increase in the interest rate, which has further negative effects. Besides, the third alternative has negative effects on employment and profits in the natural gas industry. Therefore the effects of this alternative are somewhat less positive than those of the first two alternatives, assuming the Pareto-optimum.

For the purpose of evaluating projects it is fair to assume that the government chooses the alternative which it expects to have the best effects. Suppose that one estimates the effects of one of the alternatives, disregarding the question which of the three has the best effects. The estimated effects of the selected alternative can then be regarded as a kind of minimum estimate of the benefits of the increase in the natural gas reserves (because one of the other alternatives may have better effects). In the next section an estimate will be given which is based on increasing natural gas exports. This alternative has been selected for practical reasons, so that at first sight one might regard this estimate as a minimum estimate. However, there is only one alternative (increasing domestic natural gas consumption) which could perhaps have more positive effects, and that at most to a limited extent. Therefore it seems justifiable to call the estimate based on natural gas exports a satisfactory estimate instead of a minimum estimate.

It can be concluded that Dutch projects saving on Dutch natural gas need not have less positive effects than projects saving on imported fuels. The reader can verify for him or herself that a similar conclusion can be drawn for projects saving on other types of fuel from domestic sources (apart from the effect on the environment, which is more ambiguous). Thus, the proposition that fuel-saving projects have positive macroeconomic effects because they lead to an increase in domestic spending at the cost of imports is not as general as it could be. A better proposition is that these projects have positive effects because they involve a substitution of unemployed labour for scarce fuels.

2.2.5. The results of quantitative studies

This section discusses some quantitative studies about the effects of a policy of saving on fuels in the Netherlands. These studies concern situations of unemployment that have the same characteristics as the one described in Section 2.2.1.

The first study is that of Driehuis et al. (1983). This study paid attention to the macroeconomic effects of a policy aiming at a reduction of the use of energy with about 20% in the year 2000. The main instrument was a tax on energy. Subsidies were also used as an instrument, but to a limited extent. The analysis was based on the assumption that the Netherlands would be a net importer of natural gas by the year 2000 (in 1983 the estimates of the reserves of Dutch natural gas were lower than they are at present). In relation to this, it was assumed that savings on natural gas lead to a decrease in the imports of natural gas. The effects of the policy were calculated with the help of the SECMON-C model, a combination of a macroeconomic and a mesoeconomic model which takes account of demand as well as supply factors.

In the base-run, which concerned the economic development with unchanged policy, there were high levels of unemployment. Partly in relation to this, the calculations showed that the policy had a positive impact on national income, private consumption and employment. In the first instance the effects on the government deficit were also positive, but these effects were offset by a counterbalancing decrease in direct taxes. It should be mentioned that the energy-saving policy was part of a broader environmental policy, which included a policy to introduce shorter working hours. This broader policy led (more or less) to full employment, and to a (moderate) increase in consumption.

Despite the above, Driehuis did not conclude that the energy-saving policy, or the environmental policy in general, would lead to increases in production, consumption and employment. This needs some explanation. According to Driehuis (1982) it was also possible to reach full employment by means of an export-promoting policy. Therefore, the economic development with environmental policy should be compared to the economic development with export-promoting policy. The latter development involved higher levels of production and consumption than the development with environmental policy, and therefore it was concluded that environmental policies involved sacrifices for the citizens.

It should be noted first of all that nothing in Driehuis's study indicates that the energy-saving policy and the export-promoting policy cannot be pursued simultaneously as long as there is unemployment. This considered, Driehuis's conclusion depends on the idea that without energy-saving policy (and without environmental policy) full employment can be reached. In this context it should be noted that at present there is still unemployment in the Netherlands. This implies that either an export-promoting policy has not been pursued seriously, or that it has been pursued seriously without leading to full employment. If the latter holds, this could be related to the fact that the effects of such a policy are not as positive as predicted by

Driehuis, but it could also be related to the fact that other economic developments may have neutralized the positive effects of the export-promoting policy. Whatever the truth about this, the results of Driehuis's study indicate that as long as there is unemployment an energy-saving policy (perhaps pursued in combination with an export-promoting policy) leads to increases in consumption and employment.

The second study is that of the Central Planning Bureau (CPB, 1989). In 1989 the CPB analysed the effects of a far-reaching energy-saving policy carried out by the Netherlands on the national economy. The analysis was based on the Athena-model. This model is also a combination of a macro- and a mesoeconomic model, and it takes account of demand as well as supply factors.

The policy aims to stimulate energy-saving investments by means of subsidies, which are financed by indirect taxes and levies on fuels. The subsidies amount to 50% of the investment costs in some cases. The policy induces energy-saving investments with a total value of 160 billion guilders over the period 1990–2010, causing a 30% reduction of CO_2-emissions in the year 2010. Because it was analysed in 1989, the policy will be called the 1989 energy-saving policy. Its effects are given in Table 2.1.

Table 2.1. Macroeconomic effects of the 1989 energy-saving policy in the year 2010

Production of enterprises (%)	–0.8
Employment (thousands man-years)	–12
Private consumption (%)	0.5
Balance on current account (% NNI)	–1.1
Government budget surplus (% NNI)	–1.8

Source: CPB (1989), p. 42.

Because the Athena-model describes a situation of unemployment which has the same characteristics as the one discussed previous by, one would expect the effects of an energy-saving policy to be as positive as indicated in the previous sections. However, apart from the effect on private consumption the calculated effects are negative. This implies that either the argument in the previous sections is wrong, or that the CPB has made one or more mistakes which have nothing to do with the Athena model itself, which is indeed the case.

The first mistake is that in the 1989 study the impact of the increase in the reserves of Dutch natural gas is not taken into account. Attention will be paid below to the effects of using the increase in the reserves to increase natural gas exports. As explained earlier, estimating these effects is a satisfactory way of estimating the benefits of the increase in the natural gas reserves.

First of all, it can be noted that there is another study, viz. CPB (1990), in which the CPB analysed the effects of a different energy-saving policy. Total energy-saving investments caused by this policy were more than four times smaller than those caused by the 1989 policy. In the 1990 study it was assumed that the increase in the natural gas reserves caused by the policy is used to increase natural gas exports. (This might be a reaction to the fact that the 1989 study had been criticized on various occasions; see, e.g., Nieuwsbrief Milieu en Economie, November 1989, pp.

3–4.) The question is what the 1990 study can teach us about the extent of the effects of increasing natural gas exports.

Table 2.2. Macroeconomic effects of the 1990 energy-saving policy in the year 2010

	Effects with increased natural gas exports[a]	Effects without increased natural gas exports[b]
Production of enterprises (%)	1.1	–
Employment (thousands man-years)	12	–
Private consumption (%)	1.0	–
Balance on current account (%NNI)	–0.5	–
Government budget surplus (% NNI)	–0.9	–1.8

[a]*Source*: CPB (1990), p. 4.
[b]*Source*: Letter from the CPB of 13 February 1991.

The model used in the 1990 study is the Athena-model, which was also used in the 1989 study. The assumptions regarding energy prices are the same in both studies. Most investments in the 1990 study are stimulated by means of subsidies financed by levies and taxes, as in the 1989 study.[11] The effects of the 1990-energy-saving policy including the increase in natural gas exports are given in the first column of Table 2.2. The effect of the policy, excluding the increase in natural gas exports, on the government budget surplus is given in the second column.

It appears that the effects of the conservation policy on production, employment and consumption are more positive in the 1990 study than in the 1989 study. Regarding the effects on the balance on current account and on the government budget surplus the following can be said. Energy-saving investments in the 1990 study are about four times as small as in the 1989 study. Therefore, one would expect the effects of the 1990 policy without natural gas exports to be about one-fourth of those of the 1989 policy. Besides, because it is especially the balance on current account and the government deficit which are affected by an increase in natural gas exports, one would expect the effects on these two variables of the 1990 policy to be much more positive with natural gas exports than without natural gas exports. However, a comparison of Tables 2.1 and 2.2 shows that in the 1990 study the effects on these two variables are much more negative than one would expect. This is remarkable, and it deserves an explanation from the CPB.[12]

Let us now consider how the outcomes of the 1989 study would have changed if natural gas exports had been increased. Savings on natural gas in the 1989 study are about twice as large as in the 1990 study.[13] In the 1990 study exporting the saved natural gas leads, viewed apart, to an improvement in the government budget surplus of 0.9%. This implies that the inclusion of increased natural gas exports in the 1989 study would have improved the government budget surplus with about 1.8%. Hence, the 1989 policy including natural gas exports would have had a more or less neutral effect on the government budget surplus instead of a negative one.[14] Besides, other variables would have been affected positively as well.

The second mistake of the CPB concerns both the 1989 study and the 1990 study, but it will be explained here for the 1989 study only. This study is based on the following procedure. First, the energy prices were set equal to the so-called NEV prices.[15] Second, the number of energy-saving projects that would be implemented without the energy-saving policy was estimated, as well as the number of projects that would be implemented as a result of this policy. Third, the macroeconomic development in a base-run was simulated, which included the projects implemented without an energy-saving policy. Fourth, the macroeconomic development with the projects caused by the policy was simulated. Fifth, the effects of these projects were calculated as being equal to the difference between the latter development and the development in the base-run.

Before taking the fourth step however, the CPB made one change: for the projects analysed separately (outside the base-run) it decreased energy prices with 'about' 30% (so that the original prices were about 43% higher than those used for the final calculations). The reason why the CPB changed the energy prices at the last moment was that in previous years the energy prices had been lower than predicted in the NEV study. This correction may be justifiable in itself. However, making a certain assumption once, it should be used throughout the whole analysis. That was not done.

Let us first discuss what the outcome would have been if the high NEV prices had been used consistently. In that case the energy saving in terms of money would have been about 43% higher than the energy saving as calculated by the CPB. This means that the macroeconomic effects would have been much more positive. (In Chapter 6 investments in wind energy will be analysed by means of the Freia model of the CPB. Large positive macroeconomic effects will be shown due to a rise in energy-prices of only 20%.)

Another question is what the outcome would have been if the energy prices about 30% lower than the NEV prices had been used consistently. Well, there are projects which would be implemented without government policy at NEV prices, but which would not be implemented without government policy at 30% lower prices. These projects will be called the X projects. The energy savings per unit of investment of the X projects are high compared with the projects that would not be implemented without government policy at NEV prices. The latter will be called the Y projects. Let us assume that, given the lower energy prices, the government aims to stimulate both the X projects and the Y projects. The related policy is called the XY policy. There are two reasons why the relative macroeconomic effects (that is, the effects per unit of energy saving) of the XY policy, calculated in a correct way, will differ from the relative macroeconomic effects of the policy concerning the Y projects only as presented in the 1989 study of the CPB. First, because the energy-savings per unit of investment of the X projects are higher than those of the Y projects, the (relative) macroeconomic effects of the X projects are more positive than those of the Y projects. Taken by itself this implies that the relative macroeconomic effects of the XY policy will be more positive than those of the policy concerning the Y projects only. Second, it is not justifiable to assume that the XY policy can be based on the same amounts of subsidies per unit of investment as the ones on which the CPB study was based; the Y projects especially will need higher subsidies, because the energy prices are lower. This implies that the correct analysis of the XY policy should take account of an additional transfer of money from the government to the private sector. This could, on balance, have negative consequences for the calculated macroeconomic effects, but it is also possible that the consequences are positive on balance. If the consequences are negative on balance, however, it is possible to generate a transfer of money in the opposite direction by devising an XY policy that combines the use of subsidies with the use of levies on energy. Therefore, the second point is not as important as it may seem to be at first sight. It can be concluded that, if the lower energy prices had been used consistently, the effects of a well designed XY policy per unit of energy saving would probably have been more positive than the effects of the policy concerning the Y projects only as presented in the 1989 study by the CPB.

If the two mistakes discussed above had not been made, the sign of the effect on the government budget surplus would probably have been reversed (because if only the first mistake is corrected, the effect already changes from negative to neutral). The effect on consumption, which was already positive, would probably have been even more positive. I do not have quantitative information about the other variables, but it is not unlikely that without the two mistakes the effects on these variables would have been positive too.

2.2.6. The effects of a policy of saving on fuels and other raw materials at the level of the European Union

The effects of a policy of saving on fuels (used as an abbreviation for fuels and raw materials) at the level of the European Union are relatively more positive than the effects of a similar policy conducted by one EU country in isolation. There are two reasons for this. The first one can be explained as follows: the EU is a net importer of fuels. Therefore, the policy mentioned above will lead to a reduction in the imports of the EU. (Part of this policy will lead to savings on fuels extracted in the EU. However, this may be neglected for essentially the same reasons as the ones mentioned in the discussion about the savings on Dutch natural gas.) At the same time, the policy will lead to an increase in demand within the EU. This will have positive effects on the national incomes, employment, the government deficits and the balances of payments of the EU countries. Now, the import coefficient of the EU as a whole is considerably lower than that of an individual EU country. Therefore the effects for the EU as a whole of a certain increase in demand will be relatively more positive than the effects of a certain increase in demand for one EU country only. In relation to this, the effects for the EU as a whole of a policy of saving on fuels and other raw materials conducted by the EU as a whole are relatively more positive than the effects for one EU country in isolation of a similar policy conducted by this country in isolation.

The point is illustrated in the appendix to this chapter. In this appendix a hypothetical project, which saves on imported oil and which is implemented in the Netherlands, is analysed. Two simple models, one relating to the EU and the other to the Netherlands, are used. Both models describe situations of unemployment. The models are not based on empirical research, and the results mentioned below should therefore be handled with care. Regarding the effects for the EU as a whole, the following holds good. Suppose that the project needs a 50% subsidy in order to be profitable from the private point of view. In that case the project has a positive effect on the sum total of the national incomes of all EU countries. Moreover, despite the provision of the 50% subsidy the effect on the sum total of all government debts is neutral on balance, as well as the effect on the sum total of the balances on current account of all EU countries. Only if the project needs a higher subsidy will the effect on the government debts be negative. The conclusions regarding the effects of the project for the Netherlands are (somewhat) less positive. For instance, the effect on the government debt will be negative if the project needs a subsidy which is higher than 29%.

The second reason why the effects of a policy of saving on fuels as pursued by the EU as a whole are relatively more positive than the effects of a similar policy pursued by one country in isolation does not only apply to situations of unemployment but also to situations of full employment. As argued by Little and Mirrlees (1974), a country that has a large share in the total world imports of a certain product should take account of the fact that its purchases of this product can affect the price of this product and therefore its total import costs. Now, the EU has a large share in total world imports of certain fuels or raw materials. The most important example is oil, and the following discussion will focus on this example. If the EU reduces its oil imports, this might lead to a reduction in the oil price and to a reduction in the total costs of its oil imports. The resulting benefits will be discussed below.

To begin with, let us make for the moment the following (unrealistic) assumptions. First, the EU is the only consumer of oil in the world, and it does not produce any oil. Second, there is a situation of general equilibrium with a Pareto optimum in the EU. The following notation will be used: E_d is the elasticity of demand for oil, and E_s the elasticity of supply of oil. p denotes the oil price, and q denotes the quantity of oil which is sold. It is assumed that the reduction of the quantity of imported oil caused by the policy is large enough to have a significant effect on the oil price, but small enough to ensure that the approximations used below are justifiable; this reduction is in the order of a few percents of q.

The total benefits for the EU of a reduction in its oil imports with quantity Δq can be divided into two parts. The first part consists of the benefits which would occur if the oil price remained constant. These benefits are called the direct benefits, and they are equal to $\Delta q \cdot p$. The second part consists of the benefits caused by the price reduction, which are called the indirect benefits. It can easily be shown that these indirect benefits are equal to:

$$\frac{p \cdot \Delta q}{E_s - E_d}$$

(with the reduction Δq being positive).[16] Expressed in terms of a percentage of the direct benefits, the indirect benefits are $100/(E_s - E_d)$% of the direct benefits. (When the price reduction is very large, say over 10%, the above should be refined. However, this affects the calculated benefits only to a limited extent.)

Let us now abandon the assumption that the EU is the only consumer of oil and that it does not produce any oil. The proportion between the net oil imports of the EU (as a whole) and the world oil production is denoted as P_{eu}. When the EU reduces its oil imports with Δq, the direct benefits are still equal to $p \bullet \Delta q$. The indirect benefits for all oil consumers in the world are (still) equal to $p \bullet \Delta q \bullet 1/(E_s - E_d)$. However, $100 \bullet (1 - P_{eu})\%$ of the indirect benefits now fall to consumers outside the EU, or to consumers inside the EU who use European oil. The latter still benefit from the reduction in the oil price, but this benefit is exactly compensated by the loss of European oil producers (given the existence of a Pareto-optimum). Therefore, the indirect benefits for the EU of a reduction in its oil imports with quantity Δq are equal to $\Delta q \bullet p\{P_{eu}/(E_s - E_d)\}$. Expressed in terms of a percentage of the direct benefits, the indirect benefits are equal to $100 \bullet P_{eu}/(E_s - E_d)\%$ of the direct benefits.

In 1987 P_{eu} was about 0.12, and there are indications that it will rise slightly in the future.[17] Stoffers (1985) estimates the long-run price elasticity of the world demand for oil to be –0.35.[18] He notes that other estimates of this elasticity are in the range of –0.25 to –0.6 (or even higher). According to Van Bergeijk (1987), estimates of this elasticity vary between –0.2 and –0.7. Van Bergeijk also remarks that there are only a few publications about the price elasticity of the world supply of oil. Stoffers (1985) has estimated the long-run price elasticity of the supply of oil of non-OPEC countries that do not have a centrally planned economy. He estimates this elasticity to be 0.55 at an oil price of 30 dollars, and 0.37 at an oil price of 10 dollars,[19] but emphasizes that these estimates may be wrong. If the figures given by Stoffers are correct, then the elasticity of the world supply of oil will probably be lower than indicated by the figures from Stoffers, because the elasticity of the supply of OPEC-countries is lower than that of non-OPEC countries.

Table 2.3. The indirect benefits for different values of E_d and E_s

E_d	E_s	Indirect benefits (percentage of the direct benefits)
–0.2	0.2	30
–0.35	0.35	17
–0.7	0.55	10

Taking P_{eu} to be 0.12, the indirect benefits can be calculated for three different combinations of values for E_d and E_s. The first combination consists of values of –0.2 for E_d and 0.2 for E_s. This combination can be used to give an estimate of the indirect benefits which might be regarded as a kind of upper limit. The second combination consists of values of –0.7 for E_d and 0.55 for E_s, and yields an estimate which can be regarded as a kind of lower limit. The third combination consists of values of –0.35 for E_d and 0.35 for E_s, and is partly based on the estimates given by Stoffers. The results of the calculations are given in Table 2.3. The table shows that the indirect benefits will be between 30% and 10% of the direct benefits.

There is of course no Pareto-optimum in reality. Therefore, the question is what the consequences of the reduction in the oil price in a situation of unemployment such as experienced today in the European countries will be. A reduction in the oil price leads to a decrease in the expenditures on imported oil of firms and consumers. Therefore, the financial position of firms and consumers improves with the amount of the indirect benefits discussed above. Regarding the question what is done with this improvement there are two possibilities. First, it can be used to increase expenditures on investment and consumption. This implies that there will be an increase in expenditures which is financed by foreign oil producers in the final analysis. Given the analysis in Section 2.2.1, it will be clear that this will have positive macroeconomic effects. The second possibility is that the improvement in the financial position is not used to increase expenditures. In all probability this means that supply on the European capital market will increase, so that the interest rate will fall. This will also have positive macroeconomic effects. All this considered, it can be said that in a situation of unemployment a decrease in the price of imported oil has positive macroeconomic effects.

It can be concluded that it is likely that the effects of a policy of saving on fuels as conducted by the EU as a whole are relatively more positive than the effects of a similar policy conducted by one country in isolation: in the first place because of the larger multiplier effects, in the second place because of its impact on oil import prices.

2.2.7. Conclusions

It has been argued in a qualitative way that projects which reduce the consumption of fuels have positive macroeconomic consequences in countries that experience a situation of unemployment such as the one experienced by many western countries since the end of the seventies. Quantitative studies regarding the effects of the implementation of such projects in the Netherlands confirm this argument, at least if the outcomes of these studies are interpreted in a correct way, and if the effects of savings on Dutch natural gas are taken into account correctly. It has also been argued, in a qualitative way, that if a fuel-saving policy is conducted by the EU as a whole, the positive effects will be greater than in the case in which such a policy is pursued by one country in isolation.

It now becomes clear that the incorporation of project analysis in macroeconomic analysis would have helped in dealing with the problems related to the increase in oil prices in the seventies and in the beginning of the eighties. Because of this increase in oil prices many countries experienced a deterioration of the balance of payments, an increase in the government deficit, a decrease in the demand for domestic products, and an increase in unemployment. The recommendations made for macroeconomic policy were, to a large extent, of an aggregate nature. One was to cut government expenditure, which was thought to be positive for the balance of payments and the government deficit, but negative for total demand and employment. A different recommendation, which nevertheless reflected the same kind of aggregate thinking, was to do just the opposite. In such a situation, however, it would be sensible to launch a huge investment programme aiming at savings on oil. Such a programme would have kept effective demand high while at the same time it would have improved the balance of payments with the OPEC countries. It could or could not have been accompanied by expenditure cuts in the rest of the government budget. Thus, this section has provided a strong case for the integration of macroeconomic analysis and project analysis.

2.3. The effects of some portfolios of projects on inflation

In this section it will be argued that the policy recommendations that can be derived from some theories of inflation may be changed when one takes account of the relation between macroeconomic analysis and project analysis. The aim of this section is merely to provoke discussion on a possible new line of research; the results will not be used for the development of the improved method of project appraisal. In relation to this, only two theories of inflation will be discussed.

The first theory of inflation is Lipsey's (1960) theory of the Phillips-curve. Lipsey has developed a microeconomic theory which explains the existence of the Phillips-curve. He emphasizes that there are various labour markets, each of which relate to a specific type of labour. According to his theory, the rate of inflation is not only determined by the aggregate rate of unemployment, but also by the distribution of unemployment among different labour markets. The more equal the distribution the lower the Phillips-curve. Lipsey's theory has been used in support of regional policies, industrial intervention policies and policies to encourage the mobility of workers between labour markets (Jackman *et al.*, 1981). Of course, it can also be used to support the implementation of projects which use types of labour that are relatively abundant. In relation to this, it can be argued that, if the government stimulated the economy by a large-scale increase in expenditure on these projects, the trade-off between inflation and unemployment would be more positive than suggested by the 'aggregate' Phillips-curve.

The second theory to be discussed is the theory which says that in the long run the Phillips-curve is vertical at the natural rate of unemployment. This implies that in the long run Keynesian demand policies cannot decrease unemployment. However, it will be argued below that, even if the 'aggregate' Phillips-curve is vertical, demand policies at the micro-level might still bring down unemployment in the long run.

Let us start with some remarks of Laidner, one of the advocates of the vertical Phillips-curve:

> [The natural rate of unemployment] would be that which ruled when aggregate demand and supply in the economy were in balance, so that there was neither upward nor downward pressure upon the rate of inflation. It would be determined by the way in which the geographical distribution of job vacancies was matched up with the geographical distribution of the unemployed; by the way in which the skill mix required to fill the vacancies was matched by that among the unemployed: that is, by the rapidity of adjustment of supply to demand in the labour

> market. The age distribution of the labour force would influence it, as would the educational characteristics of the labour force. Barriers or subsidies to geographical mobility of labour and of jobs, such as trade union restrictions, council house subsidies, etc., as well as barriers or subsidies to the acquisition of new skills, such as professional examination standards, also would affect it. (Laidner, 1975, pp. 44–45)

The implications of this argument, together with the proposition that the Phillips-curve is vertical, are described by Laidner in the following way:

> The implication [. . .] is that, if higher employment levels than are consistent with a vertical long-run Phillips-curve are desired, the way to achieve them is to operate with policies directed towards the structure of the labour market and not with 'demand management' policies. [. . .] The natural rate of unemployment can be lowered by removing barriers to labour mobility, by increasing the educational attainments of the labour force, and so on. (Ibid., pp. 46–47)

Now, if the Phillips-curve is vertical and if the explanation of the natural rate of unemployment given above is correct, it is true that demand management policies should be avoided as far as aggregate demand is concerned, and that preference should be given to policies concerning the structure of the labour market. These policies are, of course, policies at micro- or meso-level. Unfortunately, policies at micro- or meso-level are almost exclusively associated with supply-side policies. To give an example, it is no coincidence that Laidner only considers the adjustment of supply to demand (at micro- and meso-level), and not the adjustment of demand to supply (at micro- and meso-level).

However, the quotations given above do not imply that it is impossible to cure structural imbalances in the labour market by changing the structure of demand. Project selection could be a major instrument to accomplish this. Logically speaking, the implication of the first quotation is broader than the one mentioned by Laidner: if unemployment is to be reduced, this should be accomplished by either supply-side policies at the micro- or meso-level, demand policies at the micro- or meso-level, or both. Thus, the rejection of demand management in the case of the existence of a vertical Phillips-curve is logical only when demand management is taken to mean aggregate demand management.

The subsequent question is whether or not a demand policy at micro- level will be at the cost of allocational efficiency. The answer to this question may vary from project to project. Let us discuss one example. Suppose that a project uses many labourers who are older than fifty and who are trained to work in a sector in which labour is relatively abundant. Suppose also that the value for consumers of the product is high in relation to the value of the leisure time of the labourers involved. It is then very well possible that this project increases allocational efficiency. Whether or not this is indeed the case is not important here. What matters is that we have reached the field of project appraisal.

2.4. Conclusions

In Section 2.2 it was concluded that portfolios of projects that lead to savings on fuels and other raw materials, as compared with many other portfolios, have positive macroeconomic effects in situations of unemployment such as experienced by many western countries since the end of the seventies. In Section 2.3 it was argued that a portfolio of projects that use types of labour that are relatively abundant might also have relatively positive macroeconomic effects, especially in a situation in which the average increase in government expenditure has as (one of) its main consequence(s) a large increase in inflation. Thus, the composition of government expenditure is important for the effects of government expenditure. In relation to this, the optimal size of the government budget partly depends upon the composition of total government expenditure. This considered, one needs a method for the selection of individual projects that leads to a portfolio of government projects with a composition which is such that its macroeconomic effects are optimal.

The characteristics of a method of project appraisal depend among other things on the purpose for which it is made. In relation to the positive outcomes of Section 2.2, in this study a project in the field of wind energy will be analyzed. This implies among other things that the method of project appraisal to be used should be suited to analyse the characteristics that distinguishes such a project from other projects. Some of these characteristics were discussed in Section 2.2. The hypothesis of Section 2.3 that projects using types of labour that are relatively abundant have relatively positive macroeconomic effects in certain economic situations, will not be investigated in this study. In relation to this, the method to be used later in this study will not make a distinction between types of labour that are relatively abundant and types of labour that are not.

In order to find a suitable method of project appraisal, the next chapter will discuss the existing methods of project appraisal for situations of unemployment. Although none of these methods will turn out to be completely satisfactory, this discussion will yield many valuable insights that can be used for the development of an improved method of project appraisal.

Appendix

A simple, quantitative analysis of the effects of a policy of saving on fuels at the level of the European Union

In this appendix a simple, quantitative analysis is given of the effects of a policy of saving on fuels at the EU level. The aim of this appendix is to deepen the insight into the problem and to give an impression of the relative magnitude of the different effects. The analysis is not based on empirical research; the reader should judge for him or herself to what extent the figures given below are plausible. Also, the government is taken to include all governments of the associated countries. The word 'national' refers to all nations in the EU. Imports and exports refer to trade between the EU and other countries.

Suppose that the economy of the EU has the following characteristics:

- There is unemployment. In relation to this, an increase in government expenditure with 1 billion ECUs leads to an increase in national income of 1.5 billion ECUs.
- Part of the imports is independent of national product. Another part is dependent on national income; an increase in national income of 1 billion ECUs implies an increase in imports of 0.1667 billion ECUs.
- Part of the exports is independent of national product. Another part is dependent on national product; an increase in national product of 1 billion ECUs leads to a decrease in exports of 0.1667 billion ECUs. This decrease in exports can be regarded as being the reflection of all kinds of problems related to an increase in production. For instance, despite the existence of unemployment in general, there can be capacity constraints in specific sectors of production, implying that an increase in production for the domestic market crowds out production for exports.
- An increase in national income leads to increases in private savings and private investment, which are equal to each other. This should be regarded as a coincidence: if the propensity to save or the relation between national income and investment was different, there would be no equality between private savings and private investment. Thus, this equality is not a neo-classical assumption. The above implies that when national income increases, the resulting change in the current account of the community as a whole is equal to the change in the government debt (multiplied by –1).

There are many possible models which yield these characteristics. I have not started the analysis by giving one of these models because this would unnecessarily limit the analysis. One possible model however is the following:

$$Y = C + I + G + X - M \qquad (1)$$
$$X = C + S + T \qquad (2)$$
$$X = Y \qquad (3)$$
$$C = 0.8 \cdot (Y - T) + \bar{C} \qquad (4)$$
$$I = 0.1334 \cdot Y + \bar{I} \qquad (5)$$
$$G = \bar{G} \qquad (6)$$
$$E = -0.1667 \cdot X + \bar{E} \qquad (7)$$
$$M = 0.1667 \cdot Y + \bar{M} \qquad (8)$$
$$T = 0.334 \cdot Y \qquad (9)$$

in which:
Y = total demand; X = national product; C = consumption; I = investment; G = government expenditure; E = exports; M = imports; S = private savings; T = taxes. A line above a symbol indicates that the variable is exogenous.

Now suppose that the government increases its investments in the insulation of government buildings with 1 billion ECUs. Neglecting for the moment the yield of this investment, and assuming that the expenditures related to these investments do not differ from other government expenditures with regard to the characteristics mentioned above, this will have the following consequences: national income will increase with 1.5 billion ECUs, imports will increase with 0.25 billion ECUs, exports will decrease with the same amount, and the government debt will increase with 0.5 billion ECUs.

The yield of the additional investments consists of savings on energy. Suppose that the total yield of the investments occurs in the year of investment. Suppose also that the change in energy consumption leads to an equal change in that section of total imports that is independent of national income. This might, for example, be the case when the government buildings are heated by means of imported oil. It will be clear that a yield of saved energy of 50% of the value of the investments will then suffice to counterbalance the original changes in the trade balance and in government debt. This implies that if the investments were made by one department of the government, and if another department subsidized these investments, a maximum subsidy of 50% could be given without increasing the government debt.

To appreciate the difference between a policy at the level of the EU and a policy conducted by one country only, let us suppose that the project mentioned above is implemented by the Dutch government, and let us take the effects of the project into consideration insofar as they concern the Dutch economy only. Suppose that the model of the Dutch economy is equal to the model for the EU given above, except for the fact that M is now equal to $0.667 \cdot Y + \bar{M}$ (which implies that, if spending increases with one billion, imports will increase with 0.4 billion). It can then be deduced that the yield in terms of energy saved should be equal to 71% of the investment in order to counterbalance the original increase in the government debt. Put differently, the government could subsidize these investments with maximal 29% without increasing the government debt. This percentage is much lower than the relevant percentage for the EU.

Notes

1. Essentially, this section is based on Van der Burg (1982, 1984).
2. Classical unemployment occurs when prices and wages are such that there is excess supply on the labour market and excess demand on the goods market (Malinvaud, 1985). The words 'exclusively' and 'to a large extent' in the main text indicate that at a disaggregated level there may be some specific labour markets with excess demand.
3. Local transport costs and other details are neglected in this chapter.
4. It is assumed that (on average) investments turn out to be as profitable as expected. This assumption may not be valid, but it does not introduce a bias in favour or against the projects.
5. If the problems on the labour market are very serious, one could consider the possibility of slowing down the introduction of shorter working hours. In that case there would be a trade-off between leisure time and the positive effects of a policy of saving on fuels (which include the positive effects on the environment).
6. This has effects on the capital market, which are discussed in the next section.
7. The main text is based on the assumption that the investments are not financed by profits. However, this assumption is not a crucial one: if investments are financed by profits, they might lead to a decrease in supply on the capital market which has similar effects as an increase in demand on the capital market.
8. Another reason is that part of the increase in private savings may not be used to increase supply on the domestic capital market, for example because it is used to buy foreign equities. However, it is

also possible that part of the investments in the projects are financed abroad, which has opposite effects. Both points have been neglected in the main text.

9. There may be small differences. For instance, the present value of the improvements in the trade balance will be somewhat smaller than the present value of the benefits of the projects because part of the costs of fuels consists of local transport costs.
10. Details such as payments to the oil companies are neglected.
11. A small part of the investments in the 1990 study are induced by so-called 'covenants' (agreements between government and industry), which are assumed to involve no costs for the government. In the 1989 study this instrument does not play a role.
12. I have asked the CPB for an explanation. In my opinion, their answer is not satisfactory. See Van der Burg (1991), p. 100.
13. According to a letter of the CPB of 27 February 1991.
14. I cannot be more precise because I do not have exact information about the extent of the savings on gas.
15. The prices as predicted in the 'Nationale Energie Verkenningen'.
16. To show this, let us first discuss the following mathematical problem. Suppose we have two relations: $y = ax + b$, and $y = cx + d$ (a, b, c, and d are constants, a>0, c<0). These two relations yield one solution for y (and for x). Suppose that the second relation is converted into the following one: $y = c(x + f) + d$, with f being a positive constant. This implies that the solution for y decreases with $a \cdot | cf | / (a - c)$. With regard to the problem discussed in the main text, it has been assumed that the changes in price and quantity are in the order of a few percents. Therefore, the slope of the supply curve, which is denoted as dp/dq_s, can be taken to be constant. The same holds good for the slope of the demand curve, which is denoted as dp/dq_d. E_s and E_d can also be taken to be constant. Given this, the question how much the price will decrease as a result of savings on oil with a (positive) amount Δq can then be answered with the help of the mathematical analysis given above. Thus, the decrease in the price of oil which results from savings on oil with a (positive) quantity Δq is equal to:

$$\Delta p = \frac{dp}{dq_s} \cdot \frac{\frac{dp}{dq_d} \cdot \Delta q}{\frac{dp}{dq_s} - \frac{dp}{dq_d}} = \frac{1}{E_s} \cdot \frac{\frac{dp}{dq_d} \cdot \Delta q}{\frac{1}{E_s} - \frac{1}{E_d}}$$

which implies that $\Delta p \cdot q = \Delta q \cdot p \cdot 1/(E_d - E_s)$.

17. In 1987 the proportion between net oil imports of the EU countries excluding France and world oil requirements was 0.093 (IEA, 1990, *Energy Policies and Programmes of IEA countries, 1989 Review*, Paris, OECD, pp. 55 and 76). IEA (1990) does not give data about France. According to another study (IEA, 1987, *Annual Oil and Gas Statistics*, Paris, OECD, pp. 12–13) the proportion between French net oil imports and German net oil imports was 0.76 in 1985. On the basis of this proportion and the figure for German net oil imports in 1987 (given by IEA, 1990), I have estimated French net oil imports to be 86.3 Mtoe in 1987. This is 2.8% of world oil requirements. Consequently, I have estimated P_{eu} to be 0.121 in 1987. The projections given in IEA (1990, pp. 55 and 76) seem to indicate that P_{eu} will slightly rise in the future, due to the decrease in British oil production. I use the word 'seem' because for a number of countries no projections have been made.
18. This estimate is based on a 20-year moving average of the oil price.
19. This estimate is based on a 12-year moving average of the oil price.

CHAPTER 3

Existing methods for the social appraisal of projects in situations of unemployment

3.1. Introduction

The social appraisal of projects can be defined as an appraisal in which projects are analysed from the perspective of society as a whole. In Chapters 3 to 7 society will be taken to mean 'nation'. In Chapter 8 some remarks will be made about the international perspective.

There are two alternative starting points for the social appraisal of projects. The first one is to base the appraisal on welfare theory. The second one is not to base it on welfare theory. Let us specify the first starting point. There are two types of welfare theory which have been used as a basis for project appraisal: neo-Paretian and Pigouvian welfare theory.[1] These two types of welfare theory are based on the same general definition of social welfare. According to this definition, social welfare is equal to the sum of all individual PVUs, with the PVU of an individual denoting the present value of all the utilities related to his or her consumption of goods and leisure time. It is assumed that it is the objective of society to maximize social welfare.

Neo-Paretian and Pigouvian welfare theory differ from each other with regard to the measurement of changes in utility. Neo-Paretian welfare theory is based on the idea that it is impossible to measure changes in utility of different persons in terms of one common yardstick. This leads to the conclusion that the best possible criterion for the acceptance of a project, or of any other change, is that it provides a potential Pareto-improvement. A change provides a potential Pareto-improvement if those who gain from it could hypothetically compensate the losers for their losses, and still be better off in terms of utility.

Now suppose that the individual utilities related to the consumption of goods and leisure time of various persons are proportional to the amounts of money the individual persons want to pay for the goods and leisure time. In that case social welfare could be defined as the present value of the consumption of goods and leisure time (of all citizens), expressed in terms of willingness to pay. Given this definition the use of the criterion of maximizing social welfare leads to the same conclusions regarding the acceptability of projects and other changes as the use of the criterion of a potential Pareto-improvement. Therefore, many project analysts treat neo-Paretian welfare theory as if it were based on this definition of social welfare, although, strictly speaking, this is not correct. In this study the same procedure will be followed.

Pigouvian welfare theory is based on the idea that interpersonal welfare comparisons can be made. Among other things, it is thought to be possible to measure the proportion between the marginal utility of consumption of persons with different incomes. In relation to this, project appraisal can take into account that the utilities related to the consumption of a certain good or a certain amount of leisure time of different people who are willing to pay the same price for it can be different.

The second starting point is not to base the appraisal of projects on welfare theory. This is based on the idea that society has more or other objectives than the maximization of the sum of all individual utilities related to the consumption of goods and leisure time. For example, a decrease in the level of unemployment, or a more equal division of income, may be regarded as a 'common interest'. This second starting point could imply the use of multi-criteria analysis.

Primal and dual methods

Another important distinction is that between primal and dual methods. When a primal method is used, a project is analysed in the following way: first, its effects on one or more variables are calculated, such as changes in consumption, employment and the government deficit. In principle, all relevant effects are taken into account, including for example multiplier effects. In practice some effects are sometimes neglected. Second, the calculated effects are evaluated on the basis of one or more criteria, reflecting the objective(s) of society.

When a dual method is used, a project is evaluated as follows: first, an inventory is made of the quantities of inputs and outputs needed or produced in various years. Second, these inputs and outputs are evaluated on the basis of shadow prices, including a shadow discount rate. The present value of all inputs and outputs at shadow prices is calculated, and the project is accepted if this present value is positive. The shadow prices reflect the way in which the use of one additional input or the availability of one additional output impedes or contributes to the realization of the objective(s) of society. The calculation of the shadow prices takes account of all relevant effects in principle. In practice some effects may be neglected.

The advantage of the dual approach, as compared with the primal method, is the following. The shadow prices of inputs and outputs need to be calculated only once. Once calculated they can be used for the evaluation of different projects, which makes the evaluation of individual projects efficient. The disadvantage is that in many situations it is difficult to calculate shadow prices.

Short history

Up to the sixties the theoretical basis of the social appraisal of projects was such that it could only be used in situations of full employment. Project appraisal was based on welfare theory. The methods used were dual methods. Regarding the neo-Paretian methods, the following can be said. In situations with a Pareto-optimum the prices used for the appraisal of projects were equal to the relevant market prices. When there was no Pareto-optimum as a result of distortions caused by taxes, externalities, and other market imperfections, second-best rules were used for the calculation of shadow prices. The shadow prices were then equal to the market prices plus or minus a correction because of these distortions. The Pigouvian methods were extended versions of the neo-Paretian methods which took account of differences in income. The neo-Paretian and Pigouvian methods were generally such that they could be used for the evaluation of actual projects. Furthermore, they were firmly rooted in welfare theory. Thus, theory and practice went hand in hand.[2]

In the sixties and seventies a number of methods were developed for situations of unemployment. Two lines of development can be distinguished. The first one was strongly related to the traditional approach. It was based on welfare theory, and on the use of dual methods. The second line of development was quite different; it concerned primal methods without a welfare-theoretical foundation.

The first line of development mainly concerned less developed countries, in which un(der)employment was a common occurrence. For these countries neo-Paretian and Pigouvian methods were developed that dealt with non-clearing labour markets, but also with distortions not necessarily related to unemployment, such as distortions caused by tariffs. From the end of the sixties some of these methods were based on integral models of the national economies. As these models gave a reasonable description of the actual situation, the resulting shadow prices could be used for the appraisal of actual projects.

With regard to developed market economies, in which for a long time full employment was the rule rather than the exception, progress was much slower. Some dual methods based on welfare theory were developed, but for a long time they were only based on a partial analysis of the economy. Integral dual methods were developed at the beginning of the eighties only. These methods were all based on neo-Paretian welfare theory.

The second line of development mainly related to the use of input–output models for the estimation of the effects of projects. This concerned less developed countries and, later, developed countries too. Generally the evaluation of the estimated effects of a project was based on an ad hoc procedure, but in one case the effects were evaluated in a more systematic way. The second line of development also included the use of econometric macro-models for the calculation of the effects of large projects in developed countries.

Thus, until the eighties the picture was clear. On the one hand there were dual methods based on welfare theory. On the other hand there were primal methods without a welfare-theoretical foundation. Since the beginning of the eighties, however, the picture has become more confused, due to the development of new approaches. Some new approaches concern the analysis of the effects of projects with the help of a theoretical or an empirical macroeconomic model, and the evaluation of these effects on the basis of neo-Paretian welfare theory. Thus, these approaches are primal approaches based on welfare theory. Another new approach is a dual approach without a welfare-theoretical foundation. This approach concerns the use of an econometric macro-model for the calculation of shadow prices. These approaches have not yet reached full maturity, but they provide some interesting insights.

Contents of this chapter

This Chapter discusses existing methods of project appraisal in situations of unemployment. It has two limitations. First, dual methods based on a partial analysis of the economy will not be discussed. These methods are inferior to the dual methods based on an integral analysis of the economy which will be discussed below, and they need no special attention here.[3] Second, when a method of project appraisal takes account of differences in the marginal utility of consumption, this will be neglected. This implies that when a Pigouvian method is discussed, that part of the method which is specifically Pigouvian will be neglected, and it will be described as if it were a neo-Paretian method. In relation to this, in the remainder of this study welfare theory can be regarded as a synonymn for neo-Paretian welfare theory.

The structure of this Chapter is as follows: in Section 3.2 attention is paid to methods without a welfare-theoretical foundation. Section 3.2.1 discusses primal methods based on an input-output model, and Section 3.2.2 primal methods based on an econometric macro-model. Section 3.2.3 deals with dual methods based on an econometric macro-model.

Methods based on welfare theory are the subject of Section 3.3. Section 3.3.1 pays attention to dual methods. Section 3.3.2 deals with primal methods based on a theoretical model of the economy. Section 3.3.3 deals with an attempt to evaluate the effects of large projects, as calculated by means of an econometric macro-model, on the basis of welfare theory.

In Section 3.4 special attention is paid to the problem of consistency between project apppraisal and macroeconomic analysis and policy. Section 3.5 discusses the implications of this Chapter for the development of an improved method of project appraisal.

Before discussing these points it is useful to give some definitions. Primary inputs are land and natural resources, labour and entrepreneurship, and capital goods. All other inputs are intermediate inputs. The direct spending effects of an expenditure on a certain good are the effects on the production and the use of inputs of the firm that produces this good. They exclude the further effects of the purchase of intermediate inputs by that firm. The first-round spending effects of an expenditure are the direct spending effects of this expenditure plus the backward linkage effects up to the use of the primary inputs. The second-round spending effects are the direct spending effects, plus the backward linkage effects up to the use of the primary inputs, of increases in consumption and (possibly) investment resulting from the increase in income and production in the first round of the spending process. The second-round spending effects plus the spending effects that occur in the successive rounds are called multiplier effects.

3.2. Methods without a welfare-theoretical foundation

3.2.1. Primal methods based on an input–output model

Primal methods based on the use of an input–output model have been used by many researchers. This section will be dedicated to the most advanced of these methods, the 'effects method' of project evaluation. The starting point of this method is the idea that project policy should be consistent with macro- or mesoeconomic policies. This implies that criteria for the evaluation of projects should partly depend on macro-

or mesoeconomic objectives and constraints. The method emphasizes practical application. It was developed in the late sixties by Prou and Chervel for use in developing countries (Prou and Chervel, 1970).[4] Recently the method has also been applied in France.[5]

The first part of the method consists of the study of the micro-economic viability of the analysed project. Questions about the demand for the project's output, the availability of labour at the project site, etc. are dealt with, and the private profitability of the project is estimated. If the results are too negative, the project is rejected right away.

Second, the first-round spending effects are analysed by means of an input–output model. To explain this, it is assumed for the moment that the project is an import substitution project. Two situations are compared: the situation with project, in which a product is made locally, and the situation without project, in which the same product is imported. For the situation with project, the first-round spending effects of the investment in the project itself, which is called direct investment, on government revenues, local salaries, business income and imports are calculated. Moreover, the annual first-round spending effects of the payments to labour and other inputs used for the operation of the project on the same four variables are calculated. In the situation without project there is no direct investment. The product in question is imported, which mainly leads to changes in imports, tariff revenues, and the income of the domestic transportation industry. The annual first-round spending effects of importing the product on the four variables mentioned above are calculated. The latter are deducted from the annual first-round spending effects of operating the project, which gives the net annual changes resulting from operating the project.

When the project is not an import substitution project, but a project of which the output is a consumption good sold on the domestic market, the method will take into account that selling the output of the project may lead to a decrease in the sales of other domestic producers, and that this will have negative effects on the four variables mentioned above. The method can also be used to analyse types of projects other than the ones mentioned above; for details the reader is referred to the relevant literature.

A special feature is that the calculations with the input–output model are based on the following assumption: if the total demand for a certain input is satisfied by national production in a certain proportion, then an increase in demand for this input as a result of the project will be satisfied in the same proportion by national production, even if the national productive capacity is fully employed without project. The underlying assumption is that in the latter case productive capacity will be increased by additional investment. This investment is called indirect investment.

The third part of the method concerns the evaluation of the outcomes of the calculations. The 'effects method' is especially meant to evaluate projects in the light of macroeconomic planning. The aim of macroeconomic planning is to analyse the economy, to specify objectives and constraints, and to indicate how objectives can be maximized under the existing constraints. To evaluate a project in this light means to analyse how it relates to objectives and constraints.

Very often the major macroeconomic objective is economic growth, while the availability of investment funds is regarded as the major constraint. In connection with this the 'effects method' takes as its 'preferred criterion' the ratio *a*/*I*, where '*a*' is the net change in yearly value added resulting from the operation of the project, and '*I*' is direct plus indirect investment. In addition to this criterion, differences in time spans of projects and in the time stream of changes in value added may also be taken into account. Projects are ranked according to their *a*/*I*, possibly with a correction for the time factor, and the ones ranking highest are selected. The criterion mentioned above need however not be the only one used. For example, if one of the objectives of macroeconomic policy is to diminish unemployment, the effects on unemployment can be a criterion.

The first point of criticism is that the criteria might not take all relevant considerations into account. For example, no interest rate is used for the evaluation. Of course this problem could easily be solved by adding one or more additional criteria. But then another problem arises: how to evaluate a project on the basis of more than one criterion. So far the advocates of the method have given no adequate solution to this problem.

The second point of criticism concerns some problems that are inevitably linked up with calculations that are done by means of an input–output model. One problem is that input-output models cannot take differences in economic regime into account. The use of an input–output model implicitly assumes that an increase in effective demand will increase production, which implies that there is Keynesian unemployment. Another problem is that input–output models are not capable of analysing monetary relations. Therefore, the macro-economic effects of financing a project cannot be calculated. This is probably the reason why the budget for private investment and the government budget are treated as constraints in the effects method. However, from a Keynesian point of view, in times of depression private investment is too low. Therefore, if the expenditures on a project would lead to an increase in indirect investment, this is an advantage. Consequently indirect investment should not be treated as a constraint. Moreover, because the government budget is treated as a constraint, the method cannot help answer the question whether or not the desirable level of government expenditure should be influenced by project selection. As was shown in the previous Chapter, this question can be important.

It can be concluded that the idea of first calculating the effects of a project and then evaluating them on the basis of practical criteria in a way which is consistent with macro- and mesoeconomic policies, seems sound. However, the problems connected with the calculation of the effects with an input–output model only are a serious impediment to the method, while the problem of the evaluation of the effects has not been solved adequately either.

3.2.2. Primal methods based on an econometric macro-model

A number of researchers have used econometric macro-models to calculate the effects of large projects, or of portfolios of projects. Essentially, the approach is as follows. First, the future economic development without project (portfolio) is simulated with the econometric macro-model. Second, the investments related to the project (portfolio) are inserted into the model, and other adaptations are made to take account of other specific characteristics of the project (portfolio). Third, the economic development with project (portfolio) is simulated. Fourth, the effects of the project (portfolio) are calculated as the difference between the economic development with project (portfolio) and that without project (portfolio). These effects consist of the effects on macroeconomic variables such as employment, private consumption, government deficit, trade balance, private investment, price level, etc. over a number of years. Once the calculations have been done, it is left to the decision-maker to evaluate the effects. (See, for some Dutch studies, Van den Beld and Middelhoek, 1971; Driehuis *et al.*, 1983; CPB, 1983a; NEI, 1983; LMO, 1985; Klaassen *et al.* 1987; CPB, 1989.)

A special point of interest is the calculation of the first-round spending effects. In order to calculate these effects different methods are used. One method is to attach a mesoeconomic model, which distinguishes different sectors of production, to the macroeconomic model. The spendings of the project are inserted into appropriate sectors of production. The first-round spending effects are then calculated with the mesoeconomic model, and the outcomes are automatically inserted into the macroeconomic model (e.g. Driehuis *et al.*, 1983). Another method is to calculate the first-round spending effects of the project separately. This may be done by means of specific information about the first-round spending effects of the project, and by means of an input–output model that is not linked to the macro-model. The results are then inserted into the econometric macro-model (e.g. LMO, 1985). The advantage of this method is that it pays more attention to project-specific characteristics. Furthermore, the input–output model used generally distinguishes a larger number of sectors than a mesoeconomic model attached to a macroeconomic model.

The main advantages of this conventional macroeconomic method of project appraisal are the following. First, the effects of a project are analysed in an integral way. Second, in many cases the model used is a model that is also used to help formulate macroeconomic policy. This has advantages regarding the consistency between project appraisal and macroeconomic policy, a subject which will be discussed in Section 3.4. Finally, because different base-runs can be distinguished, the analysis can relate to different economic regimes. However, the last advantage should be regarded as a theoretical advantage, as the studies mentioned above are based on one base-run only.

A first point of criticism is that in the studies mentioned above there are no good criteria for evaluating the effects. In a study which was not mentioned above an attempt has been made to develop such criteria on the basis of welfare theory. This study will be discussed in Section 3.3.3.

Another point is tied up with the fact that there are different methods of financing a government project: capital market loans, business taxes, wage taxes, other direct taxes, liquidity creation, or expenditure cuts elsewhere, each method having its own specific macro-economic effects. The macro-economic effects of a project can heavily depend upon the method of finance chosen.[6] Therefore, clear criteria for the choice of the method of finance should be established. Up to the present these criteria have not been formulated, apart from the study discussed in Section 3.3.3.[7]

Up to now the conventional macroeconometric method has only been used for the evaluation of large projects or portfolios of projects. Econometric macro-models have never been used for the evaluation of small projects. There are two studies in which some remarks regarding this point have been made. Malinvaud *et al.* (1983) state that simulations with econometric macro-models should only be made with regard to large-scale policies and projects. Simulations should not be made with regard to individual projects of small and medium size. The argument is as follows. The smaller projects are, the more specific their characteristics. In theory one can take these characteristics into account by introducing new variables into the model which reflect the differences between project-specific characteristics and characteristics of the macro-model. However, this makes less sense if there are too many new variables.[8] Zuidema (1982) states that, if the project is small, the effects of the project will not be perceptible on the national level. I have found no other studies in which this point is discussed. Apparently, it is taken for granted that it is not sensible to use econometric macro-models for the analysis of small projects.

A more thorough analysis of the problems related to the use of econometric macro-models for the analysis of small projects will be given in Chapter 4. It will be shown that, at first sight at least, these problems are serious, but that nevertheless it is sensible to use econometric macro-models for the analysis of small projects.

There are some other points of criticism concerning the conventional macro-econometric method of project appraisal, but at this stage in the argument they are less important. For purposes of a clear sequence of exposition they will not be discussed until Chapter 4.

3.2.3. A dual method based on an econometric macro-model

Malinvaud *et al.* (1983) devised a method for the calculation of shadow prices that is not based on the objective of utility maximization. This method comprises the following. First, the objective function of the government is defined. This objective function includes variables such as unemployment, the government deficit, and the balance on current account.

Second, an econometric macro-model is used to carry out three excercises. In the first excercise the optimal rate of exchange is calculated. This is the rate of exchange that leads to the macroeconomic development that is best geared to the objective function. In order to determine this optimal exchange rate, an iterative procedure is used, in which the effects of various different exchange rates on economic development and on the objective function are analysed. Two similar procedures are carried out to determine the optimal wage rate and the optimal interest rate.

Third, these three optimal prices are used to calculate the shadow prices of inputs and outputs of projects. The shadow prices of imported inputs and exported outputs are set equal to the market prices multiplied by the ratio between the optimal exchange rate and the market exchange rate. The shadow price of labour is set equal to the optimal wage rate. The shadow interest rate is set equal to the optimal interest rate. The shadow prices of intermediate inputs bought from domestic producers are set equal to the shadow costs of producing them, the latter being determined in the same way as the costs of a project at shadow prices. Fourth, government projects are analysed on the basis of these shadow prices. Projects are accepted if the present value of the benefits minus costs at shadow prices is positive.

The approach is in its initital stage. As yet only the shadow exchange rate, the shadow wage rate and the shadow interest rate have been calculated. Shadow prices for intermediate inputs bought from domestic producers have not been calculated. The objective function of the government has not been determined. Instead, intuition was used to weigh the different objectives of the government against one another. In relation to this, the researchers state that they have not calculated optimal prices, but 'satisfactory prices'.[9]

The main problem related to this approach can be explained by using the optimal wage rate as an example. The fact that a certain wage rate is the optimal wage rate means the following: if everywhere in the economy the market wage rate equalled that specific wage rate, the economic development would be optimal. This implies that the outcomes of the calculations of Malinvaud *et al.* (1983) can be used as a basis for wage policy. However, it is unrealistic to assume that both employers and labour unions would agree with a wage policy based on these calculations. Thus, in reality market wages will probably not be equal to optimal wages.

According to Malinvaud *et al.* (1983) the outcomes of their calculations can be used for project appraisal in a situation in which market wages are not equal to optimal wages. However, in my opinion this is not justifiable. This can be explained as follows. When market wages are equal to optimal wages, it is indeed justifiable to accept a certain project which is profitable at the optimal wage rate (and at other optimal prices). When market wages are not equal to optimal wages, it may be justifiable to reject the same project. For instance, consider a situation in which market wages are higher than optimal wages. This implies that labourers will be paid more than the optimal wage rate. Therefore in this situation the payment of wages to labourers employed in a public project will lead to a higher increase in the government deficit than in a situation in which market wages equal optimal wages. This higher increase in the government deficit can have negative effects. Malinvaud *et al.* (1983) do not take account of these effects (their calculations do not take account of the difference between the optimal wage rate and the market wage rate).

More in general, the method neglects various kinds of changes in the financial positions of economic actors caused by the differences between market prices and optimal prices. Because changes in financial positions can have important macroeconomic effects, this is not justifiable.

Apart from this, the fact that the calculations of Malinvaud *et al.* (1983) are completely focused on the situation in which market prices are equal to optimal prices implies that they cannot take account of a number of other effects of a project which may occur in reality. For instance, they neglect the fact that the implementation of a large number of projects may lead to an increase in the wage rate (via the Phillips-curve), and in other prices, which may have further negative macroeconomic effects.

The question is whether these problems can be solved by adapting the method. I do not see how this can be done; as far as I can see, the method of Malinvaud *et al.* (1983) cannot be used as a basis for further research.

3.3. Methods with a welfare-theoretical foundation

3.3.1. Dual methods

This section discusses existing dual methods based on an integral model of the economy. These methods have the following common characteristics. The models used are general disequilibrium models, in which at least one market does not clear by price adjustments. It is assumed that the objective of the government is to maximize social welfare. Social welfare is defined as the present value of the consumption of goods and leisure time, expressed in terms of willingness to pay. The government has different instruments at its disposal to realize its objective. Some of these instruments are tariffs and taxes. Another instrument is the selection of public projects.

The government is faced with certain constraints. Some of these follow directly from the model of the economy. Other constraints do not follow directly from the model, for instance a constraint on the government deficit. Thus, the problem is how to use the instruments such that, given the constraints, social welfare is maximized.

The use of instruments other than the selection of government projects is assumed to be given at the moment project appraisal starts. This may reflect the fact that these instruments are not analysed at all (for example because it is politically impossible to use them). It may also reflect the fact that the other instruments have been analysed first, and that it is subsequently assumed that they are used in the best possible way at the moment project appraisal starts.

The most important dual method is the Little–Mirrlees method, and it will be the first to be discussed. After that attention will be paid to some recent developments.

The Little–Mirrlees method

The Little–Mirrlees method was developed in 1968 (see Little and Mirrlees, 1974).[10] The method is Pigouvian. However, given what has been said before, that part of the method which is specifically Pigouvian will be neglected below, so that the method will be described as if it were based on neo-Paretian welfare theory. This considered, it can be said that the method is based on the assumption that the objective of the government is to maximize social welfare, the latter being defined as the present value of the consumption of goods and leisure time, expressed in terms of willingness to pay. The description of the Little–Mirrlees method given below only concerns its essentials; the method is more sophisticated than indicated below.

The model underlying the Little–Mirrlees method has, among other things, the following characteristics. The labour market does not clear; there is involuntary unemployment and underemployment. Capital goods are fully employed, and total supply is (more or less: see below) determined by the capital stock. The deficit on the trade balance is equal to the difference between domestic demand and domestic supply of goods and services. Increases in domestic demand or decreases in domestic supply will (more or less: see below) lead to an increase in this deficit.

Supply on the capital market consists of private savings plus supply from abroad. Demand on the capital market consists of the demand of private investors plus the demand of the government. The capital market clears. Both private investors and the government use all the funds they borrow immediately for investment. (Public funds can also be used for transfers of income, but this is neglected in this elementary exposition.) There is no hoarding of money.

In this exposition it is assumed that there is a constraint on foreign borrowing, which implies that there is a constraint on the balance on current account. Private investors do not borrow from abroad. The government always borrows as much money abroad as is possible given the constraint on the balance on current account. There is also a constraint on the government deficit. This constraint is at least as big as the constraint on the balance on current account. The government deficit, which equals government borrowing, is as high as possible given this constraint. Private savings do not depend on the rate of interest, and are determined by incomes. Private borrowing, which equals private investment, is determined by the rate of interest. The rate of interest is determined on the capital market in such a way that private borrowing equals the difference between private savings and government demand on the domestic capital market. Given all this, a marginal increase in private savings will lead to an equal increase in private investment.

The characteristics of the model mentioned above imply that a shortage of aggregate effective demand cannot exist. Nevertheless, an increase in spending of a specific type does have specific effects. This point needs an extensive explanation. Let us assume that the government increases its investment. Let us first look at the spending effects. In the model an increase in spending of a specific type has specific first-round spending effects. These effects consist of first-round increases in production, employment, the use of capital goods, wages, profits, taxes, tariffs, and imports in specific sectors of the economy. Taken by themselves, the increases in wages and profits lead, among other things, to an increase in the spending on consumption goods. In the second round of the spending process this will lead to further changes of the type mentioned above. In the subsequent rounds of the spending process similar effects occur, although on a smaller scale. The increases in wages and profits also lead to an increase in private savings. Other effects of the increase in spending will be discussed later. The model of the economy contains among other things an input–output model, so that the effects of the specific increase in spending mentioned above can be estimated in a precise manner.

As stated above, an increase in spending of a specific type leads to an increase in the use of capital goods in certain sectors of the economy. However, capital goods are fully employed. Furthermore, private investment is constrained. Therefore, the use of capital goods in certain sectors of the economy leads to a decrease in the availability of capital goods for other sectors. Therefore, it leads to a decrease in production, employment, wages, profits, taxes, tariffs, and imports in other sectors. This decrease has further multiplier effects, and effects on private savings, too. Furthermore, the decrease in production mentioned above implies that fewer outputs are made available. Given the model of the economy as described earlier, this decrease in available outputs leads in the final analysis to a deterioration of the trade balance via either a decrease in exports or an increase in imports.

Increases in employment in certain sectors of the economy resulting from the spending process described above lead partly to decreases in unemployment, partly to decreases in underemployment, and partly to decreases in employment elsewhere. In relation to the decreases in employment and underemployment there will be a decrease in production elsewhere. The value of this loss of production is estimated. Subsequently, it is essentially treated in the same way as the loss of production caused by the use of capital goods.

As stated above, changes in spending lead to changes in private savings and government revenues from taxes and tariffs. Both private savings and government revenues are supposed to be invested. This leads to an increase in the stock of capital goods, and therefore to an increase in future production. In relation to this, the future levels of employment, private consumption, private savings, and government revenues from taxes and tariffs are increased. The increases in future private savings and government revenues cause an increase in future investment. In the more distant future this leads to increases in employment, private consumption, private savings and government revenues, etc. The model can be used to calculate all future changes in private consumption and employment that are the result of a change in private savings and of a change in government revenues from taxes and tariffs. It is assumed for the moment that the model has an infinite time horizon.

Attention has been paid above to the spending effects of an increase in government investment. It is now time to deal with the question how this increase in investment is financed. Since the total government budget for investment is given, an increase in investment for a specific project implies that other government investments have to be curtailed. (Note that it has been assumed in this elementary exposition that government funds are only used for government investment.) The effects of this are the opposite of the effects of an increase in government revenues (see also the preceding paragraph).

As stated above, the increase in spending leads to an increase in imports. This increase in imports does not need to be discussed separately, because it can be regarded as a reflection of the fact that the original increase in the government deficit is not completely counterbalanced by increases in government revenues and private savings. Because of this (alternative) investment will be curtailed. The curtailment of investment is related to the constraints on private and public borrowing which, as discussed above, are (partly) a reflection of the constraint on the balance on current account.

What happens if a government project produces an output that is sold on the market? Two effects can be distinguished. First, government revenues increase. As will be clear by now, this has positive effects because it will lead to an increase in government investment. With regard to the second effect, two cases can be distinguished. In the first case the output is exported. In this case the second effect is an improvement of the trade balance, which does not have any effects on the rest of the economy, apart from effects that can be regarded as a reflection of the first effect (compare the discussion in the previous paragraph). In the second case the output is sold on the domestic market. Selling the output of the project on the domestic market implies that part of the budget of domestic buyers of goods and services is used for buying this output. This implies that spending on other domestic products will decrease.[11] Thus, a decrease in domestic spending occurs, which has effects which are more or less the opposite of the effects of the increase in spending discussed above. Of course the exact effects will be influenced by specific characteristics.

The description of the model of the economy and the objective of the government can be completed by emphasizing the following: the present value of all future changes in consumption resulting from an increase in investment with one guilder is greater than one guilder. This implies that the allocation of income between savings and consumption is not optimal; private savings, which are determined by income and not by the interest rate, are too low. This, in itself, implies that it would be better if demand were such that the income of people with a high propensity to save would be increased. Resources such as capital goods and certain types of labour are scarce, while other types of labour are un(der)employed. It would therefore be useful if demand were more directed to goods that are produced with resources that are relatively abundant. To summarize: there is no shortage of total effective demand, but the composition of demand is not optimal.

It is now easy to explain how shadow prices for inputs and outputs of government projects are calculated. In order to do so, it is assumed for expositional purposes that the value of leisure time is zero. Given the objective of the government mentioned before, this implies that in the final analysis only changes in consumption are important. Let us first deal with the shadow price of a certain input. The purchase of this input by the government is inserted into the model, and the effects of the purchase of this input on consumption over a long period of time are calculated. These effects will, broadly speaking, be similar to the effects of an increase in government expenditure discussed above. However, specific differences will exist because every input has its own characteristics. Subsequently, the present value of all changes in consumption caused by the purchase of the input is calculated. The changes in consumption are valued at market prices, and the discount rate used reflects the private time preference rate. A similar procedure is used with regard to all other inputs and outputs. Thus, a certain change in the present value of changes in consumption is attached to each input and output. The shadow prices of all inputs and outputs are then calculated as being equal to the relevant changes in this present value. The shadow prices are normalized by changing the numéraire.

The description given above is not a correct description of the Little–Mirrlees method yet. There is an important difference between the calculation of the shadow prices as described above and the calculation as done by Little and Mirrlees. This difference can be explained as follows. From a private point of view one can better buy an input in year 2 for 1000 guilders (in real prices) than buy the same input in year 1 for 1000 guilders (because of the existence of interest). Intuitively, the same holds good from a social point of view. In other words, it is intuitively plausible that buying a certain input in year 2 has a less negative effect on the present value (in a reference year) of all changes in consumption than buying the same input in year 1. The above will enable the reader to understand (intuitively) that the shadow price of an input or output bought or sold in a certain year, calculated as explained above, is higher than the shadow price of the same input or output bought or sold in a subsequent year. However, this is not in line with convention in project appraisal.

In the Little–Mirrlees method, which is in line with convention in this respect, the following procedure is followed: all shadow prices of a certain input or output are equated with the shadow price of the same input or output bought or sold in year 1, and the value of inputs and outputs bought or sold in later years is discounted by an appropriate accounting rate of interest. This accounting rate of interest is such that the discounted values of inputs and outputs, valued at the set of shadow prices used by Little and Mirrlees, are equal to the values of these inputs and outputs at the shadow prices calculated as explained in the previous paragraphs. Given the characteristics of the model and the objective of the government, this accounting rate of interest is the same for all types of inputs and outputs. (In Chapter 7 it will be shown that this does not hold good for all economic models.)

As stated above, in the final analysis only changes in consumption are important. All other changes are only important insofar as they affect consumption: they have an indirect value. Still assuming that the model has an infinite time horizon, it is not necessary to pay specific attention to this indirect value, because all effects of these other changes on consumption are already calculated by means of the model. In case the model has a finite time horizon, attention should be paid to the indirect value of these other changes in as far as they affect consumption levels after the period analysed by means of the model. Regarding this point the reader is referred to Little and Mirrlees (1974).

Some implications of the model for the shadow prices are the following. The shadow price of an input will tend to be low when the input consists of unskilled labour which was formerly un(der)employed. The shadow price of an input will tend to be high when its production involves an intensive use of capital goods. The shadow price of an output will tend to be high when it is exported. The shadow price of an output sold on the domestic market will tend to be low, especially if it leads to a decrease in the sale and production of goods of which the production involves the use of many formerly unemployed labourers.

A point that deserves particular attention is the following. In principle (but generally not in practice), the method is based on the idea that the government budget is not given. In principle, the method can be used in such a way that the government budget, and foreign borrowing, is made dependent upon the outcomes of project appraisal. More specifically, the method can take into account that the government budget should be increased when the marginal government project, financed by an increase in foreign borrowing, has positive effects on balance, and vice versa. In this context the following iterative procedure is used. First, project appraisal is based on the assumption that the government budget is given at a certain level. Second, the outcomes of project appraisal are used to change the level of the government budget. Third, project appraisal is based on the assumption that the government budget is given at its new level, etc. This implies that 'macroeconomic policy' is partly dependent upon the outcomes of project appraisal. This point will be discussed further at a later stage in this study.

With regard to the method, three possible lines of criticism can be distinguished. First, one might argue that the Little–Mirrlees model does not give a good description of reality because of its theoretical structure. Second, one might criticize the estimated value of the parameters of the model. Third, the method is rather complicated, which makes it difficult for a decision-maker to understand what is meant when it is stated that the present value of the net benefits of a project at shadow prices is positive.

Only the first line of criticism will be discussed in detail. Before doing this, the following must be mentioned: Little and Mirrlees did not advise using their method in developed western countries. However, in the context of this study it is useful to pose the question whether it would be possible to do so. The discussion of this question will be mixed with the criticism of the method. Of course negative answers to this question cannot be regarded as a criticism of Little and Mirrlees' work.

The model of the economy is based on some specific assumptions. All private savings are either used for private investment or for government expenditure. An increase in private savings leads to an equal increase in private investment. Given that the marginal productivity of private investment is estimated to be higher than the private time preference rate, these assumptions imply that an increase in private savings should be considered a positive point. Given these assumptions the basic Keynesian problem, which is that excess savings can lead to a decrease in national income, can never occur. For many less developed countries these assumptions may be justifiable. However, their validity may be questioned for at least some LDCs, such as the Latin-American countries which have experienced high ratios of capital flight. Furthermore, their validity may be questioned for many developed western countries. In these countries an increase in private savings may cause a decrease in growth or even a depression. Insofar as this is the case, increases in private savings should be valued negatively instead of positively.

A related point is that according to the Little–Mirrlees model an increase in effective demand does not have positive effects, except when it involves a relative shift in demand towards sectors producing at low social costs. This is related to the assumption that capital goods are always fully employed, and that the increase in the stock of capital goods is determined by private savings and the constraint on foreign borrowing, not by effective demand. Again, for some LDCs such a description may come close to reality. For other LDCs and for developed capitalist countries this may not be the case.

The value of an increase in government revenues, and the costs of an increase in government expenditures, are determined by estimating the effects on future consumption of an increase in government investment. Now it is questionable whether such a procedure can be applied to countries which have considerable government debts to foreign countries or foreign institutions, which are to be repaid in due time under penalty of losing credibility. In these countries the total amount of money used to pay foreign creditors is not fixed, but is dependent on the financial possibilities of the moment. This implies that there is another way of using an increase in government revenues, which is to use it in order to decrease foreign debt. When increases in government revenues are used in this way, the value of government revenues does not depend upon the value of future consumption resulting from government investment but on the value (in terms of consumption) of not losing credibility. A similar reasoning applies to a situation in which there is a considerable government debt which is to a large extent financed at the domestic capital market, and in which marginal increases in government revenues are used to decrease the government deficit. The benefits of increases in government revenues should then be equalled to the benefits of having a smaller government debt. The latter benefits might, for example, include the benefits of an increase in investors' confidence, or of having more room to combat future depressions by a Keynesian policy.

The Little–Mirrlees method is one of the major accomplishments of cost benefit analysis. It is based on an integral analysis of the economy, and has its roots in welfare theory. It can be used for the analysis of actual projects because the model used gives a reasonable description of the economies of a number of underdeveloped countries. However, the assumptions of Little and Mirrlees are not valid with regard to all LDCs. Furthermore, these assumptions are such that the LM-rules cannot be used for project evaluation in developed capitalist countries.

Recent developments

In recent years, a number of studies has been published about dual approaches with a welfare-theoretical foundation.[12] In relation to the fact that my criticism of the Little–Mirrlees method was essentially a criticism of the model used, attention will only be paid to approaches that are based on a model which is essentially different from Little and Mirrlees' model. I have found two such approaches.

The starting point of the two approaches is that it is the objective of the government to maximize social welfare, defined as before. The two approaches are based on different models of the economy, and distinguish different constraints. These will be described below. Given the model and the constraints, and given the objective of the government, formulae for shadow prices for inputs and outputs of government projects are derived. The procedure for the derivation of these formulae is essentially the same as the procedure used by Little and Mirrlees. Unlike the Little–Mirrlees method, these formulae are not used to derive shadow prices that can be used for the appraisal of concrete projects, which is related to the fact that the empirical values of the parameters of the model are not estimated.

The models and the constraints on which the two approaches are based can be described in the following way. That of Fourgeaud *et al.* (1986) is a one-period model, without savings and investments. Three final goods are distinguished: exportables, domestic consumption goods and imported consumption goods. Production is determined by demand as long as unemployment exists. Demand for domestic final goods equals exports plus demand for domestic consumption goods. Exports are exogenous. Demand for domestic consumption goods is a function of the income of households, and of the prices of domestic consumption goods and imported consumption goods. Domestic consumption goods are produced by private firms and by state-owned firms. Both use labour and imported inputs in fixed proportions, but the technology used may differ between them. Income of households equals wages plus transfers of income from private firms and from the public sector. These transfers may be negative. Transfers of income from private firms to households are equal to the profits of private firms or to the losses of private firms multiplied by –1, and transfers of income from the public sector to households are equal to the surplus of the public sector or to the deficit of the public sector multiplied by –1. All transfers can be realized without costs. All prices are fixed. The supply of labour is given. An important constraint is the production function. Another constraint is that the balance on current account must not be negative. Given the model, unemployment will exist if, among other things, exports are too low.

The ultimate aim of the approach is the derivation of formulae for shadow prices for inputs and outputs of state-owned firms. These firms may produce, for example, consumption goods that substitute consumption goods produced by the private sector, using a technology that differs from the one used in the private sector in that it needs relatively much labour and relatively few imported inputs.

The model of Marchand *et al.* (1984, 1985) is a two-period model of an economy without a foreign sector. In it, households consume goods and leisure time. At the beginning of the first period, households have a stock of goods that can be used as consumption goods or, alternatively, as capital goods. The part of this stock that is not consumed in the first period is supplied on the capital market in the form of loans. Households also supply labour on the labour market. Private firms and state-owned firms use capital (borrowed in the first period) and labour in order to produce consumption goods which are sold in the second period. The 'income' of the households in the second period equals wages, loan repayments and interest, and transfers of income from private firms and from the public sector. Loan repayments in the second period are equal to loans contracted in the first period. Transfers of income from private firms to households are equal to the profits of private firms or to the losses of private firms multiplied by –1, and transfers of income from the public sector to households are equal to the surplus of the public sector or to the deficit of the public sector multiplied by –1. All transfers can be realized without costs. Payments for consumption goods bought in the second period by the households equal the 'income' of the households. The price of consumption goods is flexible, and the market for consumption goods clears. The wage rate and the rate of interest are fixed. In relation to this, it is possible that the labour market, or the capital market, or both, do not clear. If both fail to clear, there are four possible regimes. For example, if both the wage rate and the rate of interest are too high to clear the market, there is 'classical unemployment'. If the wage rate is too high, and the rate of interest too low, there is 'Keynesian unemployment'. A remarkable point is the following. If the interest rate is too high, there are, initially, excess savings. However, this is immediately perceived by the households, which react at once by increasing their demand for consumption goods. This implies that excess savings cannot lead to a decline in effective demand. An important constraint is the production function.

In commenting on these approaches, it can be noted in the first place that they are based on many simplifying assumptions. Transfers of money can always be realized without costs. It is not possible that excess savings lead to a decline in aggregate demand. Many macroeconomic phenomena, such as inflation, expectations, government deficits, and deficits on current account, are either not treated at all or they are treated in a way that is highly unrealistic. Because of this, the approaches, unlike the Little–Mirrlees method, do not provide useful rules for the evaluation of concrete projects. Of course, the authors mentioned above clearly recognize this. Marchand *et al.* (1985) conclude their paper by remarking that extensions of their model would be worthwhile. Fourgeaud *et al.* (1986) are rather vague about the implications of the fact that the model they use is based on many simplifying assumptions.

Before supplying extensions to the models mentioned above, the question can be asked whether this would make sense. More specifically, can approaches like the ones described above be regarded as the beginning of a sensible and fruitful research programme that will ultimately lead to the calculation of shadow prices that can be used for the evaluation of concrete projects in developed capitalist economies? If the models were extended to capture more macroeconomic phenomena in a more realistic way, they would start to resemble the complicated econometric macromodels that have been constructed in the context of macroeconomics. This implies that extending the models described above would imply that one would have to undertake econometric modelling within the particular context of project appraisal. This is inefficient. Instead of occupying oneself with macroeconomic modelling in order to obtain shadow prices, it would be far more efficient to use an existing model. This point will be pursued later in this study.

3.3.2. Primal methods based on a theoretical model

This section discusses primal approaches based on an abstract model of the economy and on welfare theory. Such approaches have been developed by Johansson (1982), Johansson and Löfgren (1989), Nentjes and Zuidema (1987) and Nentjes (1989). The point of departure of these studies is that it is the objective of the government to maximize social welfare, defined as before. The effects of a government project on consumption and employment in one or more years are analysed by means of an abstract model of the economy. These changes are expressed in terms of changes in social welfare, and the project is accepted if the net change in social welfare is positive. The studies differ from one another in that different models of the economy are used.

The difference between these primal approaches and the dual approaches discussed in the previous section is the following. In the former approaches the effects of the project as a whole are analysed and evaluated. In the latter approaches the effects of individual inputs and outputs are first analysed and evaluated (expressed in terms of shadow prices) separately. After that the profitability of the project at shadow prices is calculated. In principle, the same models and the same social welfare functions can be used for both approaches. If the same models and the same social welfare functions were used, the conclusion regarding the acceptability of a project of both approaches would be the same (at least, if the models used are linear models, which holds good with regard to the models discussed in this section and the previous section). However, as will become clear below, in practice it happens that different models are used. (The social welfare functions used are essentially the same.)

Given this, and given that the dual approaches have been discussed at length, we will only pay attention to the models used. Let us first discuss the model on which the study of Johansson (1982) is based. Johansson presents a Barro–Grossman model, which is capable of analyzing certain aspects of the economy under different regimes of disequilibrium (orthodox Keynesian unemployment, Keynesian unemployment, classical unemployment and repressed inflation). The model is based on rigorous assumptions, the following of which are the most important. Time and investment do not exist. Any budget deficit of the government, the firms or the households, is automatically neutralized by an income transfer. Finally, prices are fixed.

Given this model, it will be clear that the criticism on the dual approaches discussed in the previous section also applies to the approach of Johansson. Finally, it can be mentioned that the models of Johansson and Löfgren (1989), Nentjes and Zuidema (1987) and Nentjes (1989) are such that the same criticism applies.

3.3.3. A primal method based on an econometric macro-model

An interesting approach is that of Zuidema (1982, pp. 122–157). Here an attempt is made to evaluate the macroeconomic effects of (part of) a large project as calculated by means of an econometric macro-model on the basis of welfare theory. The first part of Zuidema's approach consists of the calculation of the macroeconomic effects of (part of) a large public project. This part of the approach is more or less similar to the approach discussed in Section 3.2.2. One difference is that Zuidema confines himself to the costs of the project, that is, to the expenditures on the project. The benefits of the project (e.g. improved recreational facilities) are not analysed by means of the econometric macro-model. Zuidema uses the model to calculate the effects of an increase in government expenditure with 1 billion guilders, and he distinguishes between four different methods of finance. The effects are calculated for the year in which the increase takes place and for the four subsequent years.

The second part of the approach concerns the evaluation of the calculated effects. This evaluation is based on neo-Paretian welfare theory. It is assumed that the utility from leisure time is zero. Therefore, the only effects that are important in the final analysis are the effects on consumption. Bearing this in mind, the 'alternative costs' of a project that costs 1 billion guilders in market prices are equalled to the sum of the following three variables: the present value of the calculated changes in private consumption, the present value of the calculated changes in investment multiplied by a correction factor which expresses the value of 1 guilder of investment in terms of private consumption, and the present value of the calculated changes in the trade balance multiplied by a correction factor which expresses the value of a unit of foreign exchange which is worth 1 guilder in terms of private consumption. Present values are obtained by discounting the changes in the different years at the social time preference rate. The correction factors are obtained from neo-classical welfare theory. The correction factor for capital is equal to the present value of the output produced with the marginal capital good during its lifetime (per guilder of capital good). This correction factor reflects the fact that the yearly returns on capital may be greater than the private time preference rate. The correction factor for foreign exchange mainly reflects the extent of over- or undervaluation of the domestic currency.

The alternative costs thus defined are calculated for all four methods of finance, and the method with the lowest alternative cost is selected. The alternative costs based on this method of finance should ultimately be compared with the benefits of the project. According to Zuidema, these benefits are equal to the present value of the output produced in terms of private consumption.

In commenting upon Zuidema's method attention will only be paid to the evaluation of the effects. The first point of criticism is that the macroeconomic effects of increasing government expenditure will stretch over a period of more than five years. For example, increases in government expenditure will lead to increases in government debt, which will cause changes in consumption over a long period.

Second, the effects of a change in investment are not evaluated in a correct way. An example is the value of a change in investment in the first year. On the one hand this value is, outside the model, calculated by multiplying the change in investment (in guilders) by the correction factor for capital. This correction factor is calculated on the basis of neo-classical assumptions. On the other hand the following procedure is used. The change in investment in the first year has effects that are calculated by means of the model. For example, according to the model this change in investment will lead to a change in capital stock, and consequently, among other things, to changes in consumption in the subsequent years. These changes in consumption are calculated by means of the model, and are also valued by Zuidema. Thus, the effects of a change in investment in year 1 are calculated with two different methods: a neo-classical method and a method that is based on the econometric macro-model, which has certain Keynesian characteristics. This implies that Zuidema's method is inconsistent, and that there is double-counting.

Third, the correction factor for foreign exchange is equalled to one, which is based on the following: first, the Dutch guilder is neither overvalued nor undervalued; second, a change in receipts of foreign exchange implies an equal change in the wealth of the country as a whole, and third, an increase in wealth can be used to increase consumption with an equal amount, so that it can be valued as being equal to a change in consumption of an equal amount. In this line of reasoning the following point is neglected. Suppose that one unit of foreign exchange worth 1 guilder is lost. This implies that the wealth of the country as a whole decreases with 1 guilder, and that there is 1 guilder (plus interest) less to spend on consumption in the future. According to the econometric macro-model, and as a result of multiplier-relations, national consumption decreases with more than 1 guilder when spendings on consumption decrease with 1 guilder. Therefore, the correction factor for foreign exchange should in fact not only depend on the degree of over- or undervaluation of the currency, but also on multiplier and other macroeconomic effects that will occur when the decreases in wealth lead to decreases in spendings on consumption.

My criticism can also be formulated in more general terms. The effects of a project as calculated by means of an econometric macro-model consist of changes in variables such as private consumption, government debt, foreign assets, and capital stock. If these changes are evaluated on the basis of neo-Paretian welfare theory, it is necessary to recalculate all these changes in terms of private consumption and (possibly) leisure time in a way which is consistent with the model used. Furthermore, attention should be paid to the fact that the effects of the project may stretch over a period that is longer than the period to which the econometric macro-model refers. Zuidema's method does not fully meet these conditions.

It may be remarked at this point that econometric macro-models such as the ones discussed in this section and in Section 3.2.2 are relatively complicated models. Therefore, it is relatively difficult (or perhaps even impossible) to use such a model to express changes in variables such as private investment and the balance on current account in terms of consumption (and possibly leisure time). This is an important difference with a model such as the Little–Mirrlees model, which is simpler and which therefore makes it relatively easy to express all changes caused by a project in terms of consumption (and leisure time) in the final analysis.

3.4. The consistency between project appraisal and macroeconomic analysis and policy

At this point attention can be paid to the problem of the consistency between project appraisal and macroeconomic analysis and policy. Two aspects of consistency can be distinguished. In order to explain the first one, it is helpful to discuss a method of project appraisal used (among others) by Dutch researchers (Jeuring and Tijsma, 1982; Van den Bosch and Veerman, 1984; Van der Vlies, 1989). This method is not as sophisticated as the methods discussed before, and it is only introduced here because it can help explain a more general point.

This method has been used to analyse certain projects which are not profitable at market prices. Essentially, it consists of the analysis of the first-round spending effects of the project by means of an input–output model. The conclusion of this analysis is always that the project's expenditures cause certain increases in employment, national income, and government revenues, and a certain decrease in unemployment benefits. Given these results, the conclusion of all studies is that the project should be undertaken, despite the fact that the private profitability is negative. In relation to this, government grants should be given.[13]

Now the spending effects of a project, as calculated with an input–output model, will be positive for any project. Therefore, if a large number of projects is analysed in the way described above, this will lead to the conclusion that many projects should be implemented, or in other words that at macro-level total government expenditure should be increased. However, macroeconomic analyses regarding the optimal level of total government expenditure generally lead to the conclusion that increases in government expenditure have certain negative consequences too. For instance, a large increase in government expenditure can cause an increase in wages and prices of goods and services. In case the expenditure is financed on the capital market, it can also cause an increase in the interest rate. These increases in prices will have further negative effects. In relation to these, in many countries, among which the Netherlands are included, the government aims to reduce the total level of government expenditure. Input–output models neglect these effects.

Here we are confronted with an interesting problem. From an econometric point of view one could argue that it is justifiable to neglect these effects when analysing a single, small project. For instance, it is not likely that in reality a small project of, say, 100,000 guilders leading to a decrease in unemployment of one man-year will cause a rise in wages, or that financing such a project will lead to an increase in the interest rate. Given this, one could argue that, as far as the effects on prices are concerned, from an econometric point of view the analysis of the spending effects of a small project with an input–output model is justifiable. At first sight this argument is correct. But from the above it then follows that an analysis of an individual project that at first sight is correct from an econometric point of view can, if it is used for many projects, ultimately lead to a wrong policy at macro-level.

In a more general way the problem can be explained as follows: in an economic system the whole can be different from the sum of the parts (Weintraub, 1979). In the 'micro-foundations literature' this point has sometimes been used to argue that one should not look for a micro-foundation for macroeconomics, but that, in order to explain the occurrence of disequilibria, one must try to formulate a macro-foundation for individual decisions (Kregel, 1987). In the context of this study it is more important that, because of the difference between the whole and the sum of the parts, the method of project appraisal discussed above is not consistent with the analyses of the effects of macroeconomic policies. Given this, what is needed is a macro-foundation for project appraisal: one should try to develop a method for the appraisal of individual small projects which takes account of the way the economy functions at the macro-level.

The second aspect of consistency between project appraisal and macroeconomic analysis and policy has been discussed in the previous Chapter. In case all government expenditures have average characteristics, the effects of an increase in total expenditures will be less positive than when individual projects are selected in such a way that the total portfolio of projects has non-average characteristics that lead to relatively positive macroeconomic effects. This implies that the conclusions with regard to the optimal total level of government expenditure could be dependent upon the question which portfolio of projects constitutes government expenditure. This implies that macroeconomic policy should be dependent on the results of project appraisal: there should be a micro-foundation for macroeconomic policy.

The question is now to what extent the methods of project appraisal discussed earlier are consistent with macroeconomic analysis and policy. Let us first discuss the 'effects method' of project appraisal. This method consists of two stages: one of analysis, and one of evaluation. The stage of analysis is based on an input–output model. Therefore, in this stage the method neglects the fact that the analysis of changes at macro-level differs from the analysis of changes at micro- or meso-level. For example, it is impossible to use the method to analyse the effects of a project on inflation or on the interest rate. The stage of evaluation however is based on the idea that project appraisal should be consistent with macroeconomic policy. In relation to this, the criteria for the evaluation of the effects partly depend on macroeconomic objectives and constraints. Because growth is considered to be an important macroeconomic objective, and because investment funds are considered to be an important macroeconomic constraint, the 'preferred criterion' is the proportion between the increase in annual value added caused by the project and the investment needed for the project.

Now one might argue that the fact that the effects of a project on prices are not taken into account during the stage of analysis is not a serious problem because these effects are implicitly taken into account when the effects of the project are evaluated. When investment is regarded as a constraint, this means that it may implicitly be acknowledged that investments can cause an increase in the interest rate. When growth is considered to be a macroeconomic objective, this might be done while aware of the effects of growth on inflation. However, this argument is only partly correct. For instance, the effect of financing a large portfolio of government projects on the interest rate does not only depend on the amount of investment, but also depends on other factors. First, the operating costs of the projects need to be financed too, and therefore they can also cause an increase in the interest rate. Second, the annual financial returns of the project will have the opposite effect. Third, the spending effects of the projects may lead to a decrease in the government deficit and therefore to a decrease in the interest rate. Because of these and other factors two portfolios having the same investment costs may have a different effect on the interest rate. This implies that when one only looks at investment costs when evaluating individual projects, one may end up with a portfolio which has more or less negative effects on the interest rate than the effects which are implictly taken into account by taking investment as a constraint. For instance, it is not impossible that the use of the 'preferred criterion' mentioned above leads to the selection of projects with low investment costs and high operating costs. In that case the effects on the interest rate are less favourable than the effects which are implictly taken into account. A similar point can be made with regard to the effects of a project on inflation. Thus, there are still some problems regarding the first aspect of consistency.

If the point regarding the interest rate mentioned above were taken into account in a systematic way, one could select a portfolio of projects that has a relatively small effect on the interest rate, because the constituent projects taken by themselves have a relatively favourable effect on demand and supply on the capital market. In that case one could perhaps come to the conclusion that government expenditure should be increased, because increasing government expenditures need not lead to a large increase in the interest rate. However, the 'effects method' does not take this possibility into account. Similar remarks can be made with regard to the effects on inflation. Thus, the 'effects method' does not score regarding the second aspect of consistency.

Primal methods based on an econometric macro-model have not been used for the analysis of small projects. The reasons for this are generally not stated explicitly, but they seem to be related to the idea that a number of effects which figure in econometric macro-models (such as inflation) are not important at the level of individual projects.

Thus, as yet a solution to the problem discussed in this section (which concerns small projects) has not been sought in the development of a primal method based on an econometric macro-model.

The Little–Mirrlees method is based on an integral model of the economy, which implies that it is based on a kind of macroeconomic analysis. Thus, there is a certain consistency between project appraisal and macroeconomic analysis. However, the model is not capable of dealing with a number of typically macroeconomic phenomena. For instance, it does not take account of the possible existence of a Phillips-curve, or of the fact that wages and prices may affect each other such that inflation accelerates. No attention is paid to expectations (such as expectations of inflation, or of the ability of the government to repay its debts). Macroeconomic policies in some less developed countries, and in all developed countries, are based on analyses which are different from the analysis of the economy which underlies the Little–Mirrlees method. This implies that the application of the Little–Mirrlees rules for project appraisal in developed countries (which is, by the way, not advocated by Little and Mirrlees) would lead to a situation in which project appraisal is not consistent with macroeconomic analysis. The Little–Mirrlees method scores regarding the second aspect of consistency; it is devised in such a way that the government budget can in principle be made dependent on the outcomes of project appraisal.

The primal and dual methods based on theoretical macroeconomic models are consistent in themselves. However, because these methods cannot be applied in practice, this cannot be considered a great accomplishment. Moreover, the following can be said: in many cases these models have their roots in the so-called micro-foundations theory. There are economists who doubt whether the development of models based on this theory can ultimately lead to macroeconomic models which describe all phenomena that are important at the macro-level in a satisfactory way (e.g. Kregel, 1987). Furthermore, even if this were possible, the specific models used in the approaches mentioned above are far from accomplishing this. For example, they are all based on the assumption that prices on markets which are in disequilibrium are fixed. This implies that they do not pay attention to one of the most important questions in the micro-foundations literature, which is why prices do not change in a situation of disequilibrium, or, in other words, why at the level of the economy as a whole coordination is not perfect (Weintraub, 1979, Van Ees and Garretsen, 1990). The counter-argument that the analysed projects are too small to affect prices is not valid, as this point precisely neglects the problem discussed in this section. It can be concluded that the resulting rules for project appraisal are not consistent with the macroeconomic models used to help formulate macroeconomic policies, so that there are still problems regarding the first aspect of consistency. Regarding the second aspect of consistency, it can be remarked that the theoretical methods discussed above have not paid attention to the possibility of making macroeconomic policy dependent upon the results of project appraisal.

3.5. Implications for the development of an improved method

It was argued above that project appraisal should be consistent with macroeconomic analysis. In this study an attempt will be made to develop a method for the appraisal of both small and large projects that is based on the use of an existing econometric macro-model.

The first choice to be made then concerns the question whether this development should be in the direction of a primal or a dual method. It has been argued that the dual method of Malinvaud *et al.* (1983), which is based on an econometric macro-model, cannot be used as a basis for further research. The other dual methods are not based on an econometric macro-model. These methods are all based on the following procedure: first, the effects of an input or output are calculated, and second, these effects are expressed in terms of one numéraire so that a shadow price can be calculated. Now it may be difficult to express all effects of an input or output, as calculated with an econometric macro-model, in terms of one numéraire. In relation to this, the development of a new method will in the first instance be directed towards a primal method.

Thus, in Chapter 4 it will be attempted to develop a primal method for the appraisal of both small and large projects that is based on an econometric macro-model. This implies that we will be confronted with a fundamental problem: a number of effects which play a part at the macro-level, and which therefore play a part in econometric macro-models, are not perceptible at the level of the individual project. A related problem is that it is still an open question whether it is basically possible to analyse the effects of a small project with an econometric macro-model with an acceptable degree of uncertainty. A solution to these problems will therefore be attempted.

If it is possible to find such a solution, there is still another problem: how to evaluate the effects. In Chapter 4 an attempt will be made to solve it. This attempt however will not be based on the idea that all effects should be expressed in terms of one numéraire.

Once the primal method has been developed, the question arises whether it is possible and sensible to convert this method into a dual method. The advantage of a dual, as compared to a primal, method is that the shadow prices of inputs and outputs need to be calculated only once. This makes a dual method more efficient than a primal method in a situation in which many projects have to be analysed. Therefore, in one of the last Chapters, Chapter 7, an attempt will be made to change the primal method of Chapter 4 into a dual method. This implies that a solution has to be found for the problem of expressing all effects of buying an input or selling an output in terms of one numéraire.

For the time being, however, the focus will be on the development of a primal method that is based on an econometric macro-model.

Notes

1. Paretian and Bergsonian welfare theory have not been used as a basis for project appraisal, and therefore they will not be discussed.
2. For a detailed description see Boadway (1974) and Lesourne (1975).
3. These methods, notably that of Haveman-Krutilla and the 'efficiency method' of the World Bank, are discussed in Van der Burg (1991).
4. An interesting discussion between an advocate of the effects method and one of the Little–Mirrlees method, which will be discussed in Section 3.3, is provided by Balassa (1976), Chervel (1977) and Balassa (1977).
5. Chervel (1984), Durufle (1984), Moulignat (1984), and Thibault (1984).
6. Zuidema (1982).
7. For example, the study of the CPB (1983a) on the Markerwaardpolder only considers financing on the capital market, without any explicit justification. The study of the NEI (1983) on the same project analyses the effects of the project with four different methods of finance, but pays no attention to the question which method should be selected.
8. 'La multiplication des variables d'écart aboutirait à une négation de l'instrument'.
9. I have not found any literature showing that the method has been improved in recent years, but my knowledge of recent French literature is rather limited.
10. The Little–Mirrlees method is essentially similar to the method devised by Dasgupta, Marglin and Sen at the same time (see UNIDO, 1972); the main difference concerns the choice of the numéraire (Lal, 1974). The Little–Mirrlees method will be discussed because it has found the widest application. Basically, this discussion is at the same time a discussion of the Dasgupta–Marglin–Sen method.
11. It is also possible that spending on imported goods will decrease. This implies that selling the output will lead to an improvement in the trade balance, just like in the first case.
12. For an overview see Drèze and Stern (1987).
13. See, for a more detailed discussion of these studies, Van der Burg (1991).

CHAPTER 4

A method to calculate and evaluate the macroeconomic effects of projects, including small projects

4.1. Introduction

The aim of this chapter is to develop a new method of project appraisal. In view of the conclusions of the previous chapter, this method should have the following characteristics. First, it is a primal method based on the use of an econometric macro-model. Second, it combines the analysis of project-specific characteristics with the analysis of the macro-model. Third, it can be applied to both small and large projects. Fourth, it pays attention to the evaluation of the effects.

The first two characteristics are also characteristics of the conventional macroeconometric method of project appraisal. Therefore, the question is why, as far as the estimation of the effects of projects is concerned, it is necessary to develop a new method. This question not only concerns the analysis of large projects, but the analysis of small projects as well; although as yet the conventional macroeconometric method has not been applied to small projects, it is sensible to ask whether this could be done. For reasons of a clear sequence of explanation, however, this question will not be answered until the new method has been explained.

This chapter consists of four parts. In the first part (Section 4.2) the procedure for the calculation of the macroeconomic effects of projects is explained. Special attention is given to the linkages between project-specific characteristics and the macroeconomic model. In the second part (Sections 4.3 and 4.4), the uncertainties related to the outcomes of the calculations are discussed. Section 4.3 discusses the uncertainties that occur when the method is applied to large projects, or portfolios of projects. Section 4.4 deals with the uncertainties that are specifically linked to the analysis of small projects. This section will show, among other things, that it is justifiable to use an econometric macro-model for the appraisal of small projects. The third part (Section 4.5) deals with the question why a new method has been developed instead of using the conventional macroeconometric method. The fourth part (Section 4.6) deals with the evaluation of the calculated effects. To avoid misunderstandings, when I talk about the calculation of the macroeconomic effects of a project, I mean the estimation of these effects. The difference between the calculated or estimated effects and the actual effects is called an error. Uncertainty related to the outcomes of the calculations concerns the possibility that errors are made.

Regarding the relation between this chapter and Chapter 5, the following can be said. This chapter deals with the method of project appraisal in the most general way. The description of the method is such that, in principle, different econometric macro-models can be used. Chapter 5 discusses the consequences of using the Freia-model of the Dutch Central Planning Bureau.

4.2. The calculation of the effects of a project

4.2.1. Introduction

Section 4.2 will give a complete description of a method for the calculation of the effects of both large and small projects. Initially at least this method concerns government projects only.

Throughout this study, the term 'macroeconomic effects of a project' will be used. Now, the method is, among other things, intended for the analysis of small projects. Thus, implicitly, the term 'macroeconomic effects of a small project' is used. The use of this term is not completely correct. As will be explained in Section 4.4, it is better to talk about 'the contribution of a small project to the macroeconomic effects of a portfolio of projects'. However, using the correct term would occupy much space, and therefore the term 'macroeconomic effects of a small project' will (implicitly) be used in this section, and at many other points in this study. A similar remark applies to the term 'macroeconomic effects of a small change'.

Throughout this chapter it will be assumed that the lifetime of the project is 15 years. The first investment is done in year 1 and the last output is produced in year 15. Another assumption is that the macroeconomic effects of the project can be estimated by the macroeconomic model for year 1 up to year 20. These assumptions are made to avoid the use of too many characters; in principle, any number of years could have been chosen. Vectors will be denoted by one or more bold small letters. Matrices will be denoted by capital letters. In reading Section 4.2, the list of symbols (pp. 93–94) may be helpful.

The method consists of two parts. First, the project is divided into parts, and the effects of these parts are calculated separately. In relation to this, different types of effects are distinguished, each type of effect being related to a specific part of the project. Second, the separate effects are added up to get the effects of the project as a whole.

The first type of effect concerns the effects of financing the expenditures. More precisely, it concerns the effects of raising money and paying the expenditures. The phrase 'paying the expenditures' is not without meaning, because raising money in itself does not imply a financial loss, whereas raising money and paying the expenditures does. The first type of effect excludes the spending effects of the expenditures on other economic actors. Thus, the effects of financing a certain expenditure can be regarded as being equal to the effects of raising money and using it to increase development aid without further effects on the domestic economy.[1] *The second type of effect* concerns the effects of the expenditures excluding the effects of financing them. In other words, this type of effect concerns the spending effects of the expenditure, and other effects that result from these spending effects. The effects on the financial position of the actor who originally made the expenditures are excluded. These effects can therefore in principle be regarded as being equal to the effects of an increase in government investment, financed by a decrease in development aid.[2] *The third type of effect* concerns the effects of the output. These three types of effects will be discussed in the following three sections.

It is possible that the reader, when reading Section 4.2, will wonder whether it is justifiable to follow a procedure in which the effects of the parts of a project are first calculated separately and then added up to get the total effects. After all, many econometric macro-models are non-linear, which implies that the calculated effects of two changes taken together may not be equal to the sum total of the effects of the two changes calculated separately. It should be remarked here that for the Freia model which is used later in this study the problem is not as serious as it might appear at first sight. Moreover, if for another model the problem is serious, the method can be adapted to take this into account. These points will be discussed in detail in Section 4.3. As stated before, the question whether it is justifiable to apply the method to small projects will be discussed in Section 4.4. Thus, regarding the question whether the procedure described below is justifiable, the reader is asked to be patient.

4.2.2. The effects of financing the expenditures

The calculation of the effects of financing the expenditures involves three elements: the calculation of the gfn_t, the gross financial needs of the project in year t, the calculation of the V_t, the effects of financing 1 guilder of government expenditure in year t, and finally the calculation of W, the effects of financing the expenditures. The expenditures include investment expenditures as well as exploitation expenditures.

The calculation of the gfn_t

The gross financial needs of the project are defined as the payments for labour, capital goods and other inputs (including all taxes and premiums). They exclude interest payments. The gross financial needs in year t are referred to as gfn_t. They are estimated for each year t (t = 1,2,..,15).

The calculation of the V_t

This sub-section deals with the calculation of the effects of financing 1 guilder of government expenditure in different years. The effects concern changes in private consumption, private investment, employment, government budget surplus and balance on current account (which is taken to exclude the balance of unilateral transfers) over a range of 20 years. Why these five variables have been selected will be discussed in Section 4.6.

The first step is to calculate the effects of financing 1 billion guilders, in different years. As was said before, the effects of financing the expenditures of the project can be regarded as being equal to the effects of increasing development aid, provided that the spending effects of development aid do not affect the domestic economy. In relation to this, the effects of financing 1 billion guilders are calculated by calculating the effects of an increase in development aid with 1 billion guilders by means of an econometric macro-model. The model used should be such that the spending effects of development aid do not affect the domestic economy. If the model does not fulfil this condition, some adaptations should be made.

As stated in Chapter 3, there are six different methods of financing: via the capital market, business taxes, other direct taxes, indirect taxes, expenditure cuts, and liquidity creation. The question on which method of financing the calculations should be based is discussed in Section 4.6. As yet it is taken for granted that one method of financing has been selected.

The calculated effects of financing 1 billion guilders by the selected method of financing in year t are tabulated in Table 4.1.

Table 4.1. Effects over twenty years of financing 1 billion guilders by the selected method of financing in year t

Year	ΔCons.	ΔInv.	ΔEmpl.	ΔG.B.S.	ΔCurr.Acc.
1	u_{t11}	u_{t12}	u_{t13}	u_{t14}	u_{t15}
2	u_{t21}	u_{t22}	u_{t23}	u_{t24}	u_{t25}
..	....	....	....	....	....
20	$u_{t20\ 1}$	$u_{t20\ 2}$	$u_{t20\ 3}$	$u_{t20\ 4}$	$u_{t20\ 5}$

On the basis of Table 4.1, matrix U_t can be defined as the (20,5) matrix with the elements u_{tik}. For each year t (t = 1,2,..,15) such a matrix U_t is calculated. Note that the first t-1 rows of U_t contain zeros only.

The second step is to calculate for each year t (t = 1,2,..,15) the (20,5) matrix V_t, with:

$$V_t = 10^{-9} \cdot U_t$$

V_t gives the effects of financing one guilder in year t. Note that one can expect many elements of V_t to be negative.

The calculation of W

The effects of financing the expenditures are given by the (20,5) matrix W, which is calculated as follows:

$$W = \sum_{t=1}^{15} gfn_t \cdot V_t.$$

Here, two questions can be posed. First, as the gfn_t exclude interest payments, one can ask whether the calculations do not neglect interest payments. The answer is negative. The reason is that V_t includes interest payments, which should therefore not be included in gfn_t.[3]

Another question is the following: does financing development aid and financing domestic projects not differ in the way in which they affect the exchange rate, and does this not have different macroeconomic effects as a result? With regard to this question two remarks can be made. First, the question is irrelevant with regard to the Freia-model used in Chapters 5 up to 7, because the exchange rate is an exogenous variable in this model. Second, it is possible that with regard to models other than the Freia-model the question can be answered in the affirmative. However, this is not a problem because the question is too partial. One should ask the following question: is the calculation of the effects on the exchange rate of the project *as a whole* correct? This question can be answered in the affirmative, which is related to the following. An increase in development aid will deteriorate the balance of unilateral transfers, and can therefore lead to a decrease in the exchange rate. A decrease in development aid will have opposite effects. It is possible that according to the calculations described above financing the project leads to a certain decrease in the exchange rate, whereas in reality financing the project will not have such an effect. Thus, these calculations may involve errors. However, as will be explained in the next section the expenditures on the project are assumed to be financed by a decrease in development aid. Therefore, it is also possible that according to the calculations described in the next section the expenditures lead to an increase in the exchange rate, whereas in reality this effect does not occur, so that in this context errors are made too. The latter errors are counterbalanced exactly by the former errors (because the expenditures on the project are equal to the gross financial needs). Therefore, the effects on the exchange rate of the project as a whole will still be estimated correctly.[4]

4.2.3. The effects of the expenditures excluding the effects of financing them

The calculation of the effects of the expenditures excluding the effects of financing them consists of three elements: first, the calculation of the fva_t, the first-round spending effects on gross national value added in year t, and of the ni_t, the first-round spending effects on imports; second, the calculation of the J_t, the effects of a first-round increase in gross national value added of 1 guilder in year t; and third, the calculation of X, the effects of the expenditures excluding the effects of financing them.

It may be repeated that in this study primary inputs are defined as labour and entrepreneurship, land and natural resources, and capital goods. All other inputs are intermediate inputs. The terms 'national income' and 'national value added' refer to the same concept; both include indirect taxes. The first-round spending effects of an expenditure are the direct spending effects of the expenditure plus the backward linkage effects up to the use of the primary inputs.

The calculation of the fva_t and of the ni_t

This section deals with the calculation of the fva_t and of the ni_t, which are calculated for each year t (t = 1,2,..,15). fva_t is defined as the change in gross national value added in year t induced by the first-round spending effects of the expenditures. ni_t is defined as the change in imports in year t induced by the first-round spending effects of the expenditures. The sum total of fva_t and ni_t is equal to the expenditures on the project in year t. Therefore, if these expenditures and the fva_t are known, the ni_t can simply be calculated as the difference between the two. For this reason, only the calculation of fva_t will be discussed explicitly below.

One part of fva_t is calculated with the help of an input–output model. This part is called vai_t. The other part is calculated without an input–output model. This part is calculated on the basis of specific research only, and is called var_t. The following holds good: $fva_t = var_t + vai_t$. The advantage of specific research is that it can provide more precise information than an input–output model. The disadvantage is that it is time-consuming. Therefore, the relative size of var_t and vai_t depends on practical considerations.

In this place only one example of the calculation of var_t will be given. In this example var_t consists of two parts. The first part is calculated as follows. The number of labourers who will be directly employed in the project in year t is estimated on the basis of specific research. The first part of var_t is then calculated as being equal to the gross wages of these labourers. The second part of var is calculated as follows. Specific research is done to estimate to what extent a certain important intermediate input for the project bought in year t will be produced by the domestic industry. Subsequently, specific research is done to estimate how much gross national value added will be yielded in this industry as a result. This gross national value added is the second part of var_t. It is added to the first part to get the value of var_t.

For the calculation of vai_t one needs, apart from an input–output model, some specific information as well. This specific information concerns the types and amounts of capital goods and intermediate inputs that will be bought by the project authority from other domestic producers, insofar as the spending effects of the expenditures on these capital goods and intermediate inputs have not been analysed in order to calculate part of var_t. Besides, this specific information concerns the types and amounts of intermediate inputs that will be bought from other domestic producers by industries that have been the subject of specific research related to the calculation of var_t, such as the industry producing the important intermediate input mentioned in the preceding paragraph. The calculation of the increase in gross national value added by means of the input–output model is a standard procedure. In this place only the formula used to calculate vai_t is given:

$$vai_t = \mathbf{v}' \bullet [\mathrm{I} - \mathrm{A}]^{-1} \bullet \mathbf{sit},$$

where:

- $\mathbf{v}$ = (q,1) column vector with element i denoting the ratio between gross value added in sector i and total output in sector i, q being the total number of sectors in the economy.
- I = identity matrix.
- A = (q,q) matrix with intermediate input coefficients (a_{ij}).
- **sit** = (q,1) column vector: $(si_{t1}, si_{t2}, ..., si_{ti}..., si_{tq})$.
- si_{ti} = spendings in year t of the project authority on capital goods and intermediate inputs produced in domestic sector i, for which holds good that the spending effects of these capital goods and intermediate inputs have not been analysed in order to calculate part of var_t, plus spendings in year t of the industries that

have been the subject of specific research related to the calculation of var_t on intermediate inputs produced in domestic sector *i*, insofar as these spendings are caused by the project.

In this chapter the superscript *t* denotes the transpose of a vector. The superscript –1 denotes the inverse of a matrix.

The calculation of the J_t

The next step is to calculate for each year *t* ($t = 1,2,..,15$) the effects of a first-round increase in gross national value added of 1 guilder in that year. The procedure is as follows. First of all, the effects up to year 20 of an increase in government investment of 1 billion guilders in year *t*, financed by a decrease in development aid, are calculated with the macroeconomic model. These impacts are given by the (20,5) matrix H_t, the determination of the H_t being analogous to that of the U_t.

The increase in government investment will have first-round spending effects on national value added and on imports. Let m_t be the import coefficient of government investment in year *t* according to the model. This import coefficient includes the capital goods directly imported by the government, but excludes the imports of capital goods used in the private sector. Consequently, $(1 - m_t)$ is the first-round increase in gross national income, as a proportion of the increase in government investment. This implies that if government investment increases with $1/(1 - m_t)$ billion, first-round gross national income increases with 1 billion. This considered, the effects of a first-round increase in gross national income with 1 guilder in year *t* are given by the matrix J_t, with:

$$J_t = \{1/(1 - m_t)\} \bullet 10^{-9} \bullet H_t.$$

The calculation of X

This section deals with the final calculation of the effects of the expenditures excluding the effects of financing them. To begin with, matrix K is calculated:

$$K = \sum_{t=1}^{15} fva_t \bullet J_t.$$

At first sight, K gives the effects of the expenditures excluding the effects of financing them. However, this is not completely correct. One further correction should be made. This concerns the fact that all effects on imports, as represented in K, have been calculated on the basis of the import coefficients m_t of the macroeconomic model. No use has been made of the more specific information which has been used to calculate ni_t. As the reader will recall, ni_t is the first-round increase in imports resulting from the expenditures on the project, as calculated by means of specific research and by means of an input–output model.

To clarify this problem, let us first explain how the first-round effects on imports are calculated if the uncorrected method (that is, the method that results in matrix K) is used. As stated above, m_t is the import coefficient of government investment in year *t* according to the model. This implies that if government investment increases with $1/(1-m_t)$ billion, first-round gross value added increases with 1 billion. Therefore, by the uncorrected method the effects of a first-round increase in gross value added with fva_t are set equal to the effects of an increase in government investment with $fva_t \bullet 1/(1-m_t)$. Consequently, the first-round effect on imports in year t as calculated on the basis of the uncorrected method is equal to:

$$m_t \bullet [fva_t \bullet 1/(1-m_t)] = fva_t \bullet m_t/(1-m_t).$$

This estimate is not based on the specific information that was used to calculate ni_t. In relation to this, $fva_t \bullet m_t/(1-m_t)$ is an estimate of the first-round spending effects on imports in year t which is inferior to ni_t. Thus, the uncorrected method may contain errors. This can be explained by a hypothetical example. Suppose that the total costs of the project consist of labour costs only. This implies that ni_t is zero, and that fva_t is equal to the total costs. On the basis of the uncorrected method, however, the estimate of the first-round effects on imports would be positive (see the formula given above). Speaking more generally, the uncorrected method overestimates the effects on imports with the difference between the estimate of the first-round effects on imports based on the uncorrected method and the specific estimate of the first-round effects on imports. Put differently, it overestimates the effects with $[fva_t \bullet m_t/(1-m_t) - ni_t]$.

Thus, a correction must be made. A positive effect on imports is a negative effect on the balance on current account. Thus, in order to correct the balance on current account, $[fva_t \bullet m_t/(1-m_t) - ni_t]$ should be added to element $(t,5)$ of matrix K. The result is matrix X:

$$X = K + \text{corrections for imports.}$$

X gives the effects of the expenditures on the project excluding the effects of financing them.[5]

4.2.4. The effects of the output

The output is a market good

If the output of a project is sold on the market, three direct consequences can be distinguished. First, the financial position of the project authority improves. Second, the position of the buyers changes. Third, the balance on current account may (or may not) improve.

The first consequence will be discussed first. The treatment of the financial returns for the project authority is exactly the opposite of that of the gross financial needs. For each year t (t = 1,2,..,15) the financial returns are calculated. They are denoted as fr_t. The effects of the financial returns are then given by matrix T:

$$T = \sum_{t=1}^{15} -fr_t \bullet V_t.$$

With regard to the second and third direct consequence of selling the output, different types of output can be distinguished. The first case is that of an export good. In this case, the second direct consequence is a change in the position of foreign buyers. It is assumed that this will have no consequences for the domestic economy. Besides, in this case the third direct consequence is an improvement in the balance on current account, which is equal to the value of the output of the project. This improvement can be represented by the (20,5) matrix Q, which is defined as follows:

$$q_{t,5} = fr_t \text{ for } t = 1, 2,\dots,15, \text{ and}$$

$$q_{t,y} = 0 \text{ if } t > 15 \text{ or } y < 5.$$

The total effects of the output are given by the (20,5) matrix Y. In case the output is an export good, Y can be calculated as:

$$\mathrm{Y} = \mathrm{T} + \mathrm{Q}.$$

The second case is that of an import-substitution good. In this case the output is bought by domestic buyers who react to their purchases of the good by decreasing their purchases of imported goods. It is assumed that ultimately the financial position of domestic buyers remains the same.[6] It is also assumed that the decreases in the sales of foreign producers have no further consequences for the domestic economy. Given these assumptions, the second direct consequence of selling the output can be neglected. The third direct consequence is that the balance on current account improves, with the improvement being equal to the value of the output of the project. This can be taken into account, using the same principles as the ones mentioned with regard to the first case.

The third case is that of a good sold to domestic buyers who react by decreasing their purchases from other domestic producers. Again it is assumed that ultimately the financial position of the buyers remains unchanged. The question then is how to treat the impact on other domestic producers. The answer is as follows: first, specific research is carried out to estimate the direct effect on the sales of other domestic producers. The estimated decreases in sales are differentiated by sector and by year. The macroeconomic effects of these decreases in sales are then calculated in a way which resembles the procedure described in Section 4.2.3. For each year t a $(q,1)$ vector **sct** (sales crowded out in year t) will be defined as:

$$\mathbf{sct} = (sc_{t1}, sc_{t2}, \dots, sc_{tq})'$$

where: sc_{ti} = decrease in sales in sector i in year t which is a direct consequence of selling the output of the project.

The first-round spending effects of these decreases in sales on gross national value added in year t, vac_t, can be calculated as:

$$vac_t = \mathbf{v}^{t} \bullet (\mathrm{I} - \mathrm{A})^{-1} \bullet -\mathbf{sct}.$$

For the meaning of the symbols, the reader is referred to Section 4.2.3.

Subsequently, the macroeconomic effects of the decrease in sales of domestic producers which is a direct consequence of selling the output are calculated as being equal to R:[7]

$$\mathrm{R} = \sum_{t=1}^{15} vac_t \bullet \mathrm{J}_t.$$

As stated before, matrix Y gives the total effects of the output of the project. In the third case Y is calculated as:

$$Y = T + R.$$

The output is a public consumption good
In case the output is a public consumption good, it can first of all be measured in physical terms. The availability of the output will lead to an increase in the satisfaction of consumers. The evaluation of the increase in satisfaction will be discussed in Section 4.6.

The output is a public investment good
The last case is that in which public goods are produced which have a positive impact on production in the private sector, such as roads, schools, or installations for the abatement of pollution. It does not seem impossible to solve the problems related to the analysis of these goods. General proof will not be provided, but it can be mentioned that an example has been given in Van der Burg (1991).

Finally, it can be remarked that, when two projects producing the same output are compared, a cost-effectiveness analysis can be made. In that case the output can be neglected.

The total effects of the project
Matrix Z is defined as the matrix that gives the effects of the project as a whole. It is calculated as:

$$Z = W + X + Y.$$

4.2.5. Additional remarks

It is possible to extend the method to take account of more project-specific information. One extension concerns the project-specific indirect taxes. This extension is explained in the appendix to this chapter. It will be used in Chapter 6.

When the method is applied, special attention should be paid to the treatment of changes in the price level. For example, if H_t refers to the effects of an increase in government investment in year t of 1 billion in current prices, then fva_t should be expressed in current prices as well. Of course, the main rule for the treatment of changes in the price level is that it should be consistent.

The calculated effects of the project depend, among other things, on the assumptions regarding the exogenous variables in the base-run, and on the type of model used. It may therefore be desirable to investigate how the calculated effects change when different base-runs are considered and when different models are used.

The method such as described above can be applied to all types of government projects. As yet the only exception concerns government projects producing public investment goods, but, as stated above, it does not seem to be impossible to extend the method in such a way that (some) government projects producing public investment goods can be analysed too. Besides, in Chapter 6 it will be shown that the method can be adapted in such a way that it can be applied to non-government projects in the electricity sector that are subsidized by the government. It is possible that other non-government projects can also be analysed with an extended version of the method. However, awaiting further research no definite conclusions can be drawn regarding the possible extensions of the method.

The method is intended for situations of unemployment only; in situations of full employment more orthodox neo-classical methods which are less complicated are fully satisfactory. The method can be used in any situation of unemployment, provided that there is a suitable econometric macro-model available. Suitable means that the model satisfies certain conditions, which will be discussed in the following section.

4.3. Potential errors related to the estimates when large projects or portfolios of projects are analysed

4.3.1. Introduction

The outcomes of the calculations discussed in the previous section should be regarded as estimates of the effects of projects. Sections 4.3 and 4.4 deal with potential errors that are related to these estimates. Section 4.3 discusses errors that may be made when the method is applied to large projects or to (large) portfolios of projects. Section 4.4 pays attention to errors that are specifically linked with the analysis of small projects.

Section 4.3 starts – in Section 4.3.2 – with a discussion of the potential errors that are related to the fact that the analysed project may have specific characteristics which are not taken into account by the method. Sections 4.3.3 and 4.3.4 deal with potential errors that are related to the fact that the effects of various large one-off changes are first calculated separately and then added up to get the effects of the project. In Section 4.3.5 some final remarks are made. In Section 4.3 the word 'large project' is taken to mean large project or portfolio of projects.

4.3.2. Errors related to project-specific characteristics

Although large projects are analysed by the method on the basis of a number of project-specific characteristics, there may still be some specific characteristics which are not taken into account. For example, if the effects of a new polder are analysed, it is possible that the propensity to consume of labourers employed in the construction of dikes is above average. This would imply that the outcomes of the calculations on the 'polder project' underestimate the effects on consumption. Of course, from a theoretical point of view it is desirable to take all possible project-specific characteristics into account. However, for practical reasons it is not possible to comply with this theoretical ideal.

To facilitate the explanation, the next two sections will be based on the assumption that the errors discussed above do not exist.

4.3.3. *Errors related to the estimate of the effects of a project that leads to specific durable changes*

This section deals with errors related to the estimate of the effects of a more or less hypothetical project, called Project H. Project H leads to yearly increases in financial needs of 1 billion and yearly increases in first-round national income of $(1-m)$ billion over a period of fifteen years. When Project H is analysed, there is only one difference between the conventional macroeconometric method of analysing large projects, as described in Section 3.2.2, and the method of this study. With the conventional method, the effects of the project are calculated on the basis of one model run (plus the base-run). With the method of this study the effects of various large one-off changes are first calculated separately by means of the model and then added up to get the effects of the project. The question then is whether the interaction effects between the different large one-off changes that are part of the project have been taken into account correctly. Interaction effects between different changes are defined as the difference between the simultaneous effects of all these changes taken together and the sum total of the individual effects of each of the changes taken in isolation.

More in general, there are two potential causes of errors when the effects of Project H are calculated by the method of this study. The first cause, which also concerns the conventional method, is that the model is not capable of estimating the effects of large and durable changes in a perfect way. The second cause, which is specifically related to the method of this study, is that the interaction effects are not taken into account correctly.

Four conditions will be mentioned below which should be fulfilled for the subsequent argument to be valid. This chapter will be based on the assumption that these conditions are fulfilled. In Chapter 5 it will be shown that, as far as the Freia-model of the Dutch Central Planning Bureau is concerned, three of these conditions, the second, third and fourth one below, are fulfilled. In Chapter 5 attention will also be paid to the remaining condition, the first one below. The four conditions are the following:

1. The macroeconomic model used can give a satisfactory estimate of the effects of large and durable changes (on the basis of conventional procedures). Durable changes are defined as changes that last for many years and have (more or less) the same size in all these years. For instance, an increase in exports with 1 billion each year over a period of ten years is a durable change, whereas a change of 1.2 billion in 1989, of 0.6 billion in 1990, of 1.1 billion in 1991, etc., is not durable.
2. The effects of a durable increase in development aid with 1 billion a year over a period of fifteen years, which is financed on the capital market, as calculated by means of the model (in the conventional way), are more or less equal to $\sum_{t=1}^{15} U_t$.
3. The effects of a durable increase in government investment financed by a decrease in development aid with 1 billion a year over a period of fifteen years, as calculated by means of the model (in the conventional way), are more or less equal to $\sum_{t=1}^{15} H_t$. Note that both $\sum_{t=1}^{15} H_t$ and $\sum_{t=1}^{15} U_t$ are the sum of one-off changes,

and exclude interaction effects. Thus, the second and third conditions imply that the model should be additive in at least two respects.

4. The effects of a durable increase in development aid that is financed on the capital market combined with a simultaneous durable increase in government investment that is financed by a decrease in development aid,[8] both increases being 1 billion a year and stretching over a period of fifteen years, as calculated by means of the model (in the conventional way), are more or less equal to $\sum_{t=1}^{15}(U_t + H_t)$. Thus, the model should be additive in one more respect.

If the last three conditions are fulfilled (which is assumed in this chapter), then the calculations with the model regarding the effects of project H do not incorrectly exclude interaction effects. If the first condition is also fulfilled (which is assumed in this chapter), then the outcomes of the calculations regarding the effects of project H are satisfactory estimates of the actual effects.

4.3.4. Errors related to the estimates of the effects of other projects

This section deals with potential errors related to the estimates of the effects of large projects other than Project H. Given that the four conditions mentioned above are fulfilled, there are three reasons why errors may be made when projects other than project H are analysed. The first reason will only be illustrated with an example here; in Chapter 5 it will be discussed more thoroughly. The effects of a one-off increase in government investment of 1 billion in year 1, as calculated by means of the model, may differ considerably from the calculated effects of a one-off increase in government investment of the same size in year 2. One is inclined to think that such a difference will be caused by differences between the economic situation in year 1 and the economic situation in year 2 that, from an economist's perspective, can be expected to affect the effects of the analysed one-off changes. (To give an (exaggerated) example: there may be unemployment in year 1, and full unemployment in year 2, which implies that one can expect the effects of a one-off increase in government investment in year 1 to be more positive than the effects of a similar increase in year 2.) In that case the difference should not be regarded as an error. However, it is also possible that (part of) the difference should be regarded as an error, for instance because it is related to the cumulative effect of certain mathematical approximations.

For reasons of a clear sequence of exposition, it is assumed in this chapter that the following condition is fulfilled: if the four conditions mentioned in Section 4.3.3 are fulfilled, the model yields satisfactory estimates of the effects of the large one-off changes. This implies that errors such as the one described above cannot occur. The condition mentioned above is called the fifth condition. The assumption that it is fulfilled is a temporary assumption made to facilitate the argument. The problems that arise if the fifth condition is not fulfilled, and a solution to these problems, will be discussed in Chapter 5.

The second reason why errors may be made in analysing a project other than Project H can be explained by means of an example. Suppose that the analysed project is equal to Project H except for the following: in year 5 the increase in financial needs is not 1 billion, but 1.5 billion. The method of this study is based on the assumption that the effects of the increase in financial needs of 1.5 billion in year 5 are proportional to the effects of an increase of 1 billion in the same year. However, in reality there may be non-linearities, so that this assumption may not be justifiable.

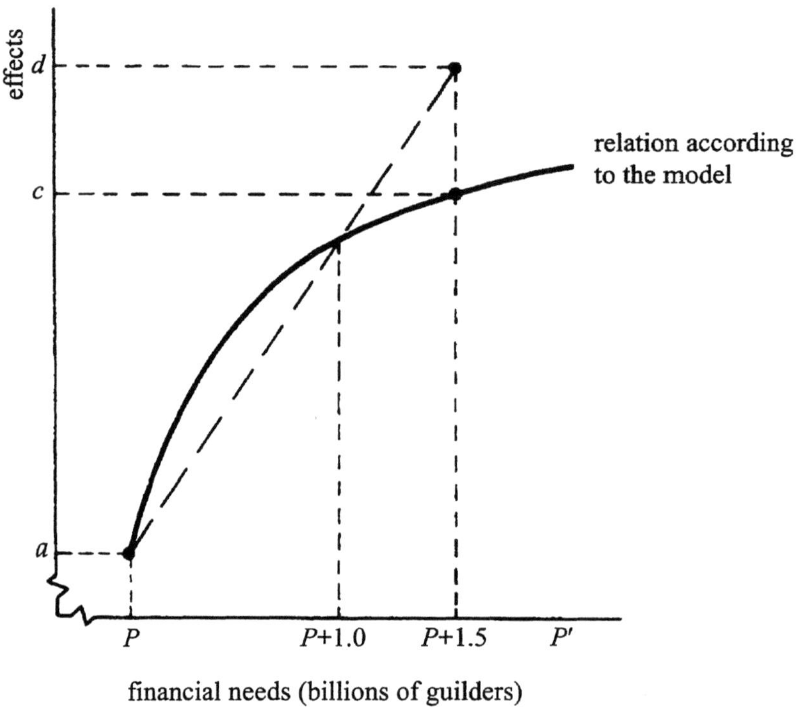

Figure 4.1. The difference between the effects of an increase in financial needs with 1.5 billion guilders as calculated by means of the method of this study and the effects of this increase according to the econometric macro-model.

The problem is illustrated in Figure 4.1. The level of the financial needs (in year 5) in the base-run is *P*. The effects (on a certain variable) of an increase in financial needs of 1.5 billion are, according to the econometric macro-model, $c - a$. According to the method of this study these effects are equal to $(d - a)$. Obviously, if the econometric macro-model gives a good description of the actual relation, and if the financial needs in the base-run are equal to the actual financial needs, then the analysis of the project by means of the method of this study will include an error that cannot be made when project H is analysed.

Now the point is that when the total amount of financial needs of the government without project is predicted, it is likely that an error greater than 1 billion is made.

For example, it is possible that the actual (future) financial needs of the government without project will be P' instead of P. Given that the five conditions mentioned earlier are fulfilled, the model gives a satisfactory estimate of the effects of the one-off increase of 1 billion. This implies that the errors related to this estimate that are caused by the incorrect prediction of the level of financial needs without project cannot be unsatisfactorily great. The errors made when the effects of a one-off increase of 1.5 billion related to the project are taken to be proportional to the effects of an increase of 1 billion should be less serious. Therefore, they can be neglected.

A similar argument can be put forward with regard to other one-off increases in financial needs that are not equal to 1 billion, as long as they do not become too large in relation to the uncertainty about the level of the financial needs without project. The same holds good for one-off increases in first-round value added that are not equal to $(1 - m)$ billion. It can be concluded that, because of the second reason, it is not impossible that the errors related to the analysis of projects other than Project H are more serious than the errors related to the analysis of Project H. However, it is justifiable to neglect this point.

The third reason why errors may arise because another project than project H is analysed will also be explained by means of an example. Just as when the second reason was discussed, the question is posed whether the calculation of the effects of an increase in financial needs in year 5 caused by the analysed project is correct. However, it is now assumed that this increase in financial needs is one billion, so that the problems related to the second reason can be neglected. The effects of the increase in financial needs in year 5 have been calculated on the assumption that in all other years the increases in financial needs caused by the project are 1 billion and that in all years the increases in first-round value added caused by the project are $(1 - m)$ billion. However, in reality the project may lead to different increases. In combination with the fact that there may be non-linearities and interaction effects, this implies that errors may be made.

Now the point is that these other changes in financial needs and in first-round value added are part of larger changes in financial needs and in first-round value added, such as changes caused by economic recessions. When the size of these changes is predicted, it is likely that errors are made which are larger than 1 billion. This implies that, even if one calculates the effects of a one-off change that is part of Project H, one cannot be sure that the calculations are based on a good estimate of the level of the financial needs without project H in other years than year 5, and of the level of the first-round value added without Project H in all years. As was established in the previous section, the method provides satisfactory estimates of the effects of Project H (under four conditions). This implies that the errors in the estimates of the effects of Project H that result from the errors made when the level of the financial needs in other years than year 5 without project H, and the level of the first-round valued added in all years without project H, are estimated, cannot be unsatisfactorily great. The errors that are related to the third reason mentioned above must be smaller. Therefore, they can be neglected.

A similar argument can be put forward with regard to the calculation of the effects of one-off increases in financial needs with 1 billion occurring in years other than year 5, and of the effects of one-off increases in first-round value added with $(1 - m)$ billion. Thus, all errors that are related to the third reason can be neglected.

4.3.5. Final remarks

In Section 4.2 it was said that the method of this study can be used in any situation of unemployment, provided that there is an econometric macro-model that fulfils certain conditions. These conditions have been specified above.

With regard to many econometric macro-models, the capability of the model to analyse large and durable changes has been the subject of much research and discussion. On the contrary, the capability of econometric macro-models to analyse large one-off changes has hardly been investigated, and it has not been the subject of a well-known discussion among economists. Therefore, it is sensible to use the calculations of the effects of large and durable changes as a benchmark. Thus, if there is a small difference between $\sum_{t=1}^{15} (U_t + H_t)$ and the effects of the relevant durable change calculated in one run, in the sense that the effects of the former can be regarded as more positive (negative), then the outcomes of the method should be seen as having a bias in favour of (against) the project.

In case the difference between $\sum_{t=1}^{15} (U_t + H_t)$ and the effects of the relevant durable change calculated in one run is large, this does not automatically imply that the method of this study is rendered worthless. For instance, let us assume that the calculations to be made in Chapter 5 show that $\sum_{t=1}^{15} (U_t + H_t)$ is 20% lower than the effects of the relevant durable change calculated in one run. In that case it might be a good idea to multiply all matrices U_t and H_t by 1.25, and to use the resulting matrices for the calculation of the effects of projects, instead of the matrices U_t and H_t. However, this idea will not be investigated in this study.

4.4. Potential errors related to the estimates when small projects are analysed

4.4.1. Introduction

In Section 3.2.2 it was noted that as yet econometric macro-models have not been used for the appraisal of small projects. Although the motivation for not doing this has not been explained extensively in the literature, in all likelihood it is something like the following: econometric macro-models are estimated on the basis of information about large-scale variables. This implies that they can (in principle) be used to analyse the effects of large changes. However, they can give no information about the effects of small changes, because they have not been estimated on the basis of information about small-scale variables.

Continuing this line of thought for a moment, one could say that the application of the method of this study to small projects is not justifiable. There is no econometric justification for taking the effects of small one-off changes to be proportional to the effects of large one-off changes as calculated by means of an econometric macro-model. This procedure could lead to errors, because in reality all kinds of discontinuities and other non-linearities exist. For instance, suppose that the model contains a downward-sloping Phillips curve. According to the method of this study, a change in unemployment with one man-year that is a direct consequence of a small project, will then have a small effect on the wage-rate, and through the wage-rate on other variables such as exports. These effects are not negligible in relation to the size of the project. However, the Phillips curve is related to the behaviour of labour unions, which do not react to every small change in the unemployment level. This implies that the best estimate of the effects of the small project, taken in isolation, includes a zero increase in the price-level. Thus, the method leads to errors.

Thus far, I have considered the arguments which could be used by opponents of the application of the method of this study to small projects. In this section it will be argued that despite these arguments such an application is sensible.

To begin with, let us specify the question to be answered in this section. Essentially, the method of this study consists of three steps. First, the effects of one-off changes of 1 billion and of $(1-m)$ billion are calculated with the econometric macro-model. Second, the effects of one-off changes caused by the project are set proportional to the effects of the relevant one-off changes of 1 billion or $(1-m)$ billion. Third, the effects of the different one-off changes caused by the project are added up to obtain the effects of the project. In the previous section it was established that, if five specific conditions are fulfilled, the effects of the large one-off changes, as calculated by means of the econometric macro-model, can be regarded as acceptable estimates of the actual effects. It was also established that, if these conditions are fulfilled, the second and third steps are justifiable with regard to large projects. It is left to Chapter 5 to prove that these conditions are fulfilled. The question to be answered in this section is whether, if the five conditions mentioned above are fulfilled, the second and the third steps are justifiable with regard to small projects. Small projects include projects with investments below 1 million guilders.

The structure of this section is as follows: Sections 4.4.2 and 4.4.3 prepare the ground for the following sections. In Section 4.4.2 attention is paid to the concept of risk-pooling. In Section 4.4.3 one of the problems related to the second step is discussed in the context of a specific hypothetical setting. Section 4.4.4 gives a more realistic treatment of all problems related to the second step. The third step is discussed in Section 4.4.5, which can be rather short. The limitation of Sections 4.4.4 and 4.4.5 is that they are based on one specific assumption. This assumption will be the subject of Section 4.4.6, which also completes the discussion of the method of this study. In Section 4.4.7 a widely accepted principle, which is not related to this method, will be criticized on the basis of the foregoing sections.

4.4.2. The concept of risk-pooling

An important topic in the cost–benefit literature is the evaluation of risks and uncertainties. Risk and uncertainty are related to decisions that may have various outcomes. They can be distinguished from each other: risk occurs in situations in which it is possible to attach probabilities to the various outcomes, whereas uncertainty occurs in situations in which this is not possible (Pearce and Nash, 1981). This section will discuss a concept that is, initially, related to the occurence of risk.

The meaning of risk neutrality and risk aversion is well-known, and need not be explained here. Attention will only be paid to an implication of risk neutrality and of risk aversion. Assume that an economic actor must decide about a project with uncertain returns. Assume that there are various possible returns, and that to each of them a probability can be attached. If the actor is risk-neutral, he will invest in the project if the expected value of the net benefits is positive. If he is risk-averse, he will invest if the expected value of the net benefits minus some value that represents the cost of risk-bearing is positive.

In cost–benefit analyses, it is generally assumed that people are risk-averse. When government projects are analysed, it is usually assumed that the profits or losses of the government are passed on to the tax payers. In many cases it is also assumed that the preference function of the government can be derived from the preference functions of the tax payers. These three assumptions imply that, in principle, the government is also risk-averse.

However, the costs of risk-bearing related to a project are lower when the government invests in the project than when an individual invests in it. This arises from two aspects of government projects. First, each government project is only one out of many, so that, if certain conditions regarding the composition of the portfolio are fulfilled (see below), we can expect those which turn out to have lower net benefits than expected (or even losses) to be more or less counterbalanced by those which happen to secure higher net benefits than expected. This is known as risk-pooling. There are two conditions for risk-pooling to occur. The first one is that the portfolio should not be dominated by one or more large projects (or large uniform sub-portfolios of projects) in such a way that the risk of these projects (or sub-portfolios) dominates the general risk structure of the portfolio. The second condition is that there should be no interdependence among projects, or, if there is, it should be such that this interdependence reduces the overall risk attached to the portfolio (Samuelson and Vickrey, 1964; Arrow and Lind, 1970; Pearce and Nash, 1981).

The second reason why the costs of risk-bearing are lower for a government than for an individual has to do with the spreading of risks among people. Essentially the argument is that there are many taxpayers who share the profits or losses of government projects. Therefore, the risk per taxpayer for any single project is small (Arrow and Lind, 1970).

With regard to the following discussion, three points are relevant. First, the discussion above was based on the idea that in the preference function of the government only the expected value of the net benefits of the total portfolio of government projects and the risk attached to the total portfolio play a part. The remainder of this chapter will also be based on this idea. In some cases the phrase 'the expected value of the net benefits' will be replaced by 'the expected value of the effects', because the question how to translate the effects of a project in terms of net benefits will not be answered until Section 4.6. Second, it is generally assumed (or argued on the basis of some other assumptions) that the government is risk-averse. The discussion below will also be based on this assumption.[9]

Third, in the following sections the concept of risk-pooling will be used. This concept concerns the following principle *only*: insofar as risks related to some projects are cancelled out by risks related to other projects, they can be neglected by the decision-maker. In order to prove that risks are cancelled out, I will use an argument which differs somewhat from the argument given above; to avoid confusion, I suggest that for now the reader forgets what has been said above about the two conditions for risk-pooling to occur. (Of course, the reader can check whether the argument below is not inconsistent with the argument concerning the two conditions for risk-pooling to occur given above. However, the point is that this could best be done after Section 4.4.)

4.4.3. One of the problems related to the principle of proportionality, in the context of a hypothetical setting

The method of this study is based on the principle that the effects of small one-off changes in financial needs and in first-round value added can be taken to be proportional to the effects of large one-off changes. This principle is called the principle of proportionality. In this section one of the problems related to this principle will be discussed within a hypothetical setting. The aim of this section is to prepare the ground for the next one, which provides a more general discussion.

This hypothetical setting is the following. The 'macroeconomic model' used consists of one relation only: the direct relation between incomes and consumption, with 'incomes' being an exogenous variable. All other relations in the economy can be neglected, except for the relation between government projects and income discussed below. According to the model, the relation between income and consumption is a linear one. For every individual the true relation between these variables is also a linear one. In other words, for every individual the marginal propensity to consume is constant. The marginal propensities to consume differ between individuals. An individual's marginal propensity to consume is independent of his or her economic position.

All government projects consist of an increase in expenditure only. Outputs are not produced. All projects are financed by a decrease in development aid, without further consequences for the domestic economy. All projects last one year only, and are implemented in the same year. The project expenditures lead to an increase in incomes that is equal to these expenditures multiplied by the difference between one and the relevant import coefficient. The estimate of this increase in incomes is based on project-specific information. This estimate is perfect. At the time a potential project is evaluated, there is no information regarding the question which individuals will experience an increase in income as a result of the project. However, the number of individuals who will experience an increase in income can be determined, as well as the size of the individual increases in income.

In this hypothetical setting the method for the estimation of the effects of a project consists of two steps. The first step is to carry out specific research to estimate the effect of the project on incomes. The second step is to use the 'macroeconomic model' to estimate the effects of the increase in incomes on consumption.

In this study the concept 'probability' is regarded as synonymous with 'objective probability'. An (objective) probability distribution is a probability distribution that is based on a large number of observations of individual elements or relations. The concept 'subjective probability' will not be used in this study.[10] Probability distributions are generally estimated by human scientists. In this study, however, the possibility is left open that a probability distribution is estimated by some kind of demi-god. This demi-god is capable of doing the individual observations needed to establish a probability distribution in situations in which human scientists are not capable of doing so. However, the demi-god is not perfect, and cannot predict the future with absolute certainty, which is why he works with probability distributions.

The 'macroeconomic model' discussed earlier is constructed by human beings. With regard to the estimation of this model, two alternative assumptions can be made. The first is that the estimate of the consumption coefficient is based on information on consumption and income of a large number of individuals. For each of these individuals, figures for consumption and income are available over a long period. On the basis of this information the propensity to consume is estimated for each of them. The consumption coefficient of the model is then set equal to the (weighed) average of these propensities to consume. The assumption described above is called *assumption A1*. It implies that for human beings it is possible to give a probability distribution of the propensity to consume of individuals. Given the assumptions underlying elementary statistics, the following can be said. If the increase in incomes caused by the project is large, and if, in relation to this, many consumers experience an increase in income, then the 95% confidence interval of the resulting increase in consumption will be relatively small (that is, small in relation to the project). If the project is small, and if only few consumers experience an increase in incomes, then the 95% confidence interval will be relatively large. A similar conclusion can be drawn for any other confidence interval.

The alternative assumption is that human beings do not have the information needed to make a probability distribution of the propensity to consume of individuals, and that the consumption coefficient of the model is based on information about aggregate consumption and aggregate income over a long period. This assumption is called *assumption A2*. Assumption A2 implies that the estimate of the consumption coefficient can be expected to be equal to the estimate based on assumption A1. The fact that human beings cannot make a probability distribution of the propensity to consume of individuals does not imply that such a distribution does not exist. It does exist, because it can be estimated by the demi-god. If the demi-god used his probability distribution to analyse the uncertainties related to the estimated effects of the project, he would come to the following conclusion: the smaller the project, the greater these uncertainties (in relation to the project). This considered, human beings can draw the same conclusion. Thus, we can draw this conclusion not only on the basis of assumption A1, but also on the basis of assumption A2.

The problem of this section can now be defined as follows: because of the above, the relative uncertainties related to the estimated effect of a small one-off change in incomes are greater than those related to the estimated effect of a large one-off change in incomes. This implies (by definition) that the uncertainties related to the problem

Assumption A1:	The consumption coefficient of the model is based on information on consumption and income of a large number of individuals.
Assumption A2:	This coefficient is based on information about aggregate consumption and aggregate income; human beings do not have the information needed to make a probability distribution of the consumption coefficient of individuals.
Assumption B:	The analysed project is part of a large portfolio of projects that are all analysed by means of the same method.

Figure 4.2. Some of the assumptions used for the argument.

of this section are cancelled out completely at the level of the large one-off change.[11]

The question now is how to evaluate these uncertainties. The answer will first be based on assumption A1. This assumption and some other assumptions used below are summarized in Figure 4.2. Given assumption A1, the effect of a project on consumption, calculated as explained above, is an expected value. Moreover, it is possible to estimate the probability distribution of this effect. Therefore, from the point of view of a cost-benefit analyst, the 'uncertainties' related to the problem of this section are not uncertainties, but risks.

Because the government is risk-averse, it will base its decision about the project not only on the expected value of its effects, but also on the uncertainties surrounding this expected value. In this context it is useful to introduce (for the time being) another assumption, *assumption B*. Assumption B is that the project is part of a large portfolio of government projects that are all analysed in the way explained above. This implies that the small one-off changes in incomes caused by individual projects are part of a large one-off change in incomes, and that all small one-off changes in incomes are analysed in the same way.

Given assumptions A1 and B, the following holds good: insofar as the risks relating to each small project are caused by the problem of this section, they cancel out completely at the level of the portfolio. Therefore, the concept of risk-pooling applies; the risks mentioned above can be neglected by the cost-benefit analyst.

The next question is whether the argument changes if instead of assumption A1 assumption A2 is valid. In answering this question, assumption B will be maintained. According to assumption A2 human beings do not have the information needed to make a probability distribution of the effect of a small one-off change. This has two implications. First, it is still an open question whether the calculated effect of a project is an expected value. The customary definition of expected value is $p_1.x_1 + p_2.x_2 + ... + p_n.x_n$, with p_i denoting the probability that x has the value x_i, and n denotes the number of possible values. Because the probability distribution of the effects is unknown by human beings, one might think at first sight that it is not possible for them to calculate the expected value of the effect. This is important because in the decision-making process the expected value is an important variable.

Fortunately, we know the following: if the demi-god estimated a probability distribution on the basis of information about all individual changes in income and consumption in the past, and if he used this probability distribution to calculate the expected value of the effect of a small project, then one could anticipate this expected value to be equal to the effect as calculated by human beings in the way described above (that is, as calculated on the basis of information about aggregate income and aggregate consumption). Therefore, the effect as calculated by human beings can still be regarded as an expected value, despite the fact that human beings do not know the probability distribution.

The second implication of assumption A2 is the following: the uncertainties related to the estimated effect of a small project cannot be regarded as risks by human decision-makers. Strictly speaking, this implies that the concept of risk-pooling cannot be applied.

The uncertainties related to the estimated effect of a small one-off change in case assumption A2 is valid cancel out at the level of the portfolio to the same extent as the risks cancel out in case assumption A1 is valid.[12] Thus, the question is whether the evaluation of uncertainties that cancel out at the portfolio level should differ from the evaluation of risks that cancel out at the same level. There is no reason to answer this question in the affirmative. The concept 'risk-pooling' can be extended to 'risk- and uncertainty-pooling'. According to this concept, risks and uncertainties can be neglected by a decision-maker as far as they cancel out at the portfolio level. Therefore, it is irrelevant whether assumption A1 or A2 is valid.

The question how the argument changes if assumption B is abandoned is discussed in Section 4.4.6. Here it is concluded that the concept 'risk-pooling' can be extended to 'risk- and uncertainty-pooling'. The fact that the uncertainties surrounding the estimated effects of a project are relatively larger the smaller the project can be neglected by a cost-benefit analyst – at least in the hypothetical setting of this section.

4.4.4. The principle of proportionality, considered from a more general and realistic point of view

This section gives a more general approach to the problems that may be related to the principle of proportionality, which underlies the second step of the method. As will be recalled, the second step implies that the effects of the one-off changes caused by the project are set proportional to the effects of the relevant one-off changes of 1 billion and $(1 - m)$ billion. In analysing these problems assumption B will essentially be maintained, but it will be specified in a slightly different way. In order to do so, let us first define portfolio Z as the portfolio that consists of all new government projects. The distinction between 'new' and 'not new' is an arbitrary one; here it is such that portfolio Z leads to yearly increases in financial needs and first-round value added that are in the order of one or a few billion guilders. This considered, assumption B can be specified: the analysed project is part of portfolio Z, and all projects of this portfolio are analysed with the method of this study. Note that there are no restrictions regarding the types of projects that are included in portfolio Z; nor will there be in the remainder of this chapter. In relation to this, the argument given below holds good for any composition of portfolio Z. Note that the effects of portfolio Z can, of course, be calculated with the method of this study.

The problem to be discussed in this section is whether it is justifiable to set the effects of the one-off changes caused by the small project proportional to the effects of the relevant one-off changes of 1 billion or $(1-m)$ billion. This problem can now be restated as follows: is it justifiable to set the effects of the one-off changes caused by the small project proportional to the effects of the relevant one-off changes that constitute portfolio Z, as calculated by the method of this study? Note that the way in which the problem is restated does not change the problem, because according to the method of this study the effects of the one-off changes that constitute portfolio Z are calculated as being proportional to the effects of the relevant changes of 1 billion and $(1-m)$ billion.

In order to discuss this problem, let us first of all pay attention to the objectives of the government. In general terms, it is the aim of the government to have an optimal economic development. What is meant by optimal will be discussed in Section 4.6. An important conclusion of that section is mentioned here: assuming that the government bases its decisions on neo-Paretian welfare theory, the only variables it needs to take into account when making a decision on investment projects are total consumption, total employment, total investment, the government deficit, and the balance on current account. In relation to this, it is assumed in this section that the government is only interested in (some elements of) the total economic development. This implies that the government is ultimately not interested in the effects of a project, taken in isolation. Instead it is interested in the contribution of individual projects to the total economic development. Now, in this study 'the effects of a portfolio' refer to the contribution of a portfolio to the total economic development. In other words, interaction effects between the portfolio and other economic phenomena are included. (Interaction effects between different changes were defined earlier as the difference between the simultaneous effects of all these changes taken together, and the sum total of the effects of these different changes taken in isolation.) Therefore, it can be said that the government is interested in the contribution of individual projects to the effects of portfolio Z.

The contribution of a small project to the effects of a portfolio of which it is part can be defined as follows: it is equal to the effects of the project, taken in isolation, plus the contribution of the project to the interaction effects between the different projects in the portfolio. The contribution of a project to the interaction effects between the individual projects in the portfolio is not defined exactly. However, this definition is such that the sum total of the contributions of the individual projects to the effects of the portfolio is equal to the effects of the portfolio.

This section is not concerned with the third step of the method, in which the effects of the various one-off changes that are part of a project are added up to get its total effects. Therefore, it can be assumed in this section that the analysed project consists of one small one-off change (in financial needs, or in first-round value added) only.

The contribution of a small one-off change to the effects of the large one-off change of which it is part, and the contribution of a large one-off change to the effects of the portfolio of which it is part, can be defined in a way that is similar to the way in which the contribution of a project to the effects of the portfolio was defined. In Section 4.3 it was, on the basis of the assumption that the model used fulfils certain conditions, concluded that the effects of large one-off changes, as calculated with the method of this study, are a satisfactory estimate of the actual effects, and that they do not incorrectly exclude interaction effects between different large one-off changes. This implies that this section can be based on the assumption that the contribution of a small one-off change to the effects of portfolio Z is equal to the contribution of this small one-off change to the effects of the relevant large one-off change that is part of portfolio Z. Thus, it can be said that the government is interested in the contribution of the project, or in other words of the small one-off change, to the effects of the relevant large one-off change.

The question is now, what is known about the contribution of a small one-off change to the effects of a large one-off change? In answering this question, it will be assumed in the first instance that there is no specific information about the small one-off changes that constitute the large one-off change, apart from their size in terms of first-round value added or financial needs.

The sum total of the contributions of all small one-off changes that constitute a certain large one-off change to the effects of this large one-off change is equal to the effects of this large one-off change. In Section 4.4.3 it was argued that it is possible (for human beings) to calculate expected values even if they do not know the probability distribution. This considered, the expected value of the contribution of a small one-off change is proportional to the effects of the large one-off change.

The question to be answered in this section is whether it is justifiable to set the effects of a one-off change related to a small project proportional to the effects of the relevant one-off change which is part of portfolio Z. It can now be said that this procedure involves the calculation of the expected value of the contribution of this one-off change to the effects of the large one-off change. Given the objective of the government discussed above, the government is interested in this expected value. However, because the government is risk-averse, it is also interested in the uncertainties surrounding this expected value, and therefore these uncertainties need to be evaluated too.

These uncertainties can be considerable, as can be explained by the following example. Suppose that the actual relation between financial needs and the rate of interest is discontinuous. Suppose also that in reality the rate of interest does not change when the financial needs increase with 81,763 million guilders or less, but that it increases when the financial needs increase with 81,764 million guilders or more. Then it is possible that in reality the contribution of most small one-off changes in financial needs to the increase in the interest rate is zero, whereas one small one-off change (of 1 million guilders) has a relatively large contribution. It is, however, difficult to predict exactly how the increase in the interest rate is related to the various small one-off changes. The cause of this problem is twofold. First, it is difficult to estimate the precise nature of the relation. Second, it is difficult to predict the order of implementation of the projects (and the related one-off changes in financial needs). More in generally, hardly anything is known about the uncertainties surrounding the expected value of the contribution of a small one-off change.

One thing is known however. Because the sum of the contributions of all small one-off changes is equal to the effect of the large one-off change, the uncertainties related to this expected value cancel out at the level of the large one-off change to a certain extent. The relative uncertainties related to the estimates of the contributions of small one-off changes that do not cancel out are equal in size to the relative uncertainties related to the estimate of the effects of the large one-off change. Given the argument in Section 4.3, these uncertainties are acceptable. The uncertainties that are related to the principle of proportionality cancel out at the level of the large change completely.

The final question is how to evaluate the uncertainties surrounding the expected value of the contribution of a small one-off change that are related to the principle of proportionality. The answer is simple. These uncertainties can be neglected by a cost–benefit analyst, because the concept of risk- and uncertainty-pooling applies.

The argument given above was based on the assumption that there is no specific information about the small one-off changes, apart from their size in terms of first-round value added or financial needs. However, there are situations in which more specific information is available. This problem concerns the analysis of both large and small projects. It has been discussed in Section 4.3.2 in the context of the analysis of large projects. Clearly, the remarks made in that section also apply to small projects.

4.4.5. The third step of the method

In the previous section it has been argued that the second step of the method, in which the effects of a small one-off change are taken to be proportional to the effects of a large one-off change, is justifiable. The remaining problem concerns the third step. In the third step the effects of a small project are taken to be equal to the sum total of the effects of the small one-off changes caused by the project. The question is then whether the interaction effects between the different parts of the project are incorrectly neglected. In answering this question, the assumption that the project is part of a large portfolio of new projects which are all analysed by means of the method developed in this study is maintained. This considered, the question is easy to answer. Given the objectives of the government as described above, the government is not interested in the interaction effects between the different one-off changes caused by the project, insofar as this project is analysed in isolation. Rather, it is interested in the question whether, at the portfolio level, the interaction effects between the different one-off changes have been taken into account in a correct way. In Section 4.3 this question has been answered in the affirmative. Therefore, there is no need to bother about the interaction effects between the different one-off changes caused by an individual project.

4.4.6. The justification of the method when it is used to analyse one project, or a few projects only

So far the assumption has been that the analysed project is part of a large portfolio of new government projects which are all analysed by means of the method of this study. This assumption is now abandoned. Instead, it is assumed that only one new government project is analysed with this method; the other projects of portfolio Z are analysed with another method (see below). The reader can verify for him or herself that the argument given below would not change if it were assumed that a small number of new government projects are analysed with the method of this study.

It was argued in Section 4.4.4 that, given that certain conditions to be discussed in Chapter 5 are fulfilled, the estimate of the effects of a small one-off change made with the method of this study can be regarded as the expected value of the contribution of this small one-off change to the effects of portfolio Z, which consists of a number of large one-off changes. This implies that the effects of a small project that consists of various small one-off changes, calculated with the method of this study as being equal to the sum total of the effects of these small one-off changes, can be regarded as the expected value of the contribution of this project to the effects of portfolio Z.

This section deals with the situation in which one new project only is analysed by means of the method of this study. Clearly, the estimate of the effects of this project can still be regarded as the expected value of the contribution of this project to the effects of portfolio Z. This considered, the only reason why it could not be justifiable to apply this method to one small project only is that the relative uncertainties related to the estimated effects of a project become greater as the project is smaller. This is the problem to be discussed in this section.

To begin with, it is noted that in reality there is always a large portfolio of new government projects. Let us consider the way in which new projects other than the project analysed by means of the method of this study are evaluated. If a decision is made about one of these projects, it must implicitly or explicitly be based on some estimate of its effects. This estimate will probably include some estimate of the microeconomic effects of the expenditures and the output. It could include some estimate of the macroeconomic effects, calculated in one way or the other. Part of the estimate could perhaps be regarded as an implicit estimate made by the decision-maker. For example, if the effect on the rate of interest were neglected by the decision-maker, one could say that his implicit estimate of this effect is zero. Whatever the truth about this, and whatever the procedure, the point is that a decision about a new project not analysed by means of the method of this study is, implicitly or explicitly, always based on some estimate of its effects. This estimate will be called a rudimentary estimate, and the related method will be called a rudimentary method.[13]

This leads us to the following question. If only one small project is analysed by means of the method of this study, is it then possible that (part of) the errors related to the estimate of its effects that are caused by the problem discussed in this section are cancelled out by (part of) the errors related to the rudimentary estimates of the effects of other new projects? In other words, does the concept 'risk- and uncertainty-pooling' still apply if only one project is analysed by means of the method of this study?

The (one) new project analysed with the method of this study is called project Y. The portfolio of all new government projects excluding project Y is called portfolio X. Portfolio X consists of a large number of projects, and includes many small projects. The portfolio of all new government projects including project Y is called portfolio Z (as before). These and other definitions given below are summarized in Figure 4.3.

Portfolio X	=	portfolio of new government projects that are, in reality, analysed by means of one or more rudimentary methods.
Project Y	=	new government project that is, in reality, analysed by means of the method of this study.
Portfolio Z	=	portfolio of all new government projects including project Y.

R_x	=	rudimentary estimate of effects of portfolio X (made, explicitly or implicitly, in reality).
S_y	=	estimate of the effects of project Y, based on the method developed in this study (made in reality).
S_x	=	estimate of the effects of portfolio X, based on the method developed in this study (hypothetical situation).
SR_z	=	(implicit) estimate of the effects of portfolio Z = $S_y + R_x$.
E_{rx}	=	errors related to R_x.
E_{sy}	=	errors related to S_y.
E_{sx}	=	errors related to S_x.
E_{srz}	=	errors related to $SR_z = E_{sy} + E_{rx}$.

Figure 4.3. Summary of definitions.

As was said before, the individual projects of portfolio X are, implicitly or explicitly, evaluated on the basis of rudimentary estimates of their effects. Besides, these projects are, implicitly or explicitly, evaluated on the basis of some estimate of the effects of portfolio X. This becomes clear when we realize that, when the decisions about the individual projects are explicitly based on the estimate of their individual effects only, the decision-maker implicitly assumes the interaction effects to be zero. Therefore, he or she implicitly assumes the effects of portfolio X to be equal to the sum total of the effects of the individual projects. The (explicit or implicit) estimate of the effects of portfolio X is called the rudimentary estimate of these effects, and it is denoted as R_x (which can be regarded as a matrix with various effects). The errors related to this estimate are denoted as E_{rx}. E_{rx} is equal to the difference between R_x and the actual contribution of portfolio X to the effects of portfolio Z. The effects of project Y as calculated with the method of this study are denoted as S_y. The difference between S_y and the actual contribution of project Y to the effects of portfolio Z is denoted as E_{sy}.

When the method of this study is applied to project Y only, and when the results are used by the decision-maker in the way proposed in this study, the effects of portfolio Z are implicitly taken to be equal to the sum total of S_y and R_x by the decision-maker. This implicit estimate of the decision-maker is denoted as SR_z. The total error which is related to this estimate is denoted as E_{srz}. Given the definition of the concept 'contribution to the total effects', the sum total of the actual contribution of project Y to the effects of portfolio Z and the actual contribution of portfolio X to the effects of portfolio Z is equal to the actual effects of portfolio Z. Therefore, E_{srz} is equal to the sum total of E_{sy} and E_{rx}.

When project Y is implemented, that is, when it is included in the portfolio of new government projects, the errors related to the (implicit) estimate of the effects of the portfolio of new government projects change from E_{rx} to E_{srz}. In order to answer the question whether the concept 'risk- and uncertainty-pooling' applies the values of E_{rx} and E_{srz} have to be compared.

In order to do so, it is necessary to discuss a point which may seem to be irrelevant at first sight. Given that (in reality) only one project of the portfolio of all new government projects is analysed by means of the method of this study, a situation in which all new projects are analysed by means of this method should be regarded as a hypothetical situation. Let us nevertheless consider this situation. Portfolio X still refers to the new projects analysed with one or more rudimentary methods in reality. In the hypothetical situation, however, the effects of these projects are estimated with the method of this study. The effects of portfolio X are estimated as being equal to the sum total of the estimates of these individual effects. This estimate of the effects of portfolio X is denoted as S_x. The errors related to S_x are denoted as E_{sx}, so that the actual effects of portfolio X are equal to $S_x - E_{sx}$. The following holds good:

$$E_{rx} = R_x - (S_x - E_{sx}) = (R_x - S_x) + E_{sx}.$$

$$E_{srz} = E_{rx} + E_{sy} = (R_x - S_x) + E_{sx} + E_{sy}.$$

On the basis of these formulae E_{rx} and E_{srz} can be compared. Consider the last two terms of the second formula. The sum total of E_{sx} and E_{sy} is equal to the sum total of the individual errors that would be made if the method of this study was applied to all individual projects of portfolio Z (because E_{sx} is equal to the sum total of the individual errors that would be made if the method of this study was applied to all individual projects of portfolio X). Part of these individual errors are cancelled out at the level of portfolio Z. They are not cancelled out completely however. The reason is the following: if the effects of portfolio Z are estimated as being equal to the sum total of the effects of all its individual projects as estimated by means of the method of this study, then the resulting estimate will not be perfect (but acceptable; see Section 4.3).

Let us divide E_{sy} and E_{sx} into two parts. The first part consists of the errors that are cancelled out at the level of portfolio Z. The other part consists of the errors that are not cancelled out at the level of portfolio Z. The problem discussed in this section is that the relative uncertainties related to the estimate of the effects of a change (such as a project or portfolio) become greater as the change becomes smaller. Insofar as errors are not cancelled out at the level of the large change, the relative uncertainties do not become larger as the change becomes smaller. Therefore, the problem discussed in this section concerns the first part of E_{sy} only. Clearly, as far as this part of E_{sy} is concerned, one cannot expect $|E_{srz}|$ to be larger than $|E_{rx}|$, and the concept 'risk- and uncertainty-pooling' applies.

To summarize the foregoing sections: from an econometric point of view, the errors related to the method of this study are relatively larger as the project is smaller, but from the point of view of a cost–benefit analyst this problem can be neglected.

4.4.7. A common misconception

In many studies in which a project or another change is analysed one finds the following proposition: if the change is small it has no (significant) effect on prices, and therefore price changes can be neglected. It follows from the argument above, however, that this proposition is not correct. This can be illustrated as follows. In Chapter 2 it was argued that a large-scale policy of stimulating oil-saving projects pursued by the EU can lead to a decrease in the world oil price and therefore to a decrease in the import costs of the EU. Under certain circumstances this decrease in import costs can amount to dozens of percents of the direct benefits of the projects, defined as the quantity of the oil savings multiplied by a given oil price. Many economists would say that an argument like this can only hold good for a large number of projects, because, if only one project is implemented, there is no effect on the world oil price. This conclusion however is not justifiable.

To explain this, let us assume that in the EU there is only one small government project which can lead to savings on oil. Let us also assume that all oil savings caused by this project occur in one year, called the next year. To keep the analysis simple, the supply of oil is assumed to be constant. The change in the world oil price in the next year is then determined by a large number of individual changes in demand for oil, such as the change caused by the project mentioned above, or the change caused by the decision of Mr. Jones to buy a car. It is assumed that in the preference function of the government only the following two factors play a role: the expected value of the total future economic development, and the uncertainties related to this expected value.

This considered, the 'government' of the EU is not interested in the effect of the small oil-saving project taken in isolation on the oil price, but in the contribution of this project to the total change in the oil price (in the next year). The expected value of this contribution is equal to the total change in the oil price multiplied by the proportion between the change in demand for oil caused by the project and the total change in demand for oil. There are condiderable uncertainties related to this expected value. However, as long as the total change in the oil price is estimated correctly, these uncertainties even out at the level of the total change, so that they can be neglected.

Let us assume that the decrease in the oil price caused by a large decrease in demand for oil is such that it leads to a decrease in the import costs of the EU that is 20% of the quantity of the decrease in demand for oil multiplied by the oil price. The government is interested in the contribution of the small oil-saving project discussed above to the total change in import costs caused by changes in the oil price. Given the above assumption, the expected value of this contribution is 20% of the quantity of the savings on oil of this project multiplied by the oil price. This is not negligible in relation to the size of the project, so that it should be taken into account when a decision about the project is made. There are condiderable uncertainties related to this expected value, but as long as the total change in the oil price is estimated correctly, these can be neglected by the government. It follows that price changes cannot always be neglected when the analysed project or the analysed change is small.

4.5. The advantages of the method of this study as compared with the conventional macroeconometric method

The conventional method of analysing the effects of a project by means of an econometric macro-model, which was described in Section 3.2.2, consists of the calculation of the effects of the project as a whole by means of two model runs: the base-run and the model run including the project. The question to be answered in this section is why, instead of using the conventional method, a new method has been developed. This question not only concerns the analysis of large projects, but the analysis of small projects as well; although as yet the conventional method has not been applied to small projects, it is sensible to ask whether this could be done.

There are two reasons why a new method has been developed. The first one, which is especially relevant for small projects, is that the method developed in this study is more efficient for the analysis of a large number of projects than the conventional method. Once the effects of one project have been calculated with the method of this study, the effects of other projects can be calculated relatively easy. The main reason is that an important part of the calculations is disconnected from the project-specific information. This refers to the calculations made by means of the econometric macro-model, to the calculation of the matrices that are completely based on these calculations, and to some of the calculations made by means of the input–output model. A computer program can be designed in such a way that only the project-specific information has to be typed in to get the final results. In this respect the method of this study compares favourably with the conventional method, in which for each project the project-specific information has to be inserted into the econometric macro-model and a new model run has to be made.

The second reason why a new method has been developed is related to the possible occurrence of errors in the estimates of the effects of projects. It concerns both small and large projects, but it will be explained with regard to large projects first. As an introductory remark, it can be said that the construction of an econometric macro-model causes many difficulties. In relation to this, the outcomes of simulations regarding the effects of large changes can give a wrong picture of the actual effects. Econometric macro-models are often used to analyse the effects of large durable changes. Generally, the model-builders spend much effort to ensure that the outcomes of simulations regarding the effects of these changes can be regarded as plausible. For example, when the effects of a large and durable increase in government expenditure are analysed, the outcomes of the simulations are often compared with the outcomes of similar simulations with other models, or with the opinion of a panel of experienced economists. If, for example, the panel of economists is of the opinion that the outcomes are not plausible, this may lead to a search for human mistakes or to a change in the model.

Once a certain number of simulations regarding the effects of different durable large changes has been made with a model, and once the necessary adjustments have been made, it could be argued that the model is capable of analysing the effects of durable large changes. However, this does not automatically imply that the model is also capable of analysing non-durable large changes. Most projects can be regarded as non-durable changes. Therefore one should, before analysing a large project, pay attention to the question whether the model is capable of analysing non-durable large changes. In the studies in which the macroeconomic effects of projects have been calculated in the conventional way (see Section 3.2.2), it remains unclear whether this question has been considered.

More in general, when the conventional method is used, it will be difficult to judge whether or not the calculated effects of a large project are plausible for three reasons: first, the analysed project will (generally) be a unique and non-durable change; second, it will be difficult to find a panel of economists who have knowledge regarding the macroeconomic effects of this unique and non-durable change; and third, generally projects will be analysed with one model only. Thus, it will be more difficult to detect errors. Furthermore, it will be relatively expensive to search for errors that are specifically related to the analysis of a unique project.

When the method of this study is used, the calculations made with the econometric macro-model concern certain 'standard' changes, which are not related to a specific project. In Section 4.3 it was argued that the errors related to the estimation of the effects of a project analysed by means of the method of this study that originate from the calculations with the econometric macro-model are small enough to be acceptable if the model used fulfils five conditions. The first one concerns the capability of the model to analyse large and durable changes. Generally, the model builders (or others) will have investigated to what extent the first condition is fulfilled. The four remaining conditions relate to the calculated effects of the 'standard' changes. If these four conditions are fulfilled (to a certain extent), then no errors are made that are specifically linked to the fact that the project is a unique and non-durable change and that originate from the calculations with the econometric macro-model (or such errors are only made to a certain extent). Because it is possible to investigate to what extent these four conditions are fulfilled (see also the next chapter), the method makes it possible to detect such errors. It will be shown in the next chapter that, in relation to the above, it is relatively easy for others to evaluate possible errors related to the estimation of the effects of a project. Thus, with regard to the detection and evaluation of possible errors, the method of this study compares favourably with the conventional method. Besides, because the last four conditions need to be investigated only once, the method is efficient with regard to the detection of errors when more than one project is analysed.

In the next chapter it will be shown that one of the last four conditions mentioned above is not fulfilled by the Dutch Freia model. However, the related problems can be solved by making certain adaptations to the method. If the conventional method had been used in combination with the Freia model, these problems could possibly also exist, but in that case they would have gone unnoticed.

If a small project were analysed with the conventional method, problems similar to the ones mentioned above could occur. Besides, a problem which is specifically related to the analysis of small changes could occur. This problem can be explained as follows. Usually the builders of the model used have paid attention to the question whether the model is capable of analysing the effects of large durable changes, but not to the question whether small changes can be analysed. For instance, in all likelihood no attention will have been paid to the question whether the mathematical procedure for the solution of the model is such that the effects of a small change can be calculated without relatively large errors. This may not be possible, for example because the number of iterations is too small. Should this be the case, the mathematical procedure for the solution of the model would have to be changed – if the conventional method were used. Clearly, problems such as these cannot occur when the method of this study is used.

4.6. The evaluation of the effects

As was discussed in Chapter 3, Zuidema (1982) has developed an interesting but not yet perfect method to evaluate the effects of a project as calculated by means of an economic macro-model on the basis of neo-Paretian welfare theory. This section sketches the outline of an improved neo-Paretian method. This method is based on the following formula, which defines the present value of the net benefits of a project:[14]

$$\mathrm{PVPVB}_1 = \sum_{t=1}^{\infty} \frac{\sum_i \Delta C_{it} \cdot S_{it}}{(1+\tau)^{t-1}} - \sum_{t=1}^{\infty} \frac{\Delta N_t \cdot S_{nt}}{(1+\tau)^{t-1}}$$

in which:

- PVNB_1 = present value in year 1 of the net benefits of a project, expressed in terms of willingness to pay.
- year 1 = the first year of the lifetime of the project.
- τ = private time preference rate.
- ΔC_{it} = change in consumption of marketed or non-marketed consumption good i in year t, taking all effects of the project into account.
- S_{it} = shadow price of consumption good i in year t, reflecting the willingness to pay for it.
- ΔN_t = change in employment in year t (measured in man-years), taking all effects of the project into account.
- S_{nt} = shadow price of labour in year t (per man-year), reflecting the increase in income to be given to an unemployed person to make him or her accept a job.

When projects are not mutually exclusive, a project is acceptable if and only if its PVNB is positive. When projects are mutually exclusive, the project with the highest PVNB should be accepted. The PVNB concerns the middle of a year. Any change in a variable that occurs in a certain year is assumed to be spread evenly over this year.

The formula reflects some limitations caused by the fact that the effects of a project, as calculated by means of an econometric macro-model, are expressed in terms of aggregates. The first limitation is that it is impossible to take account of consumer surpluses. In the formula this is reflected by the failure to relate the shadow price of a consumption good to the number of goods consumed. In relation to this, the shadow price of a marketed consumption good is equal to its market price. Second, it is impossible to take account of individual differences in the shadow price of labour and in the private time preference rate. Therefore, the shadow price of labour and the private time preference rate in the formula should be considered as averages. Regarding the determination of the private time preference rate and the shadow prices for non-marketed consumption goods and labour the reader is referred to the literature (Pearce and Nash, 1981; Sugden and Williams, 1978; Mishan, 1981). The shadow prices are real prices, that is, they reflect a willingness to pay measured in constant market prices. Therefore, the effects as calculated by means of the econometric macro-model should also be expressed in constant market prices.

Another limitation of the calculations with the econometric macro-model is that they cover only a limited time span. The formula above however covers an infinite time span. Therefore, another formula concerning a finite time span is presented below. This formula also takes account of the remark regarding consumption of marketed goods made above. Besides, it relates to a present value not in the first but in the last year to which the econometric macro-model relates, which has certain advantages in the context of the subsequent analysis. Thus, the following formula is presented:

$$\mathrm{PVNB}_x = \sum_{t=1}^{x} \frac{\Delta CM_t}{(1+\tau)^{t-x}} + \sum_{t=1}^{x} \frac{\Sigma_q \Delta C_{qt} \bullet S_{qt}}{(1+\tau)^{t-x}} + \sum_{t=1}^{x} \frac{\Delta N_t \bullet S_{nt}}{(1+\tau)^{t-x}} + X$$

in which:

PVNB_x = present value in year x of all net benefits of a project, expressed in terms of willingness to pay.

x = last year to which the econometric macro-model relates.

ΔCM_t = total change in consumption of marketed consumption goods in year t as calculated by means of the econometric macro-model, valued at market prices.

ΔC_{qt} = change in consumption of non-marketed consumption good q in year t, taking all effects of the project into account.

S_{qt} = shadow price of non-marketed consumption good q in year t, reflecting the willingness to pay for it.

X = present value in year x of all changes in utility following year x, expressed in terms of willingness to pay.

The most difficult part of the evaluation is the calculation of the last term of the formula, X. Below it is assumed that the lifetime of the analysed projects is shorter than time horizon x. Given this, the following argument can be formulated.

X is the present value in year x of all changes in utility (in terms of willlingness to pay) related to changes in consumption and employment following year x caused by the project. More specifically, these changes in consumption and employment are a result of the fact that, because of the project, the point of departure in year x for the economic development after year x has changed. This point of departure is mainly determined by the level of certain stock variables. In this context, three stock variables are distinguished, viz. government debt, net foreign assets, and the capital stock. These three stock variables have been selected because of the following: first, they are affected by the wind energy project analysed in this study, and second, they are very important for the economic development after year x. In principle, other stock variables could have been selected as well. For instance, one could also have selected the reserve of domestic natural resources, or the financial assets of the government. However, these variables are not affected by the project analysed in this study, and therefore they will be neglected.

The change in government debt in year x caused by the project is equal to the sum of all changes in government deficit up to year x. The change in net foreign assets in year x equals the sum of all changes in the balance on current account up to year x. Regarding the capital stock the following can be said: the project to be analysed in this study does not lead to changes in the stock of capital goods of the government in year x.[15] Therefore, the change in the capital stock in year x is equal to the change in the private stock of capital goods in year x. The latter is equal to the sum of all changes in private investment up to year x, minus a correction for wear and tear and for technological development (which will be described in later chapters).

This considered, two questions should be answered in order to calculate X. First, what are the effects of the changes in government debt, net foreign assets, and capital stock in year x caused by the project, on consumption and employment after year x? Second, how can these changes in consumption and employment (and relatedly leisure time) be converted into a present value in year x of changes in utility, expressed in terms of willingness to pay? The second question should be answered on the basis of evaluation techniques, using concepts such as the time preference rate and the shadow price of labour. The first question should be answered with the aid of macroeconomic analysis. Thus, the problem of evaluating the effects which have been calculated by means of the econometric macro-model is partly a matter of macroeconomic analysis.

As was stated above, X is expressed in terms of utility, measured in terms of willingness to pay. Thus, the calculation of X implies that the changes in government debt, net foreign assets and capital stock in year x are converted into utility. This means that when one answers the two questions mentioned above, one implicitly assigns weights to the changes in these three stock variables, these weights expressing the value of a unit change in each of the stock variables in terms of a unit change in utility.

The first alternative is to use one's own experience and knowledge, or that of some distinguished economists, to determine the weights of the three stock variables. Sensitivity analysis could then be carried out in order to establish the extent to which the acceptability of projects depends upon the weights.

The second alternative is to leave the problem of the evaluation of the effects to the decision-maker. For instance, the project analyst could only calculate the present value in year x of the changes in utility (in terms of willingness to pay) up to year x caused by the project, and the changes in government debt, foreign assets and the capital stock in year x. It could then be left to the decision-maker to judge the project on the basis of this information. If the decision-maker is instructed in such a way that he considers the weights as depending on the answers to the two questions mentioned above, the approach can still be regarded as being based (in a loose sense) on neo-Paretian welfare theory. An even more rudimentary approach is to calculate only the effects of the project on consumption, employment, government deficit, current account, and private investment up to year x, and to leave the rest to the decision-maker. In that case only the choice of the variables of which the changes are calculated can be regarded as being based on neo-Paretian welfare theory.[16]

The third alternative to determine X is to assume that from year $x + 1$ onwards a situation of general equilibrium with a Pareto-optimum exists. This implies that net foreign assets having a value of 1 guilder in year x can be used to generate changes in utility from future consumption and employment that have a present value in year x of one guilder. Thus, the weight of foreign assets is one. Similar remarks apply to the change in the capital stock. However, a change in government debt (which is not accompanied by a change in net foreign assets) will have no influence on future utility levels. Therefore, X is equal to the sum of the change in net foreign assets in year x and the change in private capital stock in year x.

The fourth alternative is to assume that from year $x + 1$ onward, general equilibrium without a Pareto-optimum prevails. The changes in the stock variables can then be valued on the basis of neo-classical insights.

In Chapter 6 the evaluation will be based on the second alternative. The third alternative will be used in Chapter 7.

Criteria for the selection of the method of financing

A point closely related to the evaluation of the effects of a project is the following. There are six different methods of financing: the capital market, business taxes, other direct taxes, indirect taxes, expenditure cuts and liquidity creation. As was explained in Chapter 3, as yet no satisfactory criteria for the selection of the method of financing have been found.

A possible solution to this problem is the following. First, with the econometric macro-model six different calculations of the effects of an increase in development aid are made, each calculation being based on a different method of financing. Using the same criteria as the ones discussed in this section, one can then select the method of financing that has the least negative effects. This method can then be used as a basis for the calculation of the effects of projects.

It may happen that the government imposes binding constraints on the way in which projects are to be financed. For example, the government may rule out the financing of projects by means of tax increases. In such a situation one may, of course, discuss the constraints. If nevertheless they cannot be changed, one should select the best method of financing available, given the constraints.

What has been said above should be regarded as a theoretical ideal. For practical reasons it will be assumed in the following chapters that the projects are financed on the capital market.

Appendix

The treatment of indirect taxes

In the Freia model used in the next chapters the indirect taxes on government investment are very low. The indirect taxes on inputs and capital goods needed for the analysed project, however, may be substantial. Therefore, it has been decided to correct the calculations for the project specific indirect tax-coefficient. In order to explain the procedure, let us give some definitions first.

$\hat{e}$ = government investment including indirect taxes.
e = government investment excluding indirect taxes.
a = first-round value added excluding indirect taxes related to government investment, according to the model.
τ = indirect tax coefficient of the model, with regard to government investment including indirect taxes.
m = import coefficient of the model, with regard to government investment excluding indirect taxes.

From these definitions the following relations can be deduced:

$$e = \hat{e} \bullet (1 - \tau)$$

$$a = e \bullet (1 - m) = \hat{e} \bullet (1 - \mathrm{m})(1 - \tau).$$

For expositional purposes m and t are assumed to be constant over the years. However, this assumption can be abandoned without serious problems. H_t is now defined more precisely than in the main text as the effects of an increase in government investment including indirect taxes with 1 billion guilders in year t. This implies that $H_t/\{(1 - \tau)(1 - m) \bullet 10^9\}$ gives the effects of a first-round increase in value added excluding indirect taxes with 1 guilder. Let us formulate the following definitions.

fit_t = increase in indirect taxes in year t caused by first-round spending effects of the project, as calculated by means of project-specific research and/or an input–output model.
$fvae_t$ = first-round effect on domestic value added excluding indirect taxes in year t of the spendings on the project, as calculated by means of project-specific research and an input–output model.
= $fva_t - fit_t$.

With regard to the spending effects, for the time being the calculation of the J_t and K is changed as follows.

$$J1_t = \frac{1}{(1-\tau)\,(1-m)} \bullet 10^{-9} \bullet H_t$$

$$K1_t = fvae_t \bullet J1_t$$

$$K1 = \sum_{t=1}^{15} K1_t$$

For the time being the effects of financing the expenditures are calculated as:

$$W^1 = \sum_{t=1}^{15} (gfn_t - fit_t) \cdot V_t$$

At first sight one might think that the total effects of the expenditures (including the effects of financing them) are equal to K1 + W^1. However, such a procedure would imply a positive bias. On the one hand the first-round effects of the project on indirect taxes, and the further consequences of this, have been taken into account as $(-fit_t \cdot V_t)$. On the other hand the first-round effects on indirect taxes of an increase in government investment, and the further effects of this, are included in the $K1_t$. It is clear that the latter should be excluded.

In order to accomplish this, the first-round increase in indirect taxes which occurs according to the model when the spending effects of the project are calculated are defined as:

$$hlp_t = fvae \cdot \frac{1}{(1-m)(1-\tau)} \cdot \tau.$$

The effects of financing the project including a correction are defined as W1:

$$W1 = \sum_{t=1}^{15} (gfn_t - fit_t + hlp_t) \cdot V_t.$$

The corrected total effects of the expenditures (including the effects of financing them) are equal to K1 + W1.

Finally, the following can be remarked. Investments in wind farms, which will be discussed in Chapter 6, involve certain increases in land rent paid to the government and in legal charges. These increases can be treated in the same way as project-specific increases in indirect taxes.

List of symbols

A = (q,q) matrix with intermediate input-coefficients (a_{ij}).

fr_t = financial returns of the project in year t, including indirect taxes.

gfn_t = gross financial needs of the project in year t related to the expenditures on the project, including indirect taxes.

fva_t = first-round effect on gross domestic value added of the expenditures on the project in year t, as calculated by specific research and the input–output model, including indirect taxes.

H_t = (20,5) matrix with the effects (on five variables in twenty years) of an increase in government investment with 10^9 guilders in year t (as calculated by the macroeconomic model).

I = identity matrix.

J_t = (20,5) matrix with the the effects of a first-round increase in gross national income of 1 guilder in year t.

K = (20,5) matrix with the effects of the expenditures, excluding the effects of financing them, excluding corrections for imports.

m_t = import coefficient of government investment in year t according to the macroeconomic model, excluding the imports of capital goods needed in the private sector.

ni_t = first-round effect on imports of the expenditures on the project in year t, as calculated by means of specific research and the input–output model.

q = number of sectors in the input–output table.

Q = (20,5) matrix with the effects of selling the output of the project, excluding the effects of the financial returns on the financial position of the project authority and the further effects of the change in this financial position, when the output is an export good or an import substitution good.

R = *idem*, but now for the case in which selling the output leads to a decrease in production of domestic producers.

sct = $(q,1)$ column vector: $(sc_{t1}, sc_{t2}, ..., sc_{ti}, ...sc_{tq})'$; the superscript t indicates the transpose of a vector.

sc_{ti} = decrease in sales of domestic producers in sector i in year t which is a direct consequence of selling the output of the project.

sit = $(q,1)$ column vector: $(si_{t1}, si_{t2}, ..., si_{ti}, ...si_{tq})'$.

si_{ti} = spendings of the project authority in year t on capital goods and intermediate inputs produced in domestic sector i, for which it holds good that the spending effects of these capital goods and intermediate inputs have not been analysed in order to calculate part of var_t, plus spendings in year t of the industries that have been the subject of specific research related to the calculation of var_t on intermediate inputs produced in domestic sector i, for which it holds good that the spending effects of these intermediate inputs have not been analysed in order to calculate part of var_t, these spendings being caused by the project.

U_t = (20,5) matrix with the effects of financing 10^9 guilders by the selected method of financing in year t (as calculated by the macroeconomic model).

v = $(q,1)$ column vector with for each sector the ratio between gross value added in that sector and total output in that sector.

vac_t = first-round effect on gross domestic value added (including indirect taxes) caused by the decrease in sales of domestic producers that is a direct consequence of selling the output of the project.

vai_t = that part of fva_t which is calculated with the help of an input–output model.

var_t = that part of fva_t which is calculated by specific research only.

V_t = (20,5) matrix with the effects of financing 1 guilder by the selected method of financing in year t.

W = (20,5) matrix with the effects of financing the expenditures of the project.

X = (20,5) matrix with the effects of the expenditures, excluding the effects of financing them, including corrections for imports.

Y = (20,5) matrix with the effects of the output.

Z = (20,5) matrix with all the effects of the project.

Notes

1. This excludes the effect of the change in development aid on unilateral transfers. These effects are discussed in the main text later on.
2. See note 1.
3. V_t includes, among other things, the following effects: first, an increase in the government deficit in year t of 1 guilder; second, an increase in the government deficit in year $t + 1$ of 1 guilder multiplied by the rate of interest; third, an increase in the government deficit in year $t + 2$ which is equal to the sum total of the increases in the deficits in year t and year $t + 1$ multiplied by the rate of interest, etc.
4. Regarding the problem of non-linearities, the reader is referred to Section 4.3.
5. Note that fva_t includes all first-round effects on gross value added, and therefore it includes the gross value added produced by the labourers directly employed in the project. H_t includes all first-round effects of an increase in government investment, so it includes the direct employment effects of this increase. Therefore, X includes an estimate of the direct effects of the project on employment. However, this is a very rough estimate; although it is based on specific research regarding the number of labourers directly employed in the project, the outcomes of this research have only been used to help determine the size of fva_t.
6. This assumption implies that the satisfaction through consumption of the domestic buyers increases, because otherwise there would be no reason for them to buy the output of the project. However, to facilitate the explanation the increase in satisfaction levels is assumed to be so small that it can be neglected. It may nevertheless be noted that the next subsection will show that changes in satisfaction levels can be incorporated into the method. If the financial position of the domestic buyers did change this might lead to changes in demand and supply on the capital market. These would then have to be analysed, at least if they were not too small in relation to the project. Analysing the effects of these changes would involve a new set of calculations with the macroeconomic model.
7. This calculation is not completely correct. Matrix R should be corrected for specific information about imports. This correction is similar to the correction of matrix K (see Section 4.2.3).
8. Note that this combined increase in development aid (financed on the capital market) and in government investment (financed by a decrease in development aid) is equal to an increase in government investment financed on the capital market.
9. The reader can easily check for him or herself that the main conclusions of this chapter will not be different if the government is risk-neutral.
10. Objective probability distributions are discussed in any textbook on statistics. Regarding 'subjective probability distributions', see e.g. Maddala (1977), pp. 15–17.
11. The fact that the relative uncertainties related to the estimated effects of a small change are greater than those related to the estimated effects of the large change implies that part of the former cancel out at the level of the large change. The relative uncertainties related to the estimate of the effects of a small change that do not cancel out at the level of a large change are equal in size to the relative uncertainties related to the estimate of the effects of the large change.
12. Thus, although we cannot talk about risks, we are dealing with a type of uncertainty about which we know much more than what is generally known about uncertainties (as opposed to risks). One wonders whether the usual distinction between risk and uncertainty is appropriate with regard to the problem at hand.
13. These names are given to clarify the issue, not to insult others. Of course, there are other methods of project analysis which are not rudimentary, but these too are only applied to a limited number of projects.
14. This formula is more or less similar to the ones presented by Zuidema (1982), Johansson (1982) and Nentjes and Zuidema (1987).
15. Because the lifetime of the project is shorter than time horizon x.
16. Basing project evaluation on welfare theory does not automatically imply that project evaluation is inconsistent with macroeconomic policy. The variables considered important by macroeconomists may, in the final analysis, only be considered important because they will sooner or later affect the levels of consumption and employment.

CHAPTER 5

The calculations done with the Freia model

5.1. Introduction

The description of the method for project appraisal in the previous chapter was such that in principle different econometric macro-models could be used. This chapter discusses the use of one specific model, the Freia model of the Dutch Central Planning Bureau (CPB). In the next chapter the outcomes of the calculations with this model will be used to analyse a specific project.

The structure of this chapter is as follows. Section 5.2 describes the Freia model. Section 5.3 gives a description of the base-run. Section 5.4 pays attention to the calculation of the matrices H_t and U_t, which relate to the effects of one-off increases in government investment and the effects of one-off increases in development aid respectively. In Section 5.5 it is demonstrated that the outcomes of the calculations fulfil the conditions of additivity mentioned in Chapter 4. Section 5.6 shows that another condition mentioned in chapter 4 is not fulfilled by the Freia model, and presents a solution for the related problems. Section 5.7 discusses the period to which the analysis refers. In Section 5.8 a comparison is made between the calculations done for this study and certain calculations done by the CPB. Section 5.9 gives a general evaluation of the errors that may be related to the calculations with the Freia model.

5.2. The Freia model[1]

The Freia model is a macroeconomic model of the Dutch economy. It was constructed in 1983 (CPB, 1983). It has been used for a number of years to analyse the effects of macroeconomic policies. Since 1987 the CPB has used another model for this purpose, the Freia–Kompas model. This model, however, resembles the Freia model in many respects (Van den Berg *et al.*, 1988). The Freia model has been composed in an eclectic manner. The supply side of the economy is modelled on the basis of a more or less neo-classical point of view, and a more Keynesian approach is followed in the specification of the demand side. Many relations in the model are non-linear.

The model consists of four main parts: the market for goods and services, the labour market, the public sector, and the financial market. In the market for goods and services a supply block and a demand block are distinguished. Potential domestic supply, i.e. capacity production, is determined with a vintage model of production with fixed technical coefficients for capital and labour. Therefore capacity production depends on the size of past and present investments and on the economic obsolescence of capital, which is determined by real labour costs.

Actual domestic production is assumed to equal demand for domestically produced goods. Endogenous components of total demand are private consumption, exports of goods, and private investment. Private consumption is explained by disposable income, the distribution of income, wealth and the interest rate. Exports depend mainly on world trade and the difference between Dutch and competing export prices. Private investment is explained mainly by the rate of return on the latest vintage versus the long-term interest rate, and by expected demand. Imports depend on demand, relative prices and the rate of capacity utilization.

Prices of goods and services are determined by the unit cost of capital and labour, by the prices of imported inputs, intermediary services and energy, by the prices of competing foreign goods and by the utilization rate. The influence of the utilization rate on prices implies that the price mechanism can contribute to equilibrium. However, the impact is relatively weak, and disequilibrium regimes can exist for long periods.

On the labour market a state of excess demand or of excess supply is a possible outcome. In the first case supply is the bottleneck and therefore the main determinant of employment, and in the second case demand. Labour supply is determined by demographic factors and by excess supply on the labour market, the latter approximating the discouraged worker effect. Labour demand is linked to labour requirements, and therefore to actual domestic production. Wages follow labour productivity and the price of private consumption. The level of direct taxes and social security contributions also has an influence on wages. Finally, wages are influenced by the so-called Phillips-curve effect.

The public sector consists of the government and the social security system. For the government, the model includes equations for tax revenues and expenditure. These, together with non-tax revenues, determine the size of the government budget deficit, which is an important variable in the financial submodel. For the social security system, both contributions and benefits are at least partly endogenous to the model.

The financial model consists of five different sectors: the government, the central bank, the banking sector, the foreign sector and the (non-bank) private sector. The private sector is highly aggregated and includes households, firms and institutional investors (pension funds, life insurance companies and social insurance funds). Different financial submarkets and corresponding assets are distinguished. The most important is the market for domestic bonds and equities, on which the long-term interest rate is determined. The long-term interest rate follows from the assumption of equilibrium between demand and supply. The same holds good with regard to the determination of the short-term interest rate. The exchange rate, as well as foreign

Table 5.1. Effects of a durable increase in government expenditure with 0.5 % of NNP, starting in 1983 and financed on the capital market. The expenditures concern government consumption and unemployment benefits

		1983	1984	1985	1986	1987	1988	1989	1990	1991
Wage rate enterprises	(%)	0.0	0.1	0.1	0.2	0.2	0.2	0.2	0.2	0.2
Price private consumption	(%)	0.0	0.1	0.1	0.1	0.1	0.1	0.2	0.2	0.2
Price exports of goods	(%)	0.0	0.1	0.1	0.1	0.0	0.1	0.1	0.1	0.1
Private consumption	(%)	0.3	0.4	0.4	0.4	0.4	0.3	0.3	0.3	0.3
Exports of goods	(%)	0.0	−0.1	−0.1	−0.1	−0.1	−0.1	−0.1	−0.1	−0.1
Private investment in buildings[a]	(%)	1.5	2.6	1.8	0.6	−0.5	−0.7	−0.6	−0.7	−0.8
Other private investment[a]	(%)	0.9	1.6	1.1	0.4	−0.3	−0.4	−0.4	−0.5	−0.6
Imports of goods	(%)	0.4	0.6	0.4	0.3	0.2	0.1	0.1	0.1	0.1
Production private sector[b]	(%)	0.4	0.4	0.4	0.3	0.2	0.2	0.2	0.1	0.1
Employment enterprises	(tmy)[c]	7.1	8.7	8.1	7.0	6.0	5.5	5.1	4.7	4.1
Unemployment	(tmy)	−6.7	−7.9	−7.2	−6.3	−5.4	−4.9	−4.6	−4.3	−3.7
Rate of capacity utilization	(% pnt)[d]	0.3	0.2	0.1	0.1	0.0	0.0	0.0	0.0	0.0
Balance on current account	(% NNP)	−0.3	−0.4	−0.4	−0.3	−0.3	−0.3	−0.3	−0.3	−0.3
Government budget surplus	(% NNP)	−0.3	−0.3	−0.3	−0.4	−0.5	−0.6	−0.6	−0.7	−0.7
Long-term interest rate	(% pnt)	0.1	0.1	0.2	0.2	0.3	0.3	0.3	0.4	0.4

[a]Excluding dwellings.
[b]Excluding production of natural gas.
[c]Thousands of man-years.
[d]Percentage points.
Source: CPB, 1983, p. 120.

interest rates, are exogenous to the model.

The main channel of influence of the financial side on the rest of the model is the long-term interest rate and, to a lesser extent, the short-term interest rate. Interest rates influence domestic expenditure components such as private investment and private consumption, and prices (the latter being influenced through capital costs). The long-term interest rate also affects interest payments of the government. There are several channels of influence of the income–expenditure submodel on the financial submodel. The most important are related to the financial surpluses of the private, public and foreign sectors, to private investment, and to non-wage income.

To illustrate the simulation properties of the model, the effects of an increase in government expenditure, as calculated by the CPB, are shown in Table 5.1. Government expenditure is increased with 0.5% of the Net National Product in 1983 and in all subsequent years. The expenditure is financed on the capital market. The base-run used by the CPB is characterized by a situation of high unemployment levels (higher than 320,000 man-years, which implies that the Phillips-curve is horizontal).

In the short run, the effects of the increase in government expenditure consist of an increase in domestic spendings and in imports, an increase in production and employment, an increase in the government deficit and a deterioration of the balance on current account. As a result of the changes in the government deficit and the balance on current account, interest rates gradually rise. The rise in the utilization rate and the increase in capital costs (caused by the rise in the long-term interest rate) lead to higher prices. Consequently exports show a gradual decline. As a result of the rise in utilization rate and the increase in domestic spendings, investment rises in the short run. In the long run, however, investment falls below the level of the base run, which is mainly caused by the rise in the interest rate. As a result of the decreases in exports and investment in the long run, production and employment start to decrease again, although after nine years they are still higher than in the base run. Through the years the increase in the government deficit gets larger.

The above shows that the capital market is an important variable in the model. An increase in government demand on the capital market leads to an increase in the rate of interest, and consequently to a decrease in private investment. Among economists there is no agreement about the question whether or not an increase in government demand on the capital market does lead to an important increase in the rate of interest (De Haan, 1989). Furthermore, according to one of the staff members of the CPB the use of an improved estimation method leads to the conclusion that the effects of an increase in demand for capital on the interest rate has been overestimated in the Freia model (Middeldorp, 1987). There may, of course, be other reasons why the effects of macroeconomic policy measures such as the one discussed above as estimated with the Freia model may differ from the actual effects. For a discussion the reader is referred to Den Butter (1985).

The Freia model has been compared with other national econometric models by Chan-Lee and Kato (1984). They evaluated fourteen different models on the basis of the calculated effects of a decrease in government expenditure. The models related to the following countries: United States, Japan, United Kingdom, France (two models), Canada, Australia, New Zealand, Belgium, Austria, Denmark, Finland, Norway and the Netherlands (the Freia model). Government expenditure was cut with 1.0% of GDP a year in the period 1976–1982. The reduction of the government deficit was assumed to lead to an equal reduction in bond financing. In the first year (1976) the decrease in GDP (as a percentage of total GDP) was 0.86% according to the Freia model. Smaller decreases were obtained only for New Zealand (0.28%), Australia (0.70%), and Belgium (0.71%). In the remaining models the decrease in GDP in the first year was larger than the 0.86% of the Freia model. In the seventh year (1982) the decrease in GDP was 0.05% according to the Freia model. In all other models the decrease was larger, varying from 0.20% to 1.60%.[2] The reason for the comparatively low decrease in GDP in the seventh year according to the Freia model is the following. A decrease in government expenditure will lead to a decrease in the rate of interest and the price level. This, in itself, will lead to an increase in GDP in the long run. Therefore, the negative effects on national income that are caused directly by the decrease in government expenditure are more or less cancelled out in the seventh year. It seems plausible that, if the simulation had referred to a longer period, the effect on GDP in later years would on balance have been negative.

The effects of a decrease in government expenditure of the same size were also analysed for the case in which an accommodating monetary policy was pursued, implying that the interest rate did not change as a result of the policy. In that case the decrease in GDP in the seventh year was 0.74% according to the Freia model. Lower percentages were obtained for Canada (0.26%), the United States (0.64%), and Denmark (0.70%), and an equal value was obtained for Norway. In all other countries the decrease in GDP was larger.[3] The figures given above show that the interest rate is very important in the Freia model. Furthermore, from the figures given above and from other information given by Chan-Lee and Kato it can be concluded that in most models the interest rate is less important than in the Freia model; in the few remaining models it is approximately equally important.

A general conclusion is that the effects of a cut in government expenditure as calculated with the Freia model are relatively positive in comparison with most other models, even if capital market effects are not taken into account. The effects of an increase in government expenditure are more or less the opposite of those of a decrease in government expenditure. Therefore, the effects of Keynesian policies will be relatively negative according to the Freia model. Of course the differences between the models will partly be caused by the differences between the economies of the countries to which they refer. Nevertheless, the results of the research of Chan-Lee and Kato indicate that the Freia model pays a great deal of attention to the repercussions of Keynesian policies.

Table 5.2. The base-run

Year	YND	UN	QY	CP	IP	BCA[a]	GBS	PCP	RL
1975	216	271	89.3	128	23.0	6.4	–11.7	12.2	8.5
1976	251	272	92.3	146	23.1	11.2	–14.6	8.3	8.4
1977	277	296	92.0	163	25.9	3.8	–12.8	7.0	7.8
1978	300	283	90.9	176	26.8	5.7	–14.4	4.9	7.3
1979	320	275	89.9	186	27.3	7.4	–17.0	3.9	8.2
1980	340	315	87.6	195	27.5	11.3	–22.6	5.9	10.7
1981	360	397	84.9	206	24.3	20.7	–27.5	7.1	12.6
1982	382	492	83.7	221	21.6	28.4	–28.5	6.3	11.3
1983	402	591	83.6	231	21.4	30.8	–32.7	3.5	9.0
1984	415	657	84.3	238	23.6	28.8	–34.0	2.3	8.7
1985	428	719	84.2	243	25.7	31.6	–33.0	2.3	8.2
1986	439	778	83.7	248	26.9	36.7	–32.2	1.9	7.6
1987	456	810	83.8	254	28.1	40.9	–35.3	1.7	7.0
1988	474	839	84.1	261	29.7	44.7	–37.2	1.8	6.4
1989	495	864	84.3	269	31.8	48.3	–38.4	1.9	5.8
1990	517	889	84.3	278	33.8	52.2	–39.4	1.9	5.1

YND = net national income at market prices (in billions of guilders).
UN = unemployment (in thousands of man-years).
QY = rate of capacity utilization (in %).
CP = private consumption (in current prices, and in billions of guilders).
IP = private investment (in current prices, and in billions of guilders).
BCA = balance on current account (in billions of guilders).
GBS = government budget surplus (in billions of guilders).
PCP = change in price private consumption (in %).
RL = nominal long-term interest rate (in %).
[a]Shows relatively large differences with data on actual development.

5.3. The base-run[4]

The version of the Freia model used for this study is the one that is available at the University of Groningen. Essentially this model is the same as the one used by the Central Planning Bureau, but because not all relevant information was available there are some differences in details.[5] The period to which the analysis refers is 1975–1990. The implications of this choice will be discussed later in this chapter. The economic development in the base-run is given in Table 5.2. The reader may note that the economic development in the last part of the eighties in the base-run differs from the actual development, which is due to the fact that the base-run was made in 1987.

The table shows, among other things, that unemployment is below 320,000 man-years during the period 1975–1980, and that it is higher in later years. This is important because the Phillips-curve has a negative slope if unemployment is below 320,000 man-years (approximately), while it is otherwise horizontal.

5.4. The calculation of the H_t and the U_t

In order to calculate the matrices H_t and U_t, a number of calculations have been made with the Freia model. Part of the results are given in Tables 5.3 and 5.4. Table 5.3 shows the effects of one-off increases in government investment with 1 billion guilders in 1975 and 1976, financed by decreases in development aid. Table 5.4 gives the effects of one-off increases in development aid with 1 billion guilders in 1975 and 1976, financed on the capital market. The effects of one-off increases in government investment and in development aid in 1977 and subsequent years have also been calculated. However, the outcomes are not presented in this study, but in Van der Burg (1991, pp. 207ff.).

In Chapter 4 it was assumed for explanation purposes that the model used calculated effects over the period from year 1 up to year 20. Consequently, all matrices H_t and U_t were (20,5) matrices. The Freia model used in this chapter calculates effects over the period 1975–1990. Therefore the matrices H_t and U_t should be (16,5) matrices. Now *t* is taken to be 1 in 1975, 2 in 1976, etc. This considered, the first part of Table 5.3, which shows the effects of an increase in government investment in 1975, gives the numerical values for all elements of H_1. The second part of Table 5.3 gives the numerical values for all non-zero elements of H_2. Similarly, Table 5.4 gives the numerical values for all non-zero elements of U_1 and U_2. The numerical values for all non-zero elements of H_3 up to H_{15} and U_3 up to U_{15} are given in Van der Burg (1991).

Table 5.3. Effects of one-off increases in government investment with 1 billion guilders (in current prices) in 1975 and 1976, financed by decreases in development aid

Private consumption	Private investment	Unemployment	Government budget surplus	Balance on current account	Year
Increase in government investment in 1975					
–0.0067	0.2410	–0.0086	0.0992	–0.4525	1975
0.0661	0.0423	0.0005	0.1808	–0.0637	1976
0.1352	–0.0989	0.0008	–0.0363	0.0864	1977
0.0994	–0.0999	0.0006	–0.0890	0.0139	1978
0.0595	–0.0789	0.0008	–0.0643	0.0532	1979
0.0442	0.0400	0.0004	–0.0223	–0.0083	1980
0.0442	0.0462	0.0001	0.0014	–0.0193	1981
0.0504	0.0183	0.0001	–0.0027	0.0041	1982
0.0516	–0.0058	0.0002	–0.0103	0.0193	1983
0.0491	–0.0158	0.0002	–0.0026	0.0300	1984
0.0453	–0.0075	0.0002	0.0106	0.0281	1985
0.0431	0.0005	0.0001	0.0271	0.0238	1986
0.0428	0.0023	0.0001	0.0400	0.0229	1987
0.0426	0.0019	0.0001	0.0517	0.0239	1988
0.0421	–0.0026	0.0000	0.0627	0.0299	1989
0.0413	–0.0038	0.0001	0.0746	0.0338	1990
Increase in government investment in 1976					
–0.0097	0.2408	–0.0077	0.1135	–0.4483	1976
0.0594	0.1151	0.0000	0.2460	–0.1287	1977
0.1366	–0.0678	0.0003	0.0579	0.0381	1978
0.1120	–0.0867	0.0003	0.0064	–0.0070	1979
0.0764	–0.0901	0.0007	0.0339	0.0423	1980
0.0598	0.0257	0.0004	0.0768	–0.0197	1981
0.0593	0.0411	0.0001	0.1085	–0.0331	1982
0.0664	0.0169	0.0000	0.1128	–0.0172	1983
0.0683	–0.0065	0.0000	0.1164	–0.0031	1984
0.0641	–0.0266	0.0001	0.1344	0.0168	1985
0.0586	–0.0212	0.0001	0.1619	0.0180	1986
0.0549	–0.0110	0.0001	0.1916	0.0112	1987
0.0530	–0.0025	0.0000	0.2229	0.0040	1988
0.0524	–0.0024	–0.0001	0.2522	0.0025	1989
0.0518	–0.0025	0.0000	0.2807	0.0009	1990

Note: Unemployment is expressed in millions of man-years. All other variables are expressed in billions of guilders. Private consumption and private investment are expressed in 1974 prices. The government budget surplus and the balance on current account are expressed in current prices.

5.5. The extent to which the calculations fulfil the conditions of additivity

As was explained in Chapter 4, the calculations have to fulfil the following three conditions of additivity. First, the (calculated) effects of a durable increase in government investment with 1 billion a year over a period of fifteen years, financed by a decrease in development aid, should be more or less equal to $\sum_{t=1}^{15} H_t$. Second, the effects of a durable increase in development aid with 1 billion a year over a period of

Table 5.4. Effects of one-off increases in development aid with 1 billion guilders (in current prices) in 1975 and 1976, financed on the capital market

Private consumption	Private investment	Unemployment	Government budget surplus	Balance on current account	Year
Increase in development aid in 1975					
–0.0204	–0.0057	0.0002	–1.0102	0.0124	1975
–0.0360	–0.0618	0.0006	–0.1228	–0.0053	1976
–0.0422	–0.1011	0.0009	–0.1311	0.0280	1977
–0.0590	–0.0798	0.0009	–0.1459	0.0192	1978
–0.0693	–0.0730	0.0008	–0.1529	0.0154	1979
–0.0759	–0.0632	0.0008	–0.1651	0.0093	1980
–0.0814	–0.0536	0.0007	–0.1840	0.0038	1981
–0.0903	–0.0487	0.0007	–0.2215	0.0095	1982
–0.0952	–0.0380	0.0007	–0.2612	0.0117	1983
–0.0971	–0.0269	0.0008	–0.3034	0.0104	1984
–0.0945	–0.0117	0.0009	–0.3499	0.0010	1985
–0.0892	0.0016	0.0011	–0.4030	–0.0124	1986
–0.0832	0.0079	0.0010	–0.4590	–0.0206	1987
–0.0766	0.0022	0.0013	–0.5266	–0.0192	1988
–0.0708	0.0045	0.0014	–0.5955	–0.0231	1989
–0.0658	–0.0043	0.0015	–0.6644	–0.0144	1990
Increase in development aid in 1976					
–0.0198	–0.0060	0.0002	–1.0110	0.0141	1976
–0.0357	–0.0624	0.0006	–0.1313	0.0063	1977
–0.0433	–0.1008	0.0008	–0.1403	0.0343	1978
–0.0599	–0.0854	0.0008	–0.1521	0.0354	1979
–0.0686	–0.0774	0.0009	–0.1602	0.0309	1980
–0.0749	–0.0627	0.0008	–0.1761	0.0239	1981
–0.0799	–0.0537	0.0007	–0.2099	0.0179	1982
–0.0859	–0.0454	0.0007	–0.2509	0.0209	1983
–0.0896	–0.0356	0.0008	–0.2925	0.0228	1984
–0.0885	–0.0199	0.0009	–0.3376	0.0149	1985
–0.0844	–0.0049	0.0011	–0.3878	0.0016	1986
–0.0790	0.0036	0.0011	–0.4410	–0.0079	1987
–0.0727	0.0000	0.0013	–0.5060	–0.0081	1988
–0.0669	0.0025	0.0014	–0.5730	–0.0122	1989
–0.0619	–0.0055	0.0015	–0.6403	–0.0044	1990

Note: See Table 5.3.

fifteen years, financed on the capital market, should be more or less equal to $\sum_{t=1}^{15} U_t$. Third, the effects of durable and simultaneous increases in development aid (financed on the capital market) and in government investment (financed by a decrease in development aid), both with 1 billion a year over a period of fifteen years, should be more or less equal to $\sum_{t=1}^{15} (H_t + U_t)$.

Table 5.5 gives the outcomes of the calculations needed to establish that these conditions are fulfilled. Table 5.5.A and 5.5.B refer to the first condition, Table 5.5.C and 5.5.D to the second, and Table 5.5.E and 5.5.F to the third. The differences between Table 5.5.A and 5.5.B, between Table 5.5.C and 5.5.D, and between 5.5.E and 5.5.F are all very small. In terms of the changes in government deficit, for in-

Table 5.5. The outcomes of the calculations needed to establish that the conditions of additivity are fulfilled

A. The sum of the separate effects of 15 one-off increases of 1 billion guilders in government investment, financed by a decrease in development aid, given in subsequent years in the period 1975–1989.

Private consumption	Private investment	Unemployment	Government budget surplus	Balance on current account	Year
–0.0067	0.2410	–0.0086	0.0992	–0.4525	1975
0.0564	0.2831	–0.0072	0.2943	–0.5120	1976
0.1846	0.2397	–0.0064	0.3252	–0.4888	1977
0.2835	0.1603	–0.0057	0.2891	–0.4983	1978
0.3493	0.0981	–0.0049	0.2592	–0.5027	1979
0.3973	0.1116	–0.0042	0.2497	–0.5295	1980
0.4295	0.1546	–0.0039	0.2361	–0.5708	1981
0.4726	0.1528	–0.0036	0.2693	–0.5656	1982
0.4916	0.1244	–0.0032	0.3067	–0.5420	1983
0.5018	0.0922	–0.0037	0.3776	–0.5226	1984
0.4940	0.0530	–0.0037	0.4695	–0.4654	1985
0.4799	0.0241	–0.0038	0.5807	–0.3962	1986
0.4678	0.0153	–0.0040	0.6882	–0.3495	1987
0.4537	0.0389	–0.0039	0.8332	–0.3294	1988
0.4435	0.0341	–0.0056	0.9860	–0.2873	1989
0.4439	–0.1363	–0.0001	1.0288	0.2849	1990

B. The effects of a durable increase in government investment with 1 billion guilders a year over the period 1975–1989, financed by a decrease in development aid

–0.0067	0.2410	–0.0086	0.0992	–0.4525	1975
0.0566	0.2815	–0.0072	0.2937	–0.5111	1976
0.1847	0.2372	–0.0065	0.3223	–0.4860	1977
0.2830	0.1573	–0.0058	0.2845	–0.4951	1978
0.3483	0.0949	–0.0047	0.2531	–0.4986	1979
0.3963	0.1364	–0.0044	0.2469	–0.5477	1980
0.4407	0.1617	–0.0039	0.2316	–0.5944	1981
0.4793	0.1577	–0.0034	0.2565	–0.5777	1982
0.4964	0.1284	–0.0032	0.2948	–0.5440	1983
0.5070	0.0976	–0.0035	0.3656	–0.5225	1984
0.5002	0.0576	–0.0035	0.4543	–0.4637	1985
0.4866	0.0259	–0.0040	0.5613	–0.3913	1986
0.4739	0.0144	–0.0040	0.6640	–0.3415	1987
0.4595	0.0369	–0.0047	0.8042	–0.3187	1988
0.4482	0.0326	–0.0052	0.9514	–0.2753	1989
0.4479	–0.1360	–0.0005	0.9892	0.2958	1990

Table 5.5 (continued)

C. The sum of the separate effects of 15 one-off increases of 1 billion guilders in development aid, financed on the capital market, given in subsequent years in the period 1975–1989

Private consumption	Private investment	Unemployment	Government budget surplus	Balance on current account	Year
–0.0204	–0.0057	0.0002	–1.0102	0.0124	1975
–0.0558	–0.0678	0.0008	–1.1338	0.0088	1976
–0.0959	–0.1687	0.0017	–1.2731	0.0480	1977
–0.1523	–0.2423	0.0024	–1.4160	0.0651	1978
–0.2156	–0.3103	0.0027	–1.5511	0.0964	1979
–0.2750	–0.3689	0.0036	–1.7057	0.1099	1980
–0.3349	–0.3823	0.0040	–1.9013	0.0834	1981
–0.3912	–0.3721	0.0041	–2.2058	0.0143	1982
–0.4381	–0.3653	0.0046	–2.5488	–0.0335	1983
–0.4807	–0.3684	0.0055	–2.9128	–0.0529	1984
–0.5096	–0.3698	0.0068	–3.3301	–0.0844	1985
–0.5295	–0.3537	0.0087	–3.7875	–0.1431	1986
–0.5452	–0.3424	0.0092	–4.2701	–0.1989	1987
–0.5543	–0.3750	0.0116	–4.8384	–0.2194	1988
–0.5604	–0.3727	0.0122	–5.4449	–0.2641	1989
–0.5573	–0.4270	0.0140	–5.0711	–0.2463	1990

D. The effects of a durable increase in development aid with 1 billion guilders a year over the period 1975–1989, financed on the capital market

–0.0204	–0.0057	0.0002	–1.0102	0.0124	1975
–0.0558	–0.0678	0.0007	–1.1338	0.0088	1976
–0.0959	–0.1687	0.0016	–1.2742	0.0477	1977
–0.1522	–0.2422	0.0023	–1.4190	0.0641	1978
–0.2153	–0.3103	0.0028	–1.5571	0.0950	1979
–0.2749	–0.3682	0.0037	–1.7155	0.1076	1980
–0.3346	–0.3820	0.0041	–1.9174	0.0804	1981
–0.3915	–0.3719	0.0043	–2.2299	0.0098	1982
–0.4383	–0.3535	0.0050	–2.5858	–0.0520	1983
–0.4802	–0.3596	0.0058	–2.9571	–0.0697	1984
–0.5069	–0.3713	0.0068	–3.3997	–0.0981	1985
–0.5282	–0.3583	0.0084	–3.8838	–0.1541	1986
–0.5450	–0.3503	0.0098	–4.4018	–0.2096	1987
–0.5550	–0.3631	0.0110	–4.9898	–0.2455	1988
–0.5607	–0.3762	0.0129	–5.6461	–0.2881	1989
–0.5590	–0.4354	0.0140	–5.3310	–0.2637	1990

Table 5.5 (continued)

E. The sum of the effects given in Table 5.5.A and 5.5.C

Private consumption	Private investment	Unemployment	Government budget surplus	Balance on current account	Year
–0.0271	0.2353	–0.0084	–0.9110	–0.4401	1975
0.0006	0.2153	–0.0064	–0.8395	–0.5032	1976
0.0887	0.0710	–0.0047	–0.9479	–0.4408	1977
0.1312	–0.0820	–0.0033	–1.1269	–0.4332	1978
0.1337	–0.2122	–0.0022	–1.2919	–0.4063	1979
0.1223	–0.2573	–0.0006	–1.4560	–0.4196	1980
0.0946	–0.2277	0.0001	–1.6652	–0.4874	1981
0.0814	–0.2193	0.0005	–1.9365	–0.5513	1982
0.0535	–0.2409	0.0014	–2.2421	–0.5755	1983
0.0211	–0.2762	0.0018	–2.5352	–0.5755	1984
–0.0156	–0.3168	0.0031	–2.8606	–0.5498	1985
–0.0496	–0.3296	0.0049	–3.2068	–0.5393	1986
–0.0774	–0.3271	0.0052	–3.5819	–0.5484	1987
–0.1006	–0.3361	0.0077	–4.0052	–0.5488	1988
–0.1169	–0.3386	0.0066	–4.4589	–0.5514	1989
–0.1134	–0.5633	0.0139	–4.0423	0.0386	1990

F. The effects of a durable increase in government investment of 1 billion guilders a year over the period 1975–1989, financed on the capital market

Private consumption	Private investment	Unemployment	Government budget surplus	Balance on current account	Year
–0.0271	0.2353	–0.0084	–0.9110	–0.4401	1975
0.0009	0.2128	–0.0065	–0.8397	–0.5012	1976
0.0888	0.0684	–0.0050	–0.9500	–0.4372	1977
0.1308	–0.0847	–0.0035	–1.1305	–0.4294	1978
0.1333	–0.2150	–0.0018	–1.2979	–0.4015	1979
0.1217	–0.2312	–0.0007	–1.4596	–0.4372	1980
0.1065	–0.2193	0.0002	–1.6731	–0.5104	1981
0.0883	–0.2124	0.0009	–1.9554	–0.5638	1982
0.0595	–0.2348	0.0015	–2.2646	–0.5790	1983
0.0274	–0.2689	0.0024	–2.5635	–0.5781	1984
–0.0078	–0.3095	0.0032	–2.9008	–0.5516	1985
–0.0412	–0.3256	0.0043	–3.2612	–0.5383	1986
–0.0698	–0.3216	0.0052	–3.6547	–0.5495	1987
–0.0930	–0.3317	0.0063	–4.0955	–0.5479	1988
–0.1107	–0.3394	0.0076	–4.5774	–0.5474	1989
–0.1084	–0.5623	0.0134	–4.1889	0.0406	1990

Note: See Table 5.3.

stance, the differences are, on average, just over 1% of the total changes, and can therefore be neglected. Thus, the conditions of additivity are fulfilled.

5.6. The differences between the effects of increases in government investment and development aid in different years

The justification of the method of project analysis used in this study, given in Chapter 4, is based on five conditions. The fist condition is that the model used is capable of analysing the effects of large durable changes. It is left to the reader to judge whether the Freia model fulfils this condition; Section 5.2 may be of some help in doing this. The second, third and fourth conditions concern the aspect of additionality. It was shown in Section 5.5 that the Freia model fulfils these conditions. The fifth condition is the following: if the four conditions mentioned above are fulfilled, then the model is also capable of analysing the effects of one-off changes in financial needs and in spending of 1 billion. This section will show that the Freia model does not fulfil this condition, and it will give a solution for the related problems.

The calculated effects of a one-off increase in government investment or development aid depend upon the year in which the increase takes place. Three types of differences between the effects of the large one-off changes occurring in different years can be distinguished. The first type concerns differences caused by factors which are taken into account by the method of this study, in such a way that these differences do not make the calculated effects of a project dependent upon the year in which (most of) the investment is done. This can first be explained for one specific difference. The tables of the effects of fifteen one-off increases in government investment in subsequent years in the period 1975–1989, which are given in Van der Burg (1991), show that the effects of a one-off increase in government investment of 1 billion on the balance on current account are, generally, more negative when the one-off increase occurs in the eighties than when it occurs in the seventies. At first sight one might conclude from this that the calculated effects on the balance on current account of a project with investments in the eighties will be more negative than those of a project with investments in the seventies. However, this conclusion is not correct. The differences between the calculated effects of one-off changes in government investment on the balance on current account are, to a large extent at least, caused by the changes in the import coefficient of government investment, which increases through the years. However, this does not affect the calculated effects of a project, because the method of this study takes account of differences between the import coefficients of the various one-off increases in government investment (see Section 4.2.3).

There are also some other differences between the effects of large one-off changes, occurring in different years, that do not make the calculated effects of a project dependent upon the year in which (most of) the investment is done. First, there are differences caused by changes in the indirect tax coefficient of government investment of the model. Second, there are differences caused by the fact that, because of the increase in the price level, the one-off increases become smaller in real prices through the years. These two differences are taken into account by the method of this study, and therefore they are also differences of the first type.

The second and third types of differences between the effects of large one-off changes occurring in different years are both differences that make the calculated effects of a project dependent upon the year in which (most of) the investment is done. The second type concerns differences that are justifiable from an econometric point of view. An example of this is the fact that the Phillips-curve has a negative slope if unemployment is below 320,000 man-years (approximately), and a zero slope if unemployment is higher. Given the characteristics of the base-run (see Table

5.2), this implies that increases in spendings that occur in the period 1975–1980 have, other things being equal, less positive effects than increases that occur later. Taken by itself, this means that the calculated effects of a project with investments in the period 1975–1980 will be less positive than the calculated effects of a project with investments after 1980. (Note, however, that this may be counterbalanced by factors other than the Phillips-curve.)

The third type of differences between the effects of large one-off changes occurring in different years are differences which are not justifiable from an econometric point of view. A number of these differences can be regarded as the result of arithmetical approximations. This can be explained by means of an example. Suppose there are three variables, A_t, B_t and C_t. Let the change in these variables between year $t-1$ and year t (in percentages) be denoted as $\dot{a}_t$, $\dot{b}_t$, and $\dot{c}_t$, respectively. Suppose that in reality A_t equals the product of B_t and C_t. Clearly, $\dot{a}_t$ is equal to $\dot{b}_t + \dot{c}_t + \dot{b}_t\dot{c}_t$. However, in order to calculate A_t the Freia model uses the following approximation in a number of formulae:

$$A_t = (1 + \dot{a}_t) \bullet A_{t-1}.$$

$$\dot{a}_t = \dot{b}_t + c_t$$

This approximation leads, in combination with the characteristics of the base-run, to errors in the calculated effects of one-off changes that occur especially in the years subsequent to the year in which the one-off change takes place. Now a one-off change lasts one year only, whereas the errors continue to play a role in all subsequent years. In relation to this the following holds good: despite the fact that for any individual year the errors are relatively small, the sum of the errors in all years can be large in relation to the size of the one-off change (Van der Burg, 1991).

To gain more insight in this problem, let us consider the effects of one-off increases in government investment with 1 billion in the years subsequent to the year in which the increase occurs. For example, the effect on the government deficit two years after the one-off increase is minus 36 million if the increase occurs in 1975, and plus 58 million if the increase occurs in 1976 (see Table 5.3). Similar differences appear when one looks at the effects that occur three or more years after the one-off increase. When one compares the effects of one-off increases in government investment in 1976 and 1977 a similar picture appears; for some other pairs of subseqeunt years the same holds good (Van der Burg, 1991). It has been shown that for the differences between the effects of an increase in government investment in 1975 on the one hand, and the effects of an increase in government investment in 1976 on the other hand the following holds good: these differences are, insofar as they occur in the years subsequent to the year in which the one-off increase in government investment takes place, for the greater part caused by mathematical approximations such as the one mentioned above. Many other differences between the effects of two one-off increases in government investment occurring in two subsequent years other than 1975 and 1976 can be explained in a similar way (Van der Burg, 1991).

It has also been shown that these errors of approximation, which are related to the calculation of the effects of individual one-off increases, cancel out for the greater part when the effects of a durable increase that lasts four years or more are calculated as being equal to the sum total of the calculated effects of the one-off increases in the different years (Van der Burg, 1991). In combination with the fact that the conditions of additivity are fulfilled, this implies that the occurrence of the errors mentioned above should not cast doubt upon the capability of the model to analyse the effects of durable changes.

It is possible that there are also differences between the effects of one-off changes in different years that are not the result of arithmetical approximations, but that are nevertheless not justifiable from an econometric point of view. This point, however, has not been analysed. Still, it can be concluded that the assumption mentioned at the beginning of this section is not justifiable: even if the model used is capable of analysing the effects of large durable changes, and even if the conditions of additivity are fulfilled, the model is not (fully) capable of analysing the effects of one-off changes in financial needs and spending with one billion.

The question is what the above means for the effects of a project as calculated by means of the method of this study. Let us consider the effects of a project of which the investments are concentrated in one year, on the present value of all the changes in government deficit up to 1990. (As will be explained in the next chapter, this present value is very important in the evaluation of the effects.) As was stated above, the calculated effects of one-off increases in government investment that occur in 1975 are less positive than those of increases occurring in 1976. Because of this the present value of all the effects of a project on the government deficit, expressed as a percentage of the present value of the investment in the project, is dozens of percents lower when the investment occurs in 1976 than when it occurs in 1975, and this is, for the greater part at least, related to the arithmetical approximations mentioned above (Van der Burg, 1991). It can be concluded that, if the method was used to calculate the effects of a project of which most expenditures are made in one particular year, one could be confronted with serious errors. The solution to this problem will be discussed below.

Before doing so, a more general remark can be made. Errors that are similar to the ones discussed above may also be related to the conventional macroeconometric method of analysing (large) projects (which, as the reader will recall, consists of calculating the effects of a project in one run). When the conventional method is used, however, these errors cannot be made visible. The fact that they are made visible by the method of this study, can be regarded as one of its advantages.

The question is now whether a solution for the problem mentioned above can be found. It has been argued that, insofar as the differences between the calculated effects of different one-off changes in different years are the result of arithmetical approximations such as the one mentioned above, they can be expected to be smaller when the variables in the base-run change in a more gradual way (Van der Burg, 1991). In relation to this, it is not unlikely that these differences would be smaller if the base-run referred to the predicted future economic development (predictions are generally based on the implicit assumption that changes will be gradual). Therefore, a solution to the problem mentioned above may be to use a base-run that refers to the future. However, this is not certain. Anyway, in this study another procedure will be followed. Note that the above implies that, perhaps, the criticism of the conventional method given above applies more to studies in which a base-run referring to the past is used (such as Klaassen *et al.*, 1987) than to other studies. However, this still has to be proved by the users of the conventional method.

The procedure used in this study can be explained as follows. It is assumed that the investments in the analysed project are spread evenly over a period of five years, with the first investment being made in 1975. It is also assumed that the expenditures for operating the project are spread evenly over the period 1976–1989. The remainder of this section will deal with the question what this procedure means for the errors that are specifically related to the calculation of the effects of one-off changes. In the next section the choice of the period in general will be discussed. The relation between the two assumptions given above and the characteristics of the analysed wind energy project will be discussed in the next chapter.

The reason why it was decided to spread the investments over the five-year period mentioned above can be explained as follows. It has been shown that the effects of a project with investments spread evenly over the period 1975–1979 and with proceeds and operating costs spread evenly over the period 1976–1989, as calculated by means of the method of this study, are almost equal to the calculated effects of a project that only differs from the first project in that the investments are spread evenly over the period 1980–1984 and in that the proceeds and the operational costs are spread evenly over the period 1981–1994. It has also been shown that the calculated effects of the first project are almost equal to the calculated effects of a project that only differs from the first one in that the investments are spread evenly over the period 1985–1989 and in that the proceeds and the operational costs are spread evenly over the period 1986–1999 (Van der Burg, 1991).[6] It should be mentioned that this result is not really surprising, because the following procedure was used. Initially, calculations were made with regard to projects that differed from each other in the number of years over which the investments were spread. Periods of three, four, five and six years were distinguished. It then turned out that the result mentioned above could be obtained by using a period of five years.

This result implies that the calculated effects of a project with investments in the period 1975–1979 are almost the same as those of a project that only differs from the first one in that the investments are spread over the fifteen-year period 1975–1989. Now, let us assume that the Freia model is capable of analysing the effects of durable changes. (As was stated above, it is left to the reader to judge the validity of this assumption. It is repeated, however, that the occurrence of the errors discussed in this section should not cast doubt upon the capability of the model to analyse the effects of durable changes.) Given this assumption, the calculated effects of a project with investments in the period 1975–1989 are a fair representation of its actual effects (because this project can be regarded as a durable change). Therefore, the calculated effects of a project with investments in the period 1975–1979 are a fair representation of the actual effects of a similar project with investments in the period 1975–1989, and the results of the next chapter should be interpreted as such. It can be concluded that the procedure used in this study implies that the errors that are specifically linked to the analysis of one-off changes are cancelled out at the level of the analysed project.

5.7. The period to which the analysis refers

It was concluded above that the calculated effects of a project with investments in the period 1975–1979 are a fair representation of the average effects of a similar project with investments in the period 1975–1989. This section deals with the question whether these effects can be regarded as a satisfactory estimate of the effects of projects that are implemented in the near future. This question can be answered in the affirmative if the following two conditions are more or less fulfilled. The first one is that the structure of the model and the value of the parameters should not only be valid with regard to the period 1975–1990, but also with regard to the period 1990–2005. The second condition is that the values of the exogenous and endogenous variables in the base-run for the period 1975–1990 are comparable to the actual values in the future. Of course, both conditions only refer to factors that affect the effects of the project.

For practical reasons this study is based on the assumption that the first condition is fulfilled. It can be noted that many models for the future are, more or less, based on a similar assumption. With regard to the second condition, it is especially the level of unemployment which is important. As shown in Table 5.2, unemployment levels in the base-run are high throughout the period 1975–1990. In relation to this it is possible that the project results in a decrease in unemployment and an increase in national income. Of course, if in the future, and especially in the period in which investments are made, a situation of full employment exists, the effects of the project could be entirely different. Thus, the calculated effects can be regarded as a conditional prediction of future effects.

5.8. Comparison of the calculations made for this study with calculations by the Central Planning Bureau

It is possible that the outcomes of the calculations presented above differ from the outcomes that would have been obtained if the CPB had made similar calculations. One possible reason is that, as was stated before, not all data necessary to run the model have been obtained from the CPB.

There are no calculations done by the CPB that relate to the same changes as the ones for which calculations have been done in this study, so that an exact comparison cannot be made. However, it is possible to compare the effects of a durable increase in government expenditure, as calculated by the CPB, with the effects of a durable increase in government investment, calculated as being equal to the sum total of the fifteen matrices H_t of Table 5.3 and the fifteen matrices U_t of Table 5.4. The former are given in Table 5.1, the latter in Table 5.5.F. Both calculations refer to spendings that are financed by means of capital market loans. The calculations of the CPB refer to increases in consumption, whereas the sum total of the matrices H_t and U_t refers to increases in investment. However, as the output of government investment is not an endogenous variable in the Freia model, the calculated effects should be the same essentially. Small differences could arise due to differences in the import coefficient of the expenditures which are stimulated, or in other characteristics. It has been shown that, if these differences were eliminated, the calculations of the CPB would not lead to outcomes that are more negative than the outcomes used in this study (Van der Burg, 1991). It even appears that the former would be slightly more positive, but the difference is small enough to be neglected.

5.9. Evaluation of the errors

This section evaluates the errors related to the estimation of the effects of a project by means of the method of this study in combination with the Freia model, insofar as these errors are directly related to the calculations with the Freia model. First of all, let us discuss the perspective from which these errors should be evaluated. As was argued in Chapter 3, project appraisal should be consistent with the macroeconomic analyses used for the formulation of macroeconomic policy. The above is one of the reasons why it has been decided to use the Freia model for project appraisal; this model has been used to help formulate macroeconomic policy in the Netherlands.

This being said, two types of errors can be distinguished. Errors of the first type are errors that are made when the effects of a project are calculated by means of the Freia model, but that are essentially also made when the Freia model is used to analyse the effects of large and durable changes. Errors of the second type are errors that are related to the specific way in which the Freia model is used in this study. When the calculated effects of a project contain errors of the first type, it holds good that similar errors are made when the Freia model is used to inform the government about the effects of macroeconomic policies. Because it is better to have a consistent policy than an inconsistent policy, errors of the first type are more acceptable than errors of the second type.

Errors of the first type can, among other things, be made when the effects of large and durable changes in the period 1975–1990, as estimated with the Freia model, differ from the actual effects. Considering that a project analyst should seek consistency with existing macroeconomic analysis, my personal opinion regarding the question whether such errors are made is not relevant. In my capacity as project analyst, I should describe the Freia model, pay attention to the literature in which this model and its differences from other macroeconomic models are discussed, and that should be all.

In the Netherlands the Freia model is well known, and Dutch decision-makers should be able to judge it for themselves on the basis of existing literature. One article, that of Chan-Lee and Kato, has received special attention in this study. On the basis of this article it can be concluded that the effects of a Keynesian policy of increasing government expenditures pursued in the seventies and eighties as calculated by means of the Freia model are generally more negative (or less positive) than the effects of this policy as calculated by other national econometric models. To a large extent this is related to the fact that the interest rate is very important in the Freia model. In this context it is also important that in a recent article of one of the staff members of the CPB it was argued that the role of the interest rate has been overestimated in the Freia model. The implications of the above for the effects of a wind energy project as calculated by means of the Freia model will be discussed in the next chapter.

Errors of the first type may also be related to the following. In this study the effects of durable changes that take place in the period 1975–1990 have been calculated. These effects should be regarded as conditional predictions of the effects of similar changes taking place in the future. Now the project analysed in the next chapter is to be implemented in the future. Thus, the estimated effects of this project, as calculated on the basis of the outcomes of this chapter, should also be regarded as conditional predictions. If, in the future, the structure of the true model and the values of its parameters differ considerably from those of the Freia model, the outcomes of this study will be less valuable. A similar statement can be made with regard to the values of the exogenous and endogenous variables. In this context, it is especially important that the effects as calculated in this study will differ from the actual effects if a situation of full employment exists in the investment phase of the analysed project.

Errors of the second type are, as stated above, specifically linked with the way in which the Freia model is used in this study. There are three reasons why such errors could occur. First, the conditions of additivity may not be fulfilled. However, as far as the Freia model is concerned, these conditions are fulfilled. Second, if the method is used to analyse a project in which the investments are concentrated in one year, the effects of the project will depend to an unacceptable extent on the year in which the investment takes place. This problem has been solved by spreading the investments of the analysed project evenly over the period 1975–1979, implying that the related erros cancel out at the project level.

Third, there may be a difference between the outcomes of the calculations of the effects of increases in government investment and development aid used in this study and the outcomes that would have been obtained if the CPB had calculated the effects of the same increases. With regard to an increase in government expenditure financed on the capital market, it was shown that if the calculations had been done by the CPB, the outcomes would have been the same, or perhaps slightly more positive.

As was stated in Section 4.5, one of the advantages of the method developed in this study concerns the detection and evaluation of errors related to the calculations with the econometric macro-model. In the above this has been illustrated for the case of the Freia model. Errors that are specifically linked with the use of this model for the particular purpose of project analysis have been distinguished from errors that are also made when more usual exercises are carried out with this model. This facilitates the detection and the evaluation of the errors. It has also been shown that certain errors, which are specifically linked with the use of the model for the purpose of project analysis, are important, and a method to eliminate these errors has been presented.

Notes

1. Parts of this section have been copied from CPB (1983) and Van den Berg *et al.* (1988).
2. Regarding the policy without accommodating monetary policy, Chan and Lee give no information on Austria, Norway and Denmark. Regarding the effects in the seventh year, no information on New Zealand is provided.
3. Regarding the policy with accommodating monetary policy, no information is given on France (one model) and Belgium. Regarding the effects in the seventh year, no information on New Zealand is provided.
4. A number of problems related to the calculations with the Freia model, which are ignored or discussed only briefly in Sections 5.3 to 5.6, are discussed in Van der Burg, 1991.
5. For more information see Van der Burg (1991).
6. A reservation is in order here: the statement in the main text only holds good with regard to the effects up to 1990; no calculations were done for other years. For some more specifics regarding this statement and, more in general, the justification of the procedure used in this study, the reader is referred to Van der Burg (1991).

CHAPTER 6

The macroeconomic effects of wind energy in the Netherlands

6.1. Introduction

At the time of writing this chapter, in 1990, about 40 MW of wind power has been installed in the Netherlands. This is around 0.2% of the total capacity of the electricity sector. The electricity produced is less than 0.1% of the total electricity production, which is related to the fact that wind is not always available. The greater part of the installed wind capacity is owned by utility companies. The remainder is owned by private investors. Some of these, particularly farmers, use part of the electricity produced for their own purposes. For the rest, the electricity produced by private investors is sold to the utility companies.

The objective of the Dutch government is to have a capacity of 1000 MW by the year 2000. To realize this objective the 'Integraal Programma Windenergie' (IPW) was launched in 1986. Under the terms of the IPW, subsidies are given to manufacturers and to proprietors of windturbines during the period 1986–1990. In 1986 it was expected that the IPW would result in a capacity of 100 to 150 MW in 1990. Moreover, it was expected in 1986 that in 1991 wind energy would be profitable without subsidies, so that its development after 1990 could continue without further financial aid from the government. At present, however, it is clear that at the end of 1990 the capacity will be below 100 MW. Furthermore, since expectations of future energy prices have been adjusted downwards, it is no longer expected that wind energy will be profitable without subsidy in 1991.

In June 1990 the Ministry of Economic Affairs stated that the government will continue to subsidize wind energy after 1990. The total yearly budget for subsidies for utilities and private investors which buy wind turbines will be 30 million guilders. This is 10 million guilders less than under the IPW. The subsidy as a percentage of the subsidized investments will be about 25%, which is lower than the 35–40% granted in 1990. Also, in the years to come the Ministry will spend 14.5 million guilders a year on research and development, pilot-projects and extension. Under the IPW, 12 million guilders a year was made available for these purposes.

Several arguments may be used in favour of government support for wind energy. First, the generation of electricity from wind is less polluting than most other forms of electricity generation.[1] Second, it may be argued that the wind industry is still in an early stage of development, so that the infant-industry argument applies. Third, the markets for energy are characterized by great uncertainties. It is not unlikely that in the future, as in the past, price shocks will occur. This could lead to considerable macroeconomic, social and political problems. To decrease the risks for the country as a whole, the dependency on certain fuels should be diminished. From this perspective it is a good policy to stimulate wind energy.[2] The fourth argument has already been explained in Chapter 2. In a situation of unemployment, investments in wind energy can have positive macroeconomic effects. Note that this argument differs from the third argument concerning the capability of the economy to cope with large and unexpected changes.

This chapter deals with the fourth argument only. Another limitation is the following: it is assumed that if the government wants to stimulate wind energy, it will do so by subsidizing investments of buyers of wind turbines. Thus, the choice of the instrument is not discussed.

The structure of this chapter is as follows: Section 6.2 describes the microeconomic characteristics of the analysed wind energy project. On the basis of these characteristics the macroeconomic effects of wind energy can be calculated. These are discussed in Section 6.3. Furthermore, Section 6.3 pays attention to the evaluation of the effects.

6.2. Characteristics of the project from a microeconomic point of view

6.2.1. Introduction

The wind energy project analysed in this chapter involves investments in a number of wind farms made by the electric utilities. These wind farms replace a certain amount of capacity and production of conventional power plants. The wind energy project is defined as the capacity and production of the wind farms minus the capacity and production of the conventional power plants which are replaced. The financial costs of the project are defined as the costs of the wind farms minus the costs of the conventional capacity and production which are replaced. The first-round spending effects of the expenditures on the project are defined as the first-round spending effects of the expenditures on wind farms minus the first-round spending effects of expenditures on conventional capacity and production which are replaced.

The project will be analysed by means of the method of project appraisal described in Chapter 4. In Chapter 4 the explanation of the method was based on the assumption that it is used to analyse government projects. However, the investments in the wind energy project are made by the electric utilities. To make it possible to apply the method to this project the following assumptions are made: first, the utilities will invest in wind farms if the present value of the net financial benefits of the project including subsidies is positive, or zero at least.[3] Second, investments in wind energy are subsidized by the government up to the point where the present value of the net financial benefits for the utilities is zero.[4] Third, the electricity price remains constant (this follows more or less from the second assumption). Fourth, the investments of the utilities are financed by capital market loans, just like the government subsidies. Fifth, the effects of an increase in capital demand of the utilities on the rate of interest, and the subsequent macroeconomic effects, are the same as those of an increase in capital demand of the government. Given all this, the wind energy project can be treated as if it were a government project.

Because the electricity price remains constant, the project does not affect the total demand for electricity. Therefore, the total electricity production remains constant. This implies that the output of the wind energy project, as defined above, is zero.

For the moment, some refinements of the method of Chapter 4, which concern the project-specific effects on imports and on indirect taxes, are neglected. These refinements will be discussed in Section 6.2.5. Thus, we now focus on the financial costs of the wind energy project and the first-round spending effects of the expenditures on this project on national value added. The financial costs of the project in year t are equal to the gfn_t of Chapter 4, and the first-round spending effects of the expenditures on the project on national value added in year t are equal to the fva_t. Together with the matrices H_t and U_t, as calculated in the previous chapter, and with the values of m_t (the import coefficient of government investment in year t according to the model), the values of the gfn_t and the fva_t provide all information needed to calculate the macroeconomic effects of the project – neglecting the refinements mentioned above.

6.2.2. Costs and benefits from a private point of view

The description of the microeconomic characteristics of the project given below draws on a more extensive report, which is Van der Burg (1989). This report provides among other things a justification for the assumptions and figures given in Section 6.2.2. On the basis of this report it can be said that the description of the wind energy project given below corresponds to reality to a reasonable extent.

Let us first delimit the analysed project. It consists of wind farms with wind turbines larger than 100 kW. A wind farm is defined (rather broadly) as a group of at least two wind turbines. It is assumed that in the year 2000 installed wind capacity will be 1000 MW. It is also assumed that 660 MW of this 1000 MW will consist of wind turbines larger than 100 kW placed in wind farms. Thus, the capacity of the analysed project is 660 MW. It is assumed that in each year of the period 1989–2000 55 MW is installed as part of the analysed project. All investments in the analysed project are assumed to be made by the electric utilities.

The private costs of the project consist of investment costs and exploitation costs. The private benefits consist of three parts. First, the project leads to fuel savings in conventional power plants. Second, it leads to savings on the capacity of conventional power plants. Third, there are savings on the operating costs of conventional power plants other than fuel costs.

To keep the analysis simple, it is assumed that all wind farms are built according to the technology of 1994–1995, and that technological development up to 1995 is moderate. It is also assumed that all capacity savings concern gas-fired combined-cycle power plants and that all savings on fuel costs and other operating costs are

Table 6.1. Private costs and benefits of the 660 MW wind energy project (in millions of guilders)

Turbine costs	–702.9
Site costs	–605.2
Capacity savings	195.7
Operating costs windfarm (annually)	–32.50
Fuel savings (annually)	85.95
Other savings on operating costs (annually)	4.30

Note: Figures are in 1989 prices. Costs have a negative sign, benefits a positive sign.

realized in the same power plants. The gas price is assumed to be constant, at a level of 27 cents per m^3. This corresponds to an oil price of \$26.5 a barrel and an exchange rate of Hfl. 1.80 a dollar. Table 6.1 gives information on the costs and benefits of the project for utilities.

With regard to the distribution of costs and benefits over the years, first of all the question is posed how this distribution would be in the hypothetical situation in which the following applies: first, total wind capacity is installed in one year, year 0, and all production starts at the beginning of year 1. Second, apart from the first point, the distribution of costs and benefits over the years is the best possible estimate of the distribution in reality. The answer to the question mentioned above is given in Table 6.2. The table shows that the lifetime of wind farms is estimated to be 15 years. It also shows that the investment phase of conventional power plants is longer than that of wind farms.

It was assumed earlier that in each year of the period 1989–2000 one-twelfth of the total capacity of 660 MW is installed. This implies that for the capacity installed

Table 6.2. Distribution of costs and benefits over the years, in the hypothetical situation in which all investments are made in the year

	Total costs and benefits (millions of guilders)[a]			Annual costs and benefits (millions of guilders a year)[a]		
	Turbine costs	Site costs	Capacity savings	Operating costs windfarm	Fuel savings	Savings on (non-fuel) operating costs
	–702.9	–605.2	195.7	–32.50	85.95	4.30
Year	Fraction of the figures above			Fraction of the figures above		
–3			0.2			
–2			0.3			
–1			0.3			
0	0.6	0.6	0.2			
1	0.4[b]	0.4[b]		1	1	1
2				1	1	1
..				..	..	..
15				1	1	1

[a]All figures in 1989 prices.

[b]The figures imply that part of the investments is made during the first year of (full) operation. This is not realistic, but the figures are justifiable for the purpose of evaluation (see the extensive report).

Table 6.3. Distribution of costs and benefits over the years, as assumed for the calculation of the macroeconomic effects

	Total costs or benefits[a] (millions of guilders)[b]			Annual costs or benefits[a] (millions of guilders a year)[b]		
	Turbine costs	Site costs	Capacity savings	Operating costs wind farm	Fuel savings	Savings on (non-fuel) operating costs
	–720	–620	216	–32.90	87.90	4.36
Year	Fraction of the figures above					
1975	0.2	0.2	0.2			
1976	0.2	0.2	0.2	1	1	1
1977	0.2	0.2	0.2	1	1	1
1978	0.2	0.2	0.2	1	1	1
1979	0.2	0.2	0.2	1	1	1
1980				1	1	1
..				..	..	..
1989				1	1	1

[a]Figures differ slightly from those of Table 6.2. For an explanation: see the extensive report.
[b]All figures in 1989 prices.

in 1989, the distribution of costs and benefits over the years is as given in the table, with 1989 being year 0, and with absolute figures for costs and benefits being one-twelfth of those in the table. Similar remarks can be made with regard to the capacity installed in the other years. Thus, for the project as a whole the first capacity savings occur in 1986, and the last costs and benefits occur in 2015.

6.2.3. *Modifications needed for the calculation of the macroeconomic effects*

To calculate the macroeconomic effects of the project described above, one would need an econometric macro-model which runs from 1986 to 2015. However, as was explained in Chapter 5, the model used actually runs from 1975 to 1990. This implies that it is not possible to analyse the wind energy project as it takes place in reality. Instead, a somewhat different project will be analysed.

The characteristics of this different project are obtained by changing the figures given in Table 6.2 in such a way that two conditions are fulfilled. First, it is possible to analyse the project with the help of a model that runs from 1975 to 1990. Second, the total change is such that its effects on the conclusions of this chapter are as small as possible. The results of the total change are given in Table 6.3.

Three points should be emphasized. First, the total change has been devised in such a way that the private profitability of the project, defined as explained in the next section, remains the same. Second, the change implies that the project starts in 1975 instead of 1989, and that the period of analysis is earlier in time than the period in which the project will actually be implemented. This has certain implications for the calculated macroeconomic effects, which will be discussed in Section 6.3. Third, some of the changes which are part of the total change mentioned above are independent of the question whether the project starts in 1989, in 1975, or in any other year. These changes concern, among other things, the following: the lifetime of the project has been shortened and the investment phase of gas-fired power plants has been made equal to that of wind farms. In the extensive report it is shown that the total of the changes that are independent of the year in which the project starts is such that, as far as the calculated macroeconomic effects are concerned, it does not lead to a bias in favour or against wind farms.

Table 6.3 provides all information needed to calculate the gfn_t. For example, taking t to be 1 in 1975, gfn_2 is equal to $\{0.2(720 + 620 - 216) + 32.9 - 87.02 - 4.36\}$ (with all figures still expressed in prices of 1989).

6.2.4. *The private profitability of the project*

The criterion for the private profitability of the project used in this study is the present value of the net benefits of the project, taken as a percentage of the present value of the investments in the wind farms. The present value of the net benefits of the project is defined as the present value of all benefits minus the present value of all costs. The above may seem somewhat unusual, as the investments in the wind farms exclude the savings on investments in conventional power plants. However, it will be shown later on that this criterion has an important practical advantage, which is related to the fact that subsidies on investments in Dutch wind farms are fixed as a percentage of these investments. At a real interest rate of 4% the private profitability of the project is minus 34%.

The private profitability of the project has also been calculated on the basis of the real interest rates of the period 1975–1989 as estimated by the Freia model. The average of these Freia real interest rates is close to 4%. The relevant calculation is based on the distribution of costs and benefits over the years as given in Table 6.3. The result of this calculation is that the private profitability is, again, minus 34%.[5] In the remainder of this chapter, the private profitability of the project will be based on the Freia interest rates. This will facilitate the comparison of the private profitability with the macroeconomic effects. Given the assumptions of Section 6.2.1, the above implies that the government gives a 34% subsidy on investments in wind farms.

6.2.5. *Input–output analysis*

The first-round spending effects of the expenditures on the wind farms and of the expenditures which are replaced have been analysed with the help of specific information, such as information about the characteristics of the wind turbine industry, and by means of an input–output model. The details are discussed in the extensive report.

The first-round effects of the different types of expenditures, expressed as a percentage of these expenditures, are given in Table 6.4. The first part of this table is based on the assumption that all wind turbines are produced in the Netherlands. Nevertheless, the effects of the expenditures on turbines on imports is relatively high. To a large extent this is related to the import of spare parts. The assumption that all turbines are produced domestically is in accordance with the present situation.

Table 6.4. First-round effects of different expenditures on the wind farms and expenditures replaced by the wind farms, expressed as a percentage of these expenditures

	Value added[a]	Indirect taxes[b] and rent paid to the government	Imports
Turbine costs[c]	56.4	0.3	43.3
Site costs	68.7	2.1	29.2
Capacity savings	39.1	0.3	60.6
Operating costs wind farm[c]	66.9	22.7	10.4
Fuel costs	0.0	0.0	100.0
Non-fuel operating costs, gas-fired plants	75.7	4.6	19.7
Alternative case[d]			
Turbine costs	28.3	0.2	71.5
Operating costs, wind farm	60.5	22.8	16.7

[a]Excludes indirect taxes and rent paid to the government.
[b]Include legal charges.
[c]In a situation in which all wind turbines are produced in the Netherlands.
[d]A situation in which 50% of wind turbines is imported.

Regarding the future, the following can be said: the Dutch wind turbine industry produces turbines which are technologically well advanced. However, the industry is small and has as yet not been able to benefit from the advantages of mass production. Therefore, it is not impossible that in future part of the turbines will be imported. In relation to this an alternative case is distinguished, in which 50% of the wind turbines is imported. Note, however, that in the first instance the calculations in Section 6.3 will be based on the assumption that all turbines are produced domestically. Finally, it can be noted that the table is based on the assumption that all savings on gas concern imported gas. Given the argument in Chapter 2, this assumption is justifiable with regard to the calculation and the evaluation of the macroeconomic effects.[6]

Tables 6.3 and 6.4 can be used to calculate the fva_t. For example, taking t to be 1 in 1975, fva_1 is equal to $0.2\{720(0.564+0.003)+620(0.687+0.021)-216(0.391+0.003)\}$.

The calculations of the macroeconomic effects will take account of certain refinements, which are related to the project-specific effects on imports and on indirect taxes and (land) rent paid to the government. The information which is necessary for this refinement is given in Table 6.4. Details about the integration of these refinements in the project analysis were supplied in Chapter 4.

A final remark is the following. In the period 1975–1989 the price level has risen with a factor of 1.78 (according to the Freia model). In relation to this, it was decided to analyse the macroeconomic effects of a project which is, in real prices, 1.78 times larger than the project described in the preceding sections. This implies that, for the project of which the macroeconomic effects are analysed, the gfn_t and the fva_t in prices of 1975 are in nominal terms equal to the gfn_t and the fva_t given in the preceding sections, which were expressed in prices of 1989. The procedure mentioned above makes no difference for the evaluation of the effects, because for this evaluation only the relative magnitude of the effects on different variables count.[7]

Table 6.5. Macroeconomic effects of the 660 MW wind energy project, at a gas price of 27 cents

Present value in 1975 of all investments in wind farms: 1305 million guilders.[a] Private profitability of the project: –34%.

Year	Private consumption[b] (million (guilders)[d]	Private investment[c] (million guilders)[d]	Unemployment (thousands man-years)	Balance on current account (million guilders)[e]	Government budget surplus (million guilders)[e]	Utilities budget surplus (million guilders)[e]
1975	–6	48	–1.70	–108	–69	–134
1976	0	55	–1.68	–45	–41	–96
1977	21	36	–1.47	–41	–44	–110
1978	38	8	–1.20	–44	–71	–123
1979	47	–19	–1.05	–42	–99	–134
1980	59	–89	0.88	122	–27	33
1981	53	–103	1.00	177	–65	27
1982	37	–53	0.82	147	–49	25
1983	31	–21	0.71	145	–44	39
1984	33	2	0.50	138	–56	57
1985	37	1	0.50	149	–66	66
1986	39	1	0.60	163	–78	75
1987	42	9	0.55	168	–86	83
1988	45	19	0.61	169	–90	92
1989	50	29	0.42	168	–90	100
1990	54	24	0.69	31	–111	0
Sum total[f]	578	–52	0.18	1298	–1087	0
Present value 75[g]				382	–320	0

[a]In 1975 guilders.
[b]Because government consumption is constant, the change in private consumption is equal to the change in total consumption.
[c]Investments in the project excluded.
[d]In 1974 prices.
[e]In current prices.
[f]This is the sum total of all changes in the period of analysis. As far as the balance on current account, the government budget surplus and the budget surplus of the electric utilities are concerned, this sum total represents a change in wealth in 1990. The sum totals of the changes in the other variables are discussed in the main text.
[g]This is the present value in 1975 of the change in wealth in 1990 mentioned in footnote 'f'. See also the main text.

6.3. The macroeconomic effects of the project

6.3.1. The macroeconomic effects

On the basis of the information given in the preceding sections and in Chapters 4 and 5, the macroeconomic effects of the project for the period 1975–1990 have been calculated. These effects are given in Table 6.5. Some of the effects are presented in an alternative way in Figure 6.1.

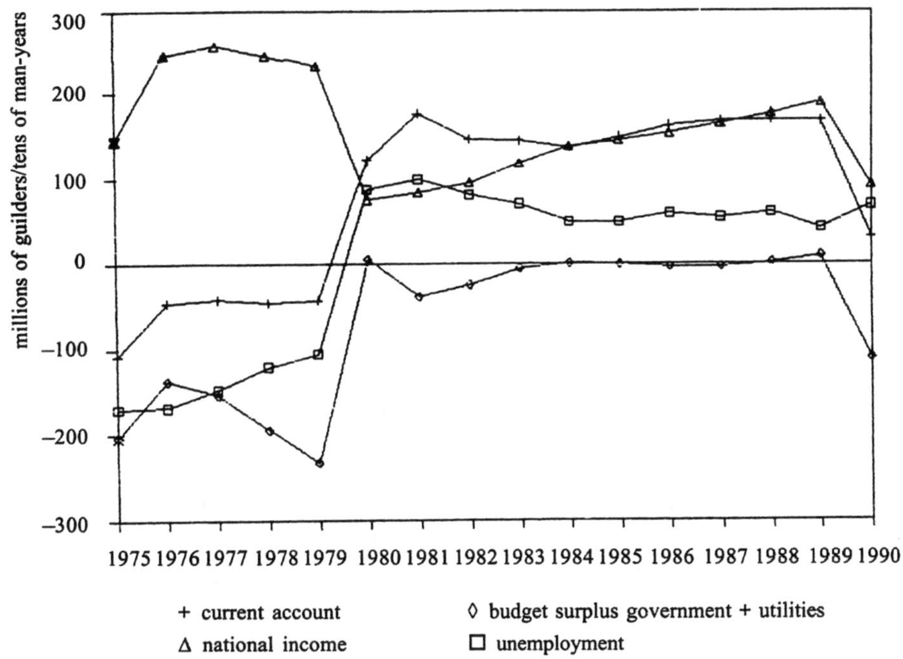

Figure 6.1. Macroeconomic effects of the 660 MW wind energy project, at a gas price of 27 cents.

First of all, two remarks which follow from Chapter 4 should be made. First, the calculated effects of the wind energy project should be regarded as the expected value of the contribution of the project to the effects of the portfolio of new government projects and projects subsidized by the government.[8] Second, although the errors related to the estimate of this contribution may be relatively larger than the errors related to the estimate of the effects of the portfolio as a whole, for purposes of evaluation it is justifiable to do as if this is not the case.

Table 6.5 only gives information about variables that are relevant from the point of view of evaluation. The choice of these variables will be discussed in the next section. It can be noted that the sum total of the changes in the government deficit in the period 1975–1990 is equal to the change in the government debt in 1990. The sum total of the changes in the balance on current account equals the change in net foreign assets in 1990. The sum total of the annual deficits and surpluses of the electricity sector is zero, which was one of the points of departure. At this point in the argument, the reader should not bother about the ‘present value 75’.

What causes the macroeconomic effects of the project? In order to answer this question, the project is divided into two parts: the project excluding fuel savings on the one hand and the fuel savings on the other hand. Regarding the project excluding fuel savings, the following can be said. During a period of five years there are large investments in wind farms, and during a longer period there are smaller expenditures on operating costs of wind farms. This is counterbalanced by the savings on investments and operating costs related to gas-fired plants to a small extent only. Consequently, the macroeconomic impact of the project excluding fuel savings is, to a large extent, the same as the impact of a Keynesian policy of increasing government consumption financed by capital market loans. Neglecting differences in scale, the most important difference is that most of the expenditures on the project are not financed by the government but by the electricity sector, implying that the deficit of the electricity sector increases. Given the assumptions mentioned in Section 6.2.1, this does not make any difference with regard to the effects on the capital market. A second specific characteristic of the project is the import coefficient of the expenditures on the project, which may differ from the import coefficient of government consumption. As will be explained in the next section, this difference is only of minor importance.

According to the Freia model the project excluding fuel savings has, just like a policy of increasing government consumption, positive as well as negative effects. A positive effect is that effective demand increases in the short run. This causes an increase in national income, and a decrease in unemployment. However, it also causes an increase in imports. The increase in national income leads to an increase in tax receipts, and the decrease in unemployment leads to a decrease in unemployment ben-

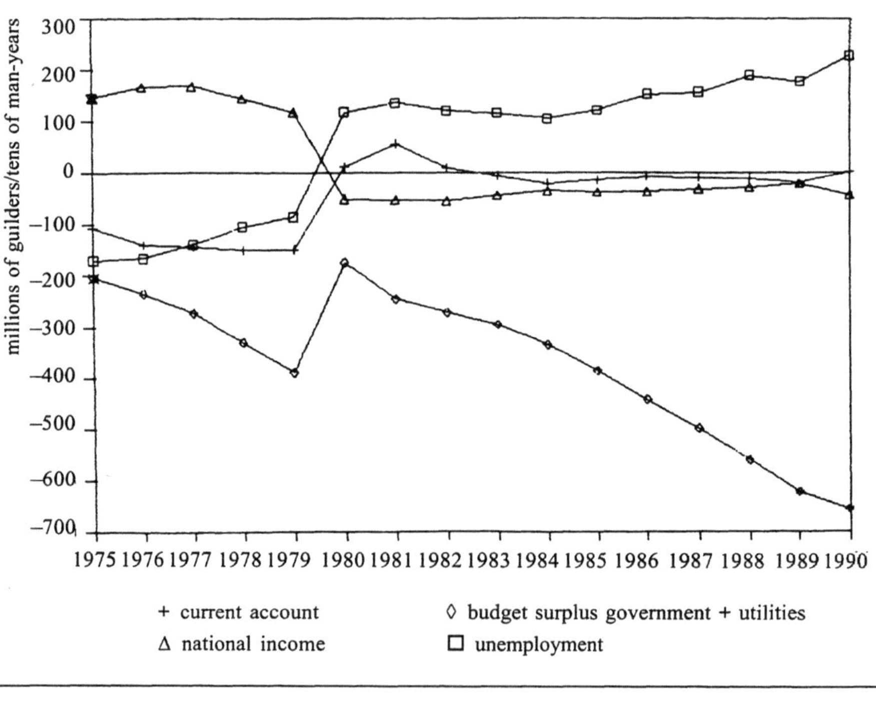

Figure 6.2. Macroeconomic effects of the 660 MW wind energy project excluding fuel savings.

efits. Consequently, the government deficit decreases. However, this decrease in the government deficit does not outweigh the increase in the joint deficits of the government and the electricity sector induced by financing the expenditures on the project. To a large extent this is related to the increase in imports, which sets a limit to the positive spending effects. Therefore, on balance the deficits of the government and the electricity sector taken together increase, implying that demand on the capital market increases. This leads to an increase in the interest rate. Furthermore, wages and prices rise as a result of the increase in effective demand and the decrease in unemployment. The increase in the interest rate and the rise of wages and prices have several negative effects, particularly in the long run. These effects consist, among other things, of decreases in exports, investments, production and employment. In the long run most of the positive spending effects of the expenditures on the project disappear, because the investment phase lasts five year only. In the long run there is a further increase in the joint deficits of the government and the electricity sector. This is partly related to the increase in the interest rate, which causes an increase in interest payments on the total government debt. The interest payments on the debt created by the earlier investments in wind farms, and the decrease in production and employment, also play a role. To illustrate the above, some of the effects of the project excluding fuel savings are presented in Figure 6.2.

The fuel savings lead to a decrease in the expenditures of the electricity sector on imported gas. This implies that imports decrease. It also implies that the electricity sector saves money and can repay the loans contracted to finance the wind farms. This has a positive effect on the capital market: the interest rate decreases. Consequently, investment, exports, production and employment increase, and the government deficit decreases. Thus, the effects of the fuel savings counterbalance the negative effects of the project excluding the fuel savings to a certain extent. On average, the fuel savings are realized later than the investments in wind farms, so that the counterbalancing effects also occur later in time. The importance of the effects of the fuel savings appear from a comparison of Figure 6.2 (project excluding fuel savings) with Figure 6.1 (project with fuel savings). It now becomes clear why the effects of the project as a whole are more or less similar to the effects of a Keynesian policy of increasing government consumption during the first years, and why they are more positive in later years.

Table 6.6 gives the macroeconomic effects of the project if the gas price is 33 cents (throughout the period of analysis). The assumption that the government subsidizes wind energy up to the point where the present value of the net financial benefits for the electricity sector is zero is maintained. At a gas price of 33 cents, the subsidy for the investments in wind farms is 17%. The gas price has been selected in such a way that the project does not affect the size of the government debt in 1990.

6.3.2. Evaluation of the effects

In Chapter 4 it was described how the evaluation of the effects could be based on neo-Paretian welfare theory. The general principles to be used were described in a theoretical way, and four alternatives for the evaluation of concrete projects were

Table 6.6. Macroeconomic effects of the 660 MW wind energy project, at a gas price of 33 cents

Present value in 1975 of all investments in wind farms: 1305 million guilders.[a] Private profitability of the project: –17%.

Year	Private consumption[b] (million guilders)[d]	Private investment[c] (million guilders)[d]	Unemployment (thousands man-years)	Balance on current account (million guilders)[e]	Government budget surplus (million guilders)[e]	Utilities budget surplus (million guilders)[e]
1975	–6	48	–1.70	–108	–25	–180
1976	0	55	–1.69	–23	13	–127
1977	22	38	–1.48	–18	19	–147
1978	40	11	–1.23	–20	1	–163
1979	50	–13	–1.09	–18	–19	–179
1980	64	–82	0.82	147	2	44
1981	59	–95	0.92	204	–27	36
1982	44	–44	0.74	178	–2	33
1983	40	–12	0.61	179	9	52
1984	43	12	0.38	173	1	77
1985	47	12	0.34	186	–1	88
1986	51	12	0.39	202	–4	100
1987	54	20	0.32	208	–3	111
1988	58	31	0.32	209	6	122
1989	63	41	0.12	210	18	133
1990	68	38	0.34	38	12	0
Sum total[f]	699	70	–1.91	1746	0	0
Present value	75[g]			515	0	0

Notes: see Table 6.5.

given. This chapter will be based on the second alternative mentioned in Section 4.6. This implies that only the choice of the variables to be taken into account will be based on neo-Paretian welfare theory. The question how the effects on the selected variables should be weighed against each other will, in this chapter, essentially be left to the decision-maker.

In Chapter 4 it was argued that the effects of the project on the following variables should be calculated: employment, consumption, government deficit, private investment and the balance on current account during the period of analysis. The effects on consumption and employment during the period of analysis are important because they have a direct effect on utility levels. The effects on the other three variables are important because they have an indirect effect on utility levels. This indirect effect can be described as follows: first, the changes in these variables during the period of analysis lead to changes in the government debt, the capital stock, and net foreign assets at the end of the period of analysis. Second, the changes in these three stock variables lead to changes in utility levels after the period of analysis. In relation to this, the effects on these stock variables should also be calculated.

There is one difference between the directions given in Chapter 4 and the choice of the variables in this chapter. Instead of calculating the effect on employment, the effect on unemployment is calculated. The sign of the effect of a project on unemployment is the opposite of that of the effect on employment. Due to the discouraged worker effect, the effect on unemployment in the Freia model is, in absolute terms, somewhat smaller than the effect on employment, but in the context of what follows this can be neglected. When evaluating the effect of a change in unemployment on utility, I will not only take account of the effect of the related change in employment on the utility of the labourer employed, but also of all kinds of external effects of unemployment, such as for instance the effect on vandalism and the related effect on the utility of spectators of football matches. Thus, some external effects are included which were not mentioned in the discussion of the shadow price of labour in Chapter 4. In relation to the above, it is assumed that a decrease in unemployment leads to an increase in utility.

Table 6.5 shows that the wind energy project leads to an increase in consumption in almost any year during the period of analysis. Although the changes in consumption have not been discounted, it will be clear that if this had been done, the present value (in any year) of these changes would have been positive for any (reasonable) rate of time preference.

The project leads to a decrease in unemployment during the first five years, and to a (smaller) increase in unemployment during later years. The sum total of the changes in unemployment over the whole period is positive. However, because this sum total is only just positive, and because unemployment decreases in the first five years, the following holds good: if a decrease in unemployment in a certain year is valued higher than an equal decrease in a later year, then the present value (in any year) of the effects of the project on utility levels related to changes in unemployment will perhaps be positive. The main conclusion, however, is that this present value is probably rather small.

The sum total of all changes in private investment shows a small decrease. In relation to this, it is likely that the value of the private capital stock in 1990 decreases slighly. However, this is not completely certain, because it is possible that wear and tear and technological development are happening so fast that increases in investment occurring before 1984 do not have much effect on the value of the capital stock in 1990. If this holds good, the change in this value will depend strongly on the changes in investment after 1984, which are all positive. In any case, the effect of the project on the private capital stock in 1990 is small.

The government debt in 1990, expressed in 1990 guilders, increases by 1087 million guilders. The increase in government debt in 1990 is also expressed in terms of the present value in 1975, in 1975 guilders. For the relevant calculation the nominal interest rates of the period 1975–1990 as estimated by the Freia model are used. The present value in 1975 (in 1975 guilders) of the change in government debt in 1990 is 320 million guilders, about 70% of the present value of the subsidies for the project.

Net foreign assets in 1990, expressed in 1990 guilders, increase by 1298 million guilders. The present value in 1975 (in 1975 guilders) of this change, calculated on the basis of Freia nominal interest rates, is 382 million guilders.

Summarizing, it can be said that the effects on the present value (in any year) of changes in consumption and the effects on net foreign assets in 1990 are positive and large, that the effects on the government debt in 1990 are unfavourable and large (although somewhat smaller in absolute terms than the effects on net foreign assets), and that the effects on the private capital stock in 1990 and on the present value (in any year) of changes in utility related to changes in unemployment are undetermined, but probably small.

As stated above, it is essentially left to the decision-maker to weigh the effects on the variables discussed above against each other. However, in order to give him at least something to go by, the outcomes of the calculations at a gas price of 33 cents are brought to the fore. Table 6.6 shows that at this price the effects on the government debt are neutral, while all other effects are positive. Assuming that a decision-maker is of the opinion that in the long run an increase in government debt is absolutely unacceptable, he can still decide to grant a subsidy of 17% for the investments in wind farms. If he is of the opinion that other variables should also be taken into account, higher subsidies can be given. In this context it can be remarked that in the long run the effects of an increase in government debt on the interest rate are counterbalanced to a certain extent by the effects of the increase in net foreign assets. This implies that there is less reason to give increases in the government debt a heavy weight in the evaluation.

6.3.3. Sensitivity analysis with regard to the microeconomic characteristics

There are many uncertainties concerning the microeconomic characteristics of the project. Therefore, it makes sense to analyse to what extent the calculated macroeconomic effects change if some of the microeconomic assumptions change. First of all it can be noted that the effects of the project have already been calculated on the basis of two different assumptions regarding the gas price. A comparison of Tables 6.5 and 6.6 shows that an increase in the gas price of 6 cents, having a substantial effect on the private profitability, also has important macroeconomic effects.

In the remainder of this section attention will be paid to the effects of changes in assumptions other than that about the gas price. It is emphasized that at least one assumption will not be changed, viz. the assumption that the government always subsidizes the project up to the point where the private profitability of the project including subsidies is zero.

The explanation of the procedure to be used can be started by repeating a conclusion of the previous section. If the assumptions of Section 6.2 hold good, and if the gas price is such that the private profitability of the project excluding subsidies is –17%, then granting a subsidy of 17% will have a neutral effect on the government debt. In that case the effects on all other variables will be positive. Therefore, it is justifiable to give a subsidy of at least 17%.

In this section, different sets of microeconomic assumptions which do not relate to the gas price, or any other relevant fuel price, will be distinguished. For each of these sets the following procedure will be used: first, the effects of the project are calculated on the basis of different prices for gas, or for any other relevant fuel.

Table 6.7. Effects of changes in assumptions about the microeconomic characteristics of the project

Case	(Main) differences with original case regarding set of assumptions[a]	Minimum justifiable subsidy (%)[a]
Original case	–	17
Case II (Alternative case of section 6.2.4)	50% of wind turbines is imported. The import coefficient of investments in wind farms is 15.1% higher, that of the operating costs 6.3% higher.	12
Case III	The support for (domestic) wind farms leads to an increase in exports of wind turbines which amounts to 50% of the turbines in domestic wind farms.	22
Case IV	The capacity savings and fuel savings concern coal-fired plants.	15
Case V	Wind energy leads to savings on the import of electricity. No capacity savings, no fuel savings.	18
Case VI	All starting points are based on the technology of 1989 rather than that of 1994–1995. The ratio between turbine costs and site costs is higher. Operating costs of wind farms are higher. Capacity savings and fuel savings are lower.	17

[a]See main text for an explanation.

Second, the fuel price which makes the effect of the project on the government debt in 1990 neutral is the price that is selected. Third, the private profitability excluding subsidies at this fuel price is examined, or, to put it differently, what the subsidy which is provided at this fuel price amounts to. In Table 6.7 this subsidy, expressed as a percentage of the investments in wind farms, is given for various sets of assumptions. In the extensive report it has been shown that for each of these sets of assumptions the following holds good: as long as the relevant fuel price is such that the project has a neutral effect on the government debt in 1990, the effects on the variables other than the government debt are essentially the same as the effects given in Table 6.6. Therefore, the subsidy given in Table 6.7 can be regarded as the minimum justifiable subsidy.

The second case presented in the table differs from the original one in that 50% of the turbines is imported. As a result, the import coefficient of the investments in the wind farm is 15% higher, and the import coefficient of the operating costs of wind farms is 6% higher. This leads to a decrease in the minimum justifiable percentage of subsidy with only 5%. From this it can be concluded that the sensitivity of the outcome on the import coefficient is not great. The other cases of Table 6.7 further support the conclusion that the outcome is not very sensitive to changes in the assumptions other than the assumption about the fuel price.

The last case, case VI, shows that the minimum justifiable subsidy does not change when all wind farms are built according to the technology of 1989. In case VI the gas price at which the government debt remains constant is 54 cents, which is 21 cents higher than in the original case. Therefore, the conclusion about the minimum justifiable subsidy does not depend on a specific assumption regarding the fuel price, but has a more general meaning.

The reader might be tempted to conclude from the remarks on case VI that if the gas price is lower than 54 cents, wind farms built around 1990 will lead to an increase in the government debt. This conclusion is wrong, mainly because wind farms built around 1990 are built on relatively favourable locations. This has a positive effect on the production of electricity, and reduces the site costs. Case VI, however, is based on the assumption that wind farms with a joint capacity of 660 MW are built, which implies that it is impossible to use only the most favourable locations. Thus, this study gives no information about the private profitability of projects built in the near future, or about the gas price at which these projects will not lead to a change in the government debt. However, because the conclusion about the minimum amount of subsidy is not very sensitive with regard to assumptions about the fuel price and other variables, it is likely that even at present the minimum justifiable subsidy is about 17%.

A final remark: it was argued in Section 6.2 that it is not impossible that in the future part of the turbines will be imported. From this point of view, the outcomes of the original calculations seem to be too optimistic, although the distortion is small (see case II). However, it is also possible that subsidizing wind farms will strengthen the position of the Dutch wind turbine industry, and that because of this the export of wind turbines will increase. This has positive effects (see case III), which are not taken into account in the original calculations either.

6.3.4. The dependency of the outcomes on macroeconomic factors

The macroeconomic effects of the wind energy project have been analysed by means of a model that simulates a timepath in the past. Therefore, the question arises whether the outcomes of the calculations can give an indication of the effects of wind farms built in the future. In Chapter 5 it was argued that the answer to this question can be affirmative, as long as the characteristics of the economy do not change in a fundamental way. In this context the situation on the labour market is of paramount importance.

If in the period in which the investments are made there is full employment instead of unemployment, there would be no reason to subsidize wind energy on the basis of the occurrence of positive macroeconomic effects such as the ones discussed above (because these effects are related to the existence of unemployment). Thus, the question is whether there will be unemployment in the Netherlands in the near future. Now, one of the basic principles underlying this study is that the evaluation of individual projects should not be influenced by the project analyst's view of the macroeconomy. Instead, it should be consistent with the macroeconomic analysis that is used to help formulate government policies. This is the reason why a macroeconomic model of the CPB has been used. Considering this, it is sensible to pay attention to the views of the CPB regarding the future situation on the labour market. At present, the CPB is of the opininon that unemployment will continue to exist in the future. With regard to the labour market, the recent analyses of the CPB of the effects of future policies are essentially based on the same point of view as the analysis made in this study by means of the Freia model.

The outcomes of the calculations also depend on the model used. In Chapter 5 the Freia model was compared with other national econometric models, which related to countries other than the Netherlands. It was concluded that the effects of a Keynesian policy concerning consumption expenditures as calculated by means of the Freia model are relatively negative, even if countries (much) larger than the Netherlands are left out of consideration. This is to a large extent related to the fact that the capital market is very important in the Freia model. It was also remarked in Chapter 5 that in a recent study one of the staff members of the CPB concludes that the influence of the capital market has been overestimated in the Freia model. Now the effects of the wind energy project excluding fuel savings are more or less equal to the effects of a Keynesian policy concerning consumption expenditures. On average the fuel savings occur later in time than the investments in the project, so that for a certain period of time the project leads to an increase in demand on the capital market. In relation to this, the negative effects of the project excluding fuel savings are only counterbalanced (more or less) completely at the end of the period of analysis. The above implies that the calculated effects of the wind energy project are influenced in a negative way by the characteristics of the capital market in the Freia model. Because of this the actual effects of wind energy in the Netherlands may be more positive than the calculated effects. It can also be noted that the outcomes of the study of Chan-Lee and Kato suggest that it is possible that in a number of other countries the actual effects of wind energy on the national economy will be more positive than the effects given in Tables 6.5 and 6.6.

A related point is the following. In Chapter 2 it was argued that projects such as the wind energy project discussed above will only lead to a short-term increase in the interest rate if, in the short run, international investors neglect the positive effects of these project on the balance of payments in the long run. Thus, the interest rate will only rise in the short run if international investors are irrational. Now the calculations with the Freia model show that the wind energy project leads to a deterioration in the balance of payments in the short run, which is more than counterbalanced by a considerable improvement in the long run. The Freia model, however, is such that during the short run international investors do not take account of the improvement of the balance of payments in the long run. If international investors were assumed to be more rational, the outcomes would have been more positive.

In this context a possible counter-argument is that the improvement in the balance of payments caused by the wind energy project is too small to be perceived by international investors, so that it should be neglected. However, on the basis of Section 4.4 it can be said that this counter-argument is not correct.

6.4. Conclusions

This chapter has shown that, in a situation of unemployment as experienced in the Netherlands in the period 1975–1990, wind energy has relatively positive macroeconomic effects, even if energy prices are such that wind energy is not profitable from the private point of view, at least not without subsidies. Among other things, it has been shown that if the investments in wind farms need to be subsidized with 17% in order to be profitable from the private point of view, the provision of the necessary subsidies will not lead to an increase in government debt, whereas the effects on other variables will be positive. This conclusion is not very sensitive to changes in microeconomic characteristics.

The conclusion is based on the use of the Freia model of the CPB. This model pays, in comparison with other models, much attention to negative effects induced by investments in wind farms. Taken by itself this implies that it is possible that the actual effects of the wind energy project are more positive than indicated by the outcomes of the calculations of this chapter. However, two reservations need to be made. First, there are great uncertainties regarding the outcomes of calculations with any econometric macro-model. Second, the calculations concern a period in the past. This does not imply that the calculations can give no indication of the effects of wind energy in the future, but one should be very careful in this respect.

It is possible that in the future (more) wind farms will be subsidized by the EU instead of by the Netherlands, so that they should be evaluated from a European point of view. Given the argument in Chapter 2, it can be said that such an evaluation would lead to (even) more optimistic conclusions.

The analysis has been based on the assumption that investments in wind energy are subsidized by the government. Whether the provision of subsidies is the most suitable instrument to promote wind energy has not been investigated. Given that the government has decided to use subsidies as an instrument, however, it is plausible that it is justifiable to give substantial grants for investments in wind energy in situations of unemployment, because of the positive macroeconomic effects related to the occurrence of unemployment. There seems to be hardly any reason at all to put a limit to the budget for subsidies as is done by the Dutch government. The above conclusions are based on an analysis that does not take account of the advantages of wind energy with regard to the environment and the dependency on foreign oil producers.

In the above, certain microeconomic factors have been neglected. For example, if presently an unlimited amount of subsidies were made available, all good locations might be occupied by turbines built at the beginning of the nineties. These locations would then not be available for more sophisticated turbines built later. This might be inefficient. Microeconomic factors such as the one discussed above have not been investigated.

Many projects which lead to savings on fuels and other raw materials have essentially the same characteristics as wind farms. On the one hand these projects involve expenditures on capital goods and operating expenditures. Just as in the case of wind farms, the effects of these expenditures are more or less the same as those of a

Keynesian policy concerning consumption expenditures. These effects are partly positive and partly negative. On the other hand, these projects lead to savings on fuels and other raw materials. These savings have effects which counterbalance, to a smaller or larger extent, the negative effects of the expenditures on capital goods and the operating expenditures. Of course the effects will vary from project to project. More research into other projects is desirable. Despite the lack of sufficient research it is at least plausible that the effects of many projects which save on fuels and other raw materials will approximately be the same as the effects of wind farms. Thus, if a large number of these projects were carried through as a result of government support, the government would probably be following an expansionist policy which not only has positive effects on consumption and employment, but also on net foreign assets, and which has no (or hardly any) negative effects on the government debt. In other words, this chapter supports the conclusions of Chapter 2.

Notes

1. For a quantitative assessment see Hohmeyer (1988), Friedrich and Vos (1989) and Van Wijk (1990).
2. Van de Klundert and Peer (1983).
3. This assumption is reasonable because of the following: if there were no uncertainties, it would be rational for the utilities to behave as described in the main text. In reality, there are great uncertainties. If the utilities do not invest in wind energy, they have to invest in fuel-driven power plants instead. Therefore, the uncertainties connected with the costs of electricity from wind have to be weighed against the uncertainties connected with the costs of electricity from fuel-driven power plants. The former are mainly caused by the fact that the wind industry is still in its development phase. The latter are mainly caused by the uncertainties regarding future energy prices. It is not implausible that the uncertainties connected with the costs of a kWh electricity from wind are smaller than those related to the costs of a kWh from fuel-driven power plants. Moreover, the uncertainty about future energy prices dominates the uncertainty related to the costs of total electricity production. This implies that investments in wind energy represent a form of risk-spreading. Considering this, the above assumption does not lead to a bias in favour of wind energy.
4. Of course, it is almost impossible to give exactly as much subsidy as is necessary to make the present value of the net benefits for the utilities zero. Therefore, the effects of giving a subsidy that is too low or too high (in relation to the goal of a zero present value of the net benefits for the utilities) should be investigated. In the situation in which the subsidy is too low the investments will not be carried through. This may not be optimal. However, if this is not optimal, then the situation in which no subsidies are offered at all will not be optimal either, so that offering subsidies will not have large negative effects. The situation in which too much subsidy is given is more complicated. Given the characteristics of the Dutch electricity sector, providing too much subsidy causes a decrease in electricity prices. This has two direct effects: an increase in the standard of living of consumers and a decrease in the production costs of firms. This will have many further effects. Electricity prices are only one component of the standard of living and the production costs. The government has certain goals with regard to the standard of living, the production costs, and other variables such as the government deficit. It has different instruments at its disposal to realize these goals. For instance, it can decrease tax rates in order to increase the standard of living and to decrease the production costs, at the cost of the goverment deficit. It may also increase subsidies to electricity producers to get the same results, or increase tax rates to get the opposite results. The government aims to use its instruments in such a way that the optimal situation with regard to the standard of living, production costs and other factors such as the government deficit will be reached. However, it can never be sure that this goal is accomplished. If the government

follows a policy that is the best possible one given the limited amount of information available, the chance that its tax rates are too high and its subsidies too low is equal to the chance that the opposite holds good. Subsidies for wind energy constitute a small fraction of the total government budget. Considering this, the chance that giving too much subsidy for wind energy moves the economy away from the optimum is just as high as the chance that the opposite occurs. Given that the related uncertainties are cancelled out at the level of the portfolio of all measures taken by the government, the above implies that there is no need to worry about subsidies for wind energy being too high.

5. This is a coincidence. Calculations based on different figures for costs and benefits show that the profitability at a real interest rate of 4% can differ a few percents from the profitability at Freia interest rates. Still, this difference is small, which is related to the fact that the average Freia interest rate is close to 4%.
6. Given the argument in Chapter 2, and given that the prices of imported gas, exported gas, and gas bought by the utilities from the Dutch gas-producer Gasunie are about equal, the following holds good: the macroeconomic effects of the project, in a situation in which all savings on gas concern imported gas, are the same as those in a situation in which all savings of gas concern Dutch gas, and in which all these savings are compensated by an increase in exports of Dutch gas.
7. In Chapter 4 it was stated that, in order to calculate the macroeconomic effects of the project, each fva_t is multiplied by (a transformation of) the relevant matrix H_t, and each gfn_t is multiplied by (a transformation of) the relevant matrix U_t. Now, the matrices H_t and U_t concern the effects of certain one-off changes that have a magnitude of 1 billion guilders in prices of year *t*. Therefore, the values of the gfn_t and the fva_t will also be expressed in prices of year *t* before the multiplication mentioned above is made.
8. Projects subsidized by the government were not mentioned in Chapter 4. However, it will be clear that these projects are included in the portfolio of which the effects are taken into consideration by the government.

CHAPTER 7

Converting the method into a dual method

7.1. General outline of the method

The primal method of Chapter 4 is based on the principle that the macroeconomic effects of each project are calculated and evaluated separately. If a large number of projects is to be analysed, this method can be time-consuming. In that case a dual method has an important advantage: once shadow prices have been calculated for all types of inputs and outputs, the evaluation of individual projects is straightforward; only the profitability of a project at shadow prices needs to be calculated to determine whether it can be accepted. However, as was concluded in Chapter 3, as yet there is no satisfactory dual method for the appraisal of concrete projects in present-day developed market economies.

In this chapter an attempt will be made to develop an improved dual method. This method will, to a large extent, be based on the primal method of Chapter 4. By this primal method the effects of the parts of a project are first calculated separately and are then added up to arrive at the total effects of the project. The parts distinguished in Chapter 4 were the (gross) financial needs in different years, the expenditures excluding financial needs in different years, and the output in different years. This primal method is only justifiable if the model used fulfils the conditions of additivity of Section 4.3. This section will be based on the assumption that this is indeed the case.[1]

The project can also be subdivided in other ways. In this chapter it will be divided into (individual) inputs and outputs. Each input and output has a volume of one; two barrels of oil bought in 1975 are two (individual) inputs. It is possible to calculate the effects of each input and output by using the same principles as the ones described in Chapter 4. This can be verified by the fact that each input and output can be regarded as a separate 'project'. Because the effects of a project can be calculated by means of the method of Chapter 4, the effects of each input and output can also be calculated by means of this method.

As an example, the effects of the purchase of a barrel of oil in 1975 can be calculated in the following way. First, the effects of the financial needs related to this barrel of oil, which equal its price, are calculated. These are calculated in the same way as the effects of the total financial needs of a project in 1975. Second, the spending effects of the expenditure on the barrel of oil are calculated. Essentially, these are calculated in the same way as the spending effects of the total expenditure on a project in 1975. However, the calculations now take account of the specific import coefficient and the specific indirect tax coefficient of the barrel of oil. Third, the total effects of the purchase of the barrel of oil are calculated as being equal to the sum total of the effects of the financial needs and the effects of the spending.

Once the separate effects of each input and output have been calculated, the total effects of the project can be calculated by adding up all these separate effects. Given the assumption that the model used satisfies the conditions of additivity as described in Section 4.3, the effects of the project calculated in this way are equal to the effects as calculated by means of the method of Chapter 4.

With regard to the evaluation of the effects, the primal method of Chapter 4 is based on neo-Paretian welfare theory. In an ideal situation this means that it consists essentially of five steps. First, the effects of the project on five variables over a certain period of years are calculated. These five variables are consumption, employment, private investment, the government deficit and the balance on current account. Second, the effects on consumption and employment (and in relation to this, on leisure time) in different years are converted into a present value (in the last year that is analysed) of changes in utility, expressed in terms of willingness to pay. Third, the effects on private investment, the government deficit and the balance on current account in different years are converted into changes in three stock variables (in the last year that is analysed). These three stock variables are the private capital stock, the government debt, and net foreign assets. Fourth, the changes in the three stock variables are converted into the present value (in the last year that is analysed) of changes in utility, expressed in terms of willingness to pay. This conversion is based on the idea that the changes in the three stock variables are only important insofar as they affect future levels of utility from consumption and employment (leisure time). Fifth, the project is accepted if the total effect on the present value of changes in utility is positive. (Note that in the previous chapter the last four steps were left to the decision-maker.)

This procedure implies that weights are assigned to the effects on different variables in different years (because the effect on any variable in any year is ultimately expressed in terms of utility). Considering this, the last four steps of the procedure could also be taken together, and then be described as follows: weights are assigned to the effects on different variables in different years. Positive weights are assigned to effects considered positive, and negative weights to effects considered negative. The sum of all effects multiplied by their weights is calculated, and the project is accepted if this sum is positive.

It is now possible to give the full outline of the dual method developed in this chapter. First, one calculates the effects of one input of the analysed project on different variables in different years in the way described above. Second, one assigns the weights mentioned in the previous paragraph to these effects, and calculates the sum of all different effects multiplied by their weights. This sum is called the PS price (preliminary shadow price) of the input. Third, the same procedure is used for every input and output of the project. Thus, each input and output is given a PS price. Note that the PS prices of two individual inputs of the same type (e.g. two barrels of oil bought in 1975) are the same, which simplifies the procedure. Fourth, one calculates the sum of the PS prices of all individual inputs and outputs. This sum is called the profitability of the project at PS prices. Fifth, the project is accepted if this profitability is positive. The reader can verify that this alternative leads to the same conclusion regarding the acceptability of the project, as did the method of Chapter 4.

The above concerns only the PS prices of inputs and outputs relating to the analysed project. However, the value of a PS price of an input or output, calculated as explained above, is independent of the analysed project. Thus, one can calculate a general set of PS prices for all types of inputs and outputs without paying attention to the question which project is analysed. When a specific project is analysed afterwards, one can select from this set the PS prices that refer to the inputs and outputs of this project.

The approach can be improved by choosing a suitable numéraire, and by normalising all PS prices on the basis of this numéraire. Besides, the effects of inputs can be regarded as costs, and in relation to this the negative sign of PS prices of inputs can be changed into a positive sign. Finally, a shadow rate of interest can be introduced. These improvements imply that the PS prices are converted into shadow prices. They will be discussed in more detail in the subsequent section.

7.2. Shadow prices based on the freia model

This section will show how shadow prices can be calculated by means of the Freia model. These shadow prices are not intended to be used for the evaluation of concrete projects. In relation to this, a number of arbitrary assumptions will be made. Also, only the shadow prices of three types of inputs of a public project will be taken into consideration: imported inputs bought in 1975, imported inputs bought in 1985, and non-traded inputs bought in 1985. In this chapter imported inputs are defined as inputs with an import coefficient of 1.0. Non-traded inputs are defined as inputs with a first-round import coefficient of 0.25. Of course, in reality there are also imported inputs and non-traded inputs with import coefficients that differ from the ones given above, but this is neglected. For an imported input one may read, for instance, a barrel of oil, which is assumed to have an import coefficient of 1.0 in this chapter. For a non-traded input one may read, for instance, a desk-lamp produced domestically with the help of imported inputs worth 25% of its total costs. It is assumed that each of the three types of inputs has a market price of 100 guilders (in 1975 prices). The purchase of the inputs is financed on the capital market. No empirical research has been carried out to estimate the effects of changes in employment (leisure time) on utility levels. Rather arbitrarily these effects are assumed to be zero, so that changes in employment can be neglected.

The calculation of the shadow prices of the three inputs involves a number of steps (which do not correspondent exactly to the steps mentioned in Section 7.1). *The first step* is to calculate, by means of the Freia model, the macroeconomic effects of

Table 7.1. Macroeconomic effects of using one unit of each of the three types of inputs

A. Effects of using an imported input in 1975 (in guilders)

Year	Private[a] consumption[b]	Private investment[b]	Balance on current account	Government budget surplus[c]
1975	–2.04	–0.57	–98.76	–101.02
1976	–3.60	–6.18	–0.53	–12.28
1977	–4.22	–10.11	2.80	–13.11
1978	–5.90	–7.98	1.92	–14.59
1979	–6.93	–7.30	1.54	–15.29
1980	–7.59	–6.32	0.93	–16.51
1981	–8.14	–5.36	0.38	–18.40
1982	–9.03	–4.87	0.95	–22.15
1983	–9.92	–3.80	1.17	–26.12
1984	–9.71	–2.69	1.04	–30.34
1985	–9.45	–1.17	0.10	–34.99
1986	–8.92	0.16	–1.24	–40.30
1987	–8.32	0.79	–2.06	–45.90
1988	–7.66	0.22	–1.92	–52.66
1989	–7.08	0.45	–2.31	–59.55
1990	–6.58	–0.43	–1.44	–66.44
Sum total			–97.43	–569.65

B. Effects of using one imported input in 1985 (in guilders)

Year	Private consumption	Private investment	Balance on current account	Govenment budget surplus
1975	0	0	0	0
–	–	–	–	–
1984	0	0	0	0
1985	–1.89	–0.70	–171.95	–175.29
1986	–3.28	–5.90	–2.95	–21.95
1987	–3.50	–9.56	1.04	–22.45
1988	–4.25	–8.44	1.08	–24.97
1989	–4.53	–7.48	0.05	–27.77
1990	–4.62	–6.43	–1.29	–31.45
Sum total			–174.02	–303.87

Notes: see next page.

using one unit of each of the three types of inputs on private consumption, private investment, the government budget surplus and the balance on current account. Table 7.1 gives the results.[2]

The second step is to calculate the present value in 1990 of the changes in utility caused by the changes in consumption up to 1990, expressed in terms of willingness to pay. In order to calculate this present value, one needs to know the private time preference rate; this is assumed to be equal to the average long-term real rate of interest in the period 1975–1989 in the Freia model, which is 4.25%. The present

Table 7.1 (*continued*)

C. Effects of using a non-traded input in 1985 (in guilders)

Year	Private consumption	Private investment	Balance on current account	Govenment budget surplus
1975	0	0	0	0
–	–	–	–	–
1984	0	0	0	0
1985	–3.38	36.29	–87.05	–154.52
1986	0.20	18.33	–32.87	14.46
1987	6.52	–22.29	20.38	–23.55
1988	2.15	–26.54	16.02	–35.05
1989	–2.36	–24.02	21.95	–28.82
1990	–4.01	–5.64	7.45	–22.82
Sum total			–54.12	–250.29

[a]Because government consumption is constant, the change in private consumption is equal to the change in total consumption.
[b]In 1974 prices.
[c]In current prices.

values in 1990 of the changes in consumption related to the use of one unit of each of the three types of inputs are given in the first row of Table 7.2.

The third step is to calculate the changes in the following three stock variables in 1990: private capital stock, government debt, and private financial wealth. The change in the private capital stock in 1990 is calculated as being equal to the sum of all changes in private investment up to 1990, minus corrections for wear and tear and for technological development. These corrections imply that capital goods lose 5% of their original value every year.[3] The changes in the private capital stock in 1990 related to using one unit of each of the three types of inputs are given in the second row of Table 7.2.[4]

The change in net financial assets of the government in 1990 is given in the third row of Table 7.2. It is equal to the sum of all changes in the government budget surplus up to 1990. The change in net private financial assets in 1990 is given in the

Table 7.2. Changes in selected variables caused by the use of one unit of each of the three types of inputs (in guilders)

	Imported input 1975	Imported input 1985	Non-traded input 1985
Present value in 1990 of changes in consumption up to 1990	–306	–48	–1
Private capital stock in 1990	–44	–69	–59
Net financial assets of the government in 1990	–570	–304	–250
Net private financial assets in 1990	+472	+130	+196

Note: All effects are now expressed in 1990 prices.

Table 7.3. Three sets of weights for the effects on the selected variables

	Set A	Set B	Set C
Present value in 1990 of changes in consumption up to 1990	1	1	1
Private capital stock in 1990	1	1.5	1.5
Net financial assets of the government in 1990	1	3	4.5
Net private financial assets in 1990	1	1.5	1.5

fourth row of Table 7.2. Net private financial assets are defined as the net financial assets of all economic agents in the country excluding the government, or, more specifically, as net foreign assets minus the net financial assets of the government. The change in net foreign assets in 1990 is equal to the sum total of the changes in the balance on current account up to 1990. Considering this, it is easy to calculate the change in net private financial assets in 1990.

The fourth step concerns the determination of the weights for the four variables discussed above. The weight for the present value in 1990 of the changes in consumption is set equal to one. Therefore, the weight of each of the three stock variables in 1990 is equal to the effect of a unit change in the relevant variable on the present value in 1990 of all changes in consumption occurring after 1990. In Section 4.6 it was explained that one possible procedure for the determination of the weights is to base the evaluation on the assumption that a situation of general equilibrium with a Pareto-optimum prevails from the end of the period of analysis onwards. This implies that the three stock variables should all have a weight of one. Thus, in set A, all weights are equal to one. The two other sets of weights to be used below have been determined arbitrarily; their function is to help analyse the sensitivity of the outcomes to the weights. These two sets of weights, together with set A, are given in Table 7.3.

The fifth step is the calculation of shadow prices. In case the weights of set A are used, the procedure can be explained as follows. The effects of buying one unit of an imported input in 1975 on the four variables discussed above, which are given in Table 7.2, are multiplied by the relevant weights of set A. This yields four products of effects and weights. Next, the sum of these four products is calculated. This sum is labelled as the PS-1 price of the imported input of 1975. The same procedure is applied to the other two types of inputs. Thus, the PS-1 price of the imported input of 1975, the imported input of 1985, and the non-traded input of 1985 are –448, –291 and –114, respectively.

Subsequently, the PS-2 prices are calculated. The imported input of 1975 is taken as the numéraire. Thus, the PS-2 price of the imported input of 1975 is 100 guilders. Given this, the PS-2 price of the imported input of 1985 is 100 guilders multiplied by –291/–448, which is 65 guilders. The PS-2 price of the non-traded input of 1985 is 25 guilders. Because these three PS-2 prices refer to inputs that are all worth 100 guilders at market prices (in prices of 1975), the PS-2 prices of these inputs divided by 100 are equal to the proportion between the PS-2 prices and market prices. This proportion is given for each of the three inputs in the first column of Table 7.4. A

Table 7.4. Proportion between PS-2 prices and market prices, for each of the three inputs and for three different sets of weights

	Set A	Set B	Set C
Imported input 1975	1	1	1
Imported input 1985	0.65	0.63	0.59
Non-traded input 1985	0.25	0.40	0.41

similar procedure can be followed with regard to sets B and C. The results are given in Table 7.4.

Two short comments can be made. First, the PS-2 price of the non-traded input bought in 1985 is (for all sets of weights) relatively lower than that of an imported input bought in the same year. This was to be expected, because according to the Freia model an increase in demand (taken by itself) has positive effects. Second, the PS-2 prices do not seem to be very sensitive to the weights for the three stock variables. This suggests that it could be fruitful to do more research along the lines of this chapter.

A further possible improvement concerns the introduction of a shadow discount rate. When a shadow discount rate is used, the shadow prices of identical goods bought in different years can be set equal. This could make the evaluation of concrete projects more efficient. Given the fact that it is justifiable to evaluate projects on the basis of the PS-2 prices mentioned above, the introduction of a shadow discount rate is subject to the following condition: the new system of shadow prices, which includes the shadow discount rate, should lead to the same conclusion regarding the acceptability of projects as does the original system of PS-2 prices. Below, the word 'shadow price' will be used exclusively for the prices in the system of shadow prices that includes a shadow discount rate.

Table 7.4 shows that the PS-2 price of an imported input bought in 1985 is 35% (set A), 37% (set B) or 41% (set C) lower than the PS-2 price of an imported input bought in 1975. Let us take the shadow price of the imported input bought in 1975 and the shadow price of the imported input bought in 1985 (in constant prices) both to be equal to the PS-2 price of the imported input bought in 1975, which is 100 guilders. Let us calculate the (real) shadow discount rate which establishes that the use of these shadow prices will lead to the same conclusions regarding the acceptability of projects as does the use of the PS-2 prices. This shadow discount rate, which applies to imported inputs only, is 4.4% (set A), 4.7% (set B) or 5.4% (set C).[5]

The next question is how to interpret this shadow discount rate. There are three factors which influence the proportion between the PS-2 price of an imported input bought in 1985 and that of an imported input bought in 1975, and which therefore influence the value of the shadow discount rate for imported inputs. First, during the period 1975–1985 interest has to be paid on the money borrowed to finance the purchase of the input in 1975. According to the Freia model, the average long-term (real) interest rate in the period 1975–1985 is 3.4%. The shadow discount rates mentioned above are 4.4%, 4.7% and 5.4%. Therefore, the value of the shadow discount rate is determined to a large extent by the long-term interest rate.

The second factor is that the economic situation in 1985 may differ from that in 1975. For instance, an increase in demand on the capital market in 1985 may lead to a higher increase in the rate of interest than it would have done in 1975, and in relation to this to a greater decrease in investment, production and the government budget surplus.

In order to explain the third factor which influences the proportion between the PS-2 prices of the two imported inputs, it is assumed that the economic situation in 1985 is exactly the same as that in 1975. Even when this assumption is made, one can still distinghuish some macroeconomic effects which can influence the proportion between the PS-2 prices of the two imported inputs. For example, if an imported input is bought in 1975, this will lead to an increase in government debt in 1975, and consequently to an increase in the interest rate, a decrease in investment and production, and a further increase in government debt in later years. Similar effects will occur when an imported input is bought in 1985, but the resulting increase in government debt will only affect the economic development from 1985 onwards. Therefore, it will affect the economic development during a shorter period than the increase in government debt caused by the purchase of an input in 1975. This will affect the proportion between the two PS-2 prices.

In the existing dual methods the set of shadow prices has the following characteristics: first, the shadow prices of identical goods bought in different years are the same. Second, the shadow discount rate is the same for all types of goods. Clearly, this increases the efficiency of the method. However, it depends on the model used whether such an efficient system of shadow prices can be achieved. It is not certain that the Freia model will generate such an efficient set of shadow prices. For example, such a set implies that the proportion between the PS-2 price of an imported input bought in 1985 and the PS-2 price of an imported input bought in 1975 is equal to the proportion between the PS-2 price of a non-traded input bought in 1985 and the PS-2 price of a non-traded input bought in 1975.[6] However, suppose that unemployment in the base-run is high in 1985 and low in 1975. This could significantly decrease the proportion between the PS-2 price of a non-traded input bought in 1985 and the PS-2 price of a non-traded input bought in 1975, but it need not have the same effect on the proportion between the PS-2 price of an imported input bought in 1985 and the PS-2 price of an imported input bought in 1975 (because the effects of buying an imported input may not be very sensitive to the situation on the labour market). Thus, it may not always be possible to obtain a system of shadow prices that is highly efficient in the sense mentioned above.

In some situations the problem mentioned above may not be too serious. For example, the base-run will generally concern a period in the future, and a predicted economic development that is more or less stable. In that case the problem mentioned above may be minor, and could perhaps be solved by using some approximations. Besides, even if it is not possible to obtain a system of shadow prices that is highly efficient in the sense mentioned above, the dual method is still efficient in the sense that once shadow prices have been calculated for inputs and outputs, they can be used for the evaluation of a large number of projects.

7.3. Conclusions

In this chapter a dual method based on an econometric macro-model has been developed. The method is not yet ready to be used for the appraisal of concrete projects. The main reason for this is that the determination of the weights has been based on ad hoc considerations.

At the beginning of this chapter it was stated that a dual method has the advantage of being efficient when a large number of projects has to be evaluated. It has been shown, however, that the system of shadow prices which can be obtained by means of an econometric macro-model may not be as efficient as one might think in the first instance, and more research regarding this point is necessary. Nevertheless, the advantage of the dual method mentioned above remains essentially valid.

Still, the following negative points should be mentioned. Although it should be possible to solve the problem of finding acceptable weights, it remains true that any solution to this problem will involve a certain subjectivity. Fortunately, the calculations of this chapter indicate that the value of the shadow prices may not be too sensitive with regard to the weights; more research regarding this point is necessary. Nevertheless, the shadow prices will always to a certain extent depend on the subjective judgments of investigators with regard to the weights. Besides, they depend on the characteristics of the macroeconomic model used. Therefore, it will always be difficult for decision-makers to understand what is meant when it is stated that a certain project is profitable at shadow prices. Of course, the outcomes of the primal method also depend on the model used, and the decisions to be made on the basis of this method also involve a subjective evaluation of the macroeconomic effects. However, the calculations with the model are clearly distinguished from the evaluation, so that the influence of the characteristics of the model used can be separated from the influence of the subjective aspects related to the evaluation. Also, it is possible to leave the evaluation of the calculated effects to the decision-maker, so that the results do not depend on the subjective judgments of investigators.

It is not yet clear whether or not the advantage of the dual method regarding the efficiency outweighs its disadvantage regarding the interpretation of the results. In relation to this, more research regarding the dual method developed in this chapter could be desirable.

Notes

1. If these conditions are not fulfilled, this can be taken into account by adapting the matrices H_t and U_t as explained in Chapter 4.
2. Using the symbols of Chapter 4, the effects of, for example, buying one unit of the imported input of 1975 are equal to $U_1 \cdot 10^{-7}$ (if the subscript 1 refers to the first year of analysis, 1975), plus a deterioration in the balance on current account of 1 billion guilders in 1975.
3. See Van der Burg (1991), p. 274 for an explanation.
4. Note that in Table 7.2 the changes in the private capital stock in 1990 are expressed in 1990 prices.
5. $(1.044)^{-10} = 0.65$, $(1.047)^{-10} = 0.63$, and $(1.054)^{-10} = 0.59$.
6. At least, if the real market prices of these goods do not change in this period.

CHAPTER 8

International aspects and the debate about import substitution

8.1. Effects on the world economy

If a situation of full employment existed everywhere, the evaluation of projects from a global perpective would be relatively easy. Essentially, projects should then be evaluated on the basis of market prices. In certain cases corrections should be made to take account of market imperfections. The main reason for stimulating projects leading to savings on fuels and other raw materials which are not profitable at market prices would then be that they lead to a decrease in pollution levels.[1]

The preceding chapters were based on the assumption that in the country in which the analysed projects are implemented, unemployment exists. This implies that there is another reason why projects leading to savings on raw materials which are not profitable at market prices could still be efficient from a global perspective: they involve a substitution of unemployed labourers for scarce raw materials. One way of taking this into account is to analyse these projects on the basis of a method which is the same as the one developed in Chapter 4, except for one point: the econometric macro-model used is a global model. However, this is beyond the scope of this study. Still, a qualitative analysis can be made.

This analysis will be based on the assumption that in some countries a policy of stimulating savings on raw materials is pursued, and that in these countries a situation of unemployment exists such as described in Chapter 2. It is also assumed that the savings on raw materials realized in these countries either lead to a decrease in their imports of raw materials, or they lead to an increase in their exports of raw materials. An example of the latter is the case in which savings on gas lead to an increase in exports of gas, which was discussed in Chapter 2. Given these assumptions, it has been shown in Chapters 2 and 6 that the effects on the economies of the countries pursuing the policy are positive – if the projects are not too unprofitable at market prices.

The above implies that the policy leads to a reduction in the exports of raw materials of countries not pursuing the policy. At the same time, however, it also leads to an increase in the exports other than exports of raw materials of these countries (because in the countries pursuing the policy, national income and imports other than imports of raw materials rise). The question to be answered is how the countries not pursuing the policy are affected on balance by the various changes in their exports.

To explain the relevant issues, attention will first of all be paid to the argumentation for a policy of import substitution by means of tariffs given by the Cambridge Economic Policy Group (CEPG) (Cripps and Godley, 1978; Fetherstone and Godley, 1978; Cripps, 1978). Essentially, this argumentation is as follows. Tariffs increase the price of imported goods. This induces a shift in demand from imports to domestic goods. It is assumed that there is unemployment in the domestic economy. Therefore, the increase in demand for domestic goods causes an increase in domestic production and employment. This leads to an increase in imports, which is, however, smaller than the original decrease in imports. The policy is to be accompanied by a policy of reducing tax rates. This causes a further increase in demand and national income, as well as an increase in imports. The decrease in tax rates should be such that, ultimately, the level of imports remains constant on balance. Under these circumstances the policy need not be a beggar-thy-neighbour policy.

According to the CEPG, such a policy could even be beneficial to the world economy. This can be explained as follows. All countries aim at full employment, but have to take account of the constraint on the balance on the current account. Other possible constraints, such as the government deficit, are not taken into account. For all countries, the minimum sustainable balance on current account equals the maximum sustainable capital inflow.[2] The maximum capital inflow is determined by the creditworthiness of the country, and by some other factors. Given the maximum capital inflow, and given the level of exports, there is a maximum capacity to import, called the import capacity. Imports are positively related to national income. For some countries the imports related to full employment national income are lower than the import capacity. These countries are not balance-of-payments constrained. Countries for which full employment imports exceed the import capacity are balance-of-payments constrained.

When faced with a reduction in exports, unconstrained countries will increase government expenditure in order to maintain full employment. This implies that they maintain their imports at the expense of changes in their net capital outflow.[3] Constrained countries, however, will reduce their imports via a reduction in national income. Therefore, world trade and world income will increase if imports from constrained countries are substituted for imports from unconstrained countries. Consequently, so long as the import substitution policy described above discriminates against imports from unconstrained countries, it will lead to increases in global levels of trade, income and employment.

A final point is the following. Godley (1982) notes that the OPEC countries (taken together) are, at the time of writing his article, unconstrained countries with a low marginal propensity to absorb. Therefore, tariffs that discriminate against imports from these countries will have a positive effect on the world economy.

An important point of criticism regarding the analysis of the CEPG concerns the assumption that government policy is only constrained by the balance of payments. In countries which are not balance-of-payments constrained there may be a constraint in the form of the government deficit. A reduction of imports from these countries may therefore also be detrimental to the world economy. In my opinion this criticism is correct. However, it does not apply to a reduction of imports from OPEC countries, because in OPEC countries that are not balance-of-payments constrained the government deficit is no constraint either.

In addition to the argument of the CEPG, I would like to emphasize the following. Whether or not a country is balance-of-payments constrained is not only related to its balance on current account, but also to its net foreign assets. For instance, a country that has a deficit on the balance on current account and large foreign assets at the same time, need not be balance-of payments constrained.[4] This considered, at the beginning of the eighties at least 60% (and to all probability more) of world net exports of oil came from countries that were not balance-of-payments constrained.[5] Moreover, it is likely that in the near future a similar situation will arise.[6]

Let us now discuss the relevance of the above for the policy advocated in this study. Part of this policy concerns oil-saving projects. If an oil-saving policy had been pursued from the end of the seventies onwards in the western countries (more seriously than has been the case), this would have led to a decrease in the quantity of their oil imports, to a decrease in the oil price (see Chapter 2), and, therefore, to a decrease in the costs of their oil imports. As was said above, at the beginning of the eighties most oil imports came from unconstrained countries with a low marginal propensity to absorb. Therefore, the policy would have led to a decrease in the net foreign assets of unconstrained oil-exporting countries. At the same time, the policy would have led to an increase in demand in the western countries. As was demonstrated in Chapters 2 and 6 this would have led to an increase in production and employment in these countries, but not to an increase in their government debts; if all western countries had pursued such a policy simultaneously, their government debts would probably have been reduced on balance. The policy would also have led to an increase in imports from less developed countries, and therefore to an increase in production and employment in these countries. As a result, the government debt in these countries would have decreased. This decrease in government debts, together with the decrease in government debts in western countries likely to occur, would be a reflection of the decrease in the net foreign assets of the oil-exporting countries. To conclude, the policy would have increased global levels of production and employment and would have decreased the government debts in less developed countries, and probably western countries as well.

As was stated above, it is likely that in the near future most oil imports will come from countries that are not balance-of-payments constrained. Therefore, it is likely that, if western countries pursue an oil-saving policy at this moment, this will more or less have similar effects on the world economy as it would have had ten years ago.

Another part of the policy advocated in this study concerns projects which lead to savings on raw materials other than oil. It is beyond the scope of this study to answer the question whether, apart from the effects on pollution levels, these projects have positive or negative effects on countries not pursuing the policy.

The following conclusions can be drawn. First, a policy of stimulating projects leading to savings on raw materials has positive effects on the environment. Second, if the countries pursuing such a policy face a situation of unemployment such as the one described in Chapter 2, this policy will have positive effects on their economies (even when the first point is neglected). Third, regarding the effects of the changes in imports and exports on the economies of countries not pursuing this policy, the following can be said. With regard to oil-saving projects the picture is positive. With regard to projects saving on other raw materials the changes in imports and exports of other countries have not been analysed. The last conclusion is that, from a global perspective, it is likely that a policy of saving on raw materials is socially efficient, even if the relevant projects are not wholly profitable from a private point of view.

8.2. Some comments on the debate about the effects of import substitution on the domestic economy

This section deals with some implications of this study for the debate about the effects of an import substitution policy on the domestic economy. Attention will only be paid to one argument for import substitution, viz. the argument that in situations of unemployment import substitution leads to an increase in demand for domestic products, and consequently to an increase in production and employment. Other arguments, such as the infant-industry argument, will not be considered. Another limitation concerns the following. There are different instruments for generating import substitution. Williamson (1983) mentions the following:[7] tariffs, quotas, state trading, exchange controls, import prohibition, buy-local laws, and non-tariff barriers. Attention will only be paid below to one of these instruments, viz. the use of tariffs. Attention will also be paid to an instrument neglected by Williamson: the use of project selection.

Let us first discuss what can be learnt from the literature regarding the question whether, in a situation of unemployment, the use of tariffs leads to an increase in domestic production and employment.[8] The main argument in favour of tariffs was mentioned above: they cause an increase in demand for domestic goods, and therefore an increase in domestic production and employment.

The main line of criticism concerns inefficiencies at the micro-level. Because of the tariffs, certain goods which were formerly imported will be produced by domestic producers at higher costs. Other goods will still be imported, but will be more expensive because of the tariffs. Thus, a number of consumption goods and inputs for the domestic industry become more expensive. The higher prices of inputs lead to increases in the prices of export goods, and to (further) increases in the prices of consumption goods. On the whole this has three direct effects. First, consumers experience a loss because of the higher prices of consumption goods. Second, exports decrease because of the higher prices of export goods. Third, government revenues from tariffs increase. However, this increase in revenues is lower than the increase in the average price of final goods multiplied by the volume of final goods (because some goods that were formerly imported are now produced by domestic producers at higher costs).

In addition to this, it is argued that there will be a number of negative macroeconomic consequences. The decrease in exports mentioned above has negative multiplier effects. The increase in consumer prices causes a wage increase, and the decrease in unemployment has the same effect. Thus, inflation rises, causing a further decrease in exports. A number of other negative macroeconomic effects could occur. It can be noted that, in the eyes of most critics of import substitution, many of the negative macroeconomic effects result from the microeconomic inefficiencies discussed above. The following quote is representative for much of the criticism:

> The basic argument [against the use of tariffs] is that there are other and superior methods of obtaining the *macroeconomic* objectives that can be furthered by tariff protection, while the latter involves accepting *microeconomic* distortions in production and consumption and limitations on competition, all of which involve a reduction in welfare (Williamson, 1983, p. 87).

The superior methods referred to are fiscal policy, monetary policy, and exchange rate policy.

Advocates of tariffs have reacted to this criticism in the following way. First, the negative effects for consumers can be counterbalanced by a decrease in tax rates. This can be financed by tariff revenues and by an increase in tax revenues caused by the increase in production. (Opponents of tariffs then argue that it is not sure that tax revenues will increase as a result of an increase in production, because production may decrease on balance, as a result of the decrease in exports.) Second, one could introduce a so-called 'tariff drawback', implying that exporters can reclaim the tariff element in their own costs. Third, exchange rate policy is inferior to a policy based on the use of tariffs in helping to realize a situation of full employment and external balance. This is mainly due to the fact that tariffs lead to a (small) improvement in the terms of trade, whereas devaluation causes a (large) deterioration in the terms of trade. A full discussion of these arguments is beyond the scope of this study.

Some advocates of tariffs acknowledge that there is some truth in the criticism mentioned above. In this context the following quote can be given:

> It is better to have an industry which is less efficient than to have no industry at all; in my opinion, it is better to have a situation in which the choice of consumers is restricted or adapted as a result of protectionism than to have a situation in which the choice of consumers is eliminated as a result of the destruction of our capacity to produce (Godley, 1982, p. 452, own translation).

It is now possible to discuss some implications of this study for the debate about import substitution. In this study a form of import substitution has been advocated which is based on project selection. The method of project selection developed takes account of both microeconomic and macroeconomic factors. This is why the proposed form of import substitution evades microeconomic distortions in production and consumption as well as limitations on competition. Therefore, the criticism of Williamson does not apply to this form of import substitution.

This point may be clarified. In Chapter 6 it was argued that the substitution of electricity from wind for electricity from conventional plants is socially efficient, even if wind energy is not wholly profitable at market prices. This implies that this substitution should not lead to an increase in the electricity price. In relation to this, it was assumed that electricity from wind is subsidized, so that consumers and exporters need not face higher electricity prices as a result of the stimulation of wind energy.[9] Thus, some of the micro- and mesoeconomic distortions resulting from the imposition of tariffs need not occur with the form of import substitution proposed in this study. Besides, the subsidies do not eliminate the incentives to produce at low costs: stimulating wind farms only implies that the competition between domestic and foreign producers of wind turbines replaces the competition between domestic and foreign producers of conventional power plants.

The form of import substitution proposed in this study pays attention to microeconomic factors. In this respect it is superior to the use of general tariffs. Like the use of tariffs, but unlike devaluation, it does not lead to a deterioration in the terms of trade. Thus, in some cases it could be a superior policy in helping to realize full employment with external balance.

Notes

1. WCED (1987), Nentjes (1988), Mäler (1990).
2. Changes in official reserves are neglected because in the long run official reserves must more or less be maintained.
3. See note 2.
4. Note that this does not contradict the argument of the CEPG, since the CEPG mentions the creditworthiness of a country as one of the factors which determines whether it is constrained or not.
5. In 1986 the IMF distinguished two types of developing countries: capital-exporting countries and other countries. Capital-exporting countries were countries recording a current account surplus during the period 1979–1981 and providing development aid over the same period. These countries were: Iran, Iraq, Kuwait, Libya, Oman, Qatar, Saudi Arabia and UAE (IMF, *World Economic Outlook*, April 1986). During the first quarter of 1982 the OPEC countries agreed that Iran, Iraq, Kuwait, Libya, Qatar, Saudi Arabia and UAE together should produce 68% of total OPEC production (Al-Chalabi, 1989). In the period 1980–1985 the share of the OPEC in world net exports of oil (excluding exports from the USSR to other CMEA countries) was 88% on average (*World Economic Outlook*, April 1989). (A decrease in oil imports of western countries would probably not have affected exports of the USSR to other CMEA countries, so that these exports can be neglected in the following.) Thus, around 1982 60% of the world net imports of oil came from capital-exporting OPEC countries. The percentage of oil imports coming from countries that were not balance-of-payments constrained was higher because of the following: first, Oman, one of the capital-exporting countries, was not a member of OPEC. Second, some oil-exporting countries outside the OPEC may not have been balance-of-payments constrained. Third, the fact that a country is not a capital exporter does not imply that it is balance-of-payments constrained. It is plausible that countries having large supplies of oil are able to finance a certain deficit on the balance on current account.
6. In 1990 the IMF made a distinction between two types of developing countries: net creditor countries and other countries. Net creditor countries were countries that were unambiguously net external creditors in 1987 or that experienced substantial cumulated current account surpluses (excluding official transfers) between 1967 (or 1968) and 1987. These countries were: Iran, Kuwait, Libya, Oman, Qatar, Saudi Arabia, UAE, Taiwan. In August 1986 the OPEC countries agreed that Iran, Kuwait, Libya, Qatar, Saudi Arabia and UAE together produce 66% of total OPEC production (excluding production of Iraq). Iraq did not participate in the agreement, but produced at that time about 16% of the production of the other OPEC countries (Al-Chalabi, 1989). Therefore, net creditor OPEC countries produced about 57% of total OPEC production. In the period 1986–1988 the share of the OPEC in world net exports of oil (excluding exports from the USSR to other CMEA countries) was 66% on average (*World Economic Outlook*, April 1989). The above implies that around 1987 approximalely 38% of the world net imports of oil came from net creditor OPEC countries. The percentage of oil imports from countries that were not balance-of-payments con-

strained was higher, for the same reasons as the ones given in the previous note. It is likely that in the nineties this percentage will increase because of the following. First, the share of the OPEC countries in world net exports of oil is expected to rise again. Second, the share of net creditor countries in total OPEC reserves is higher than the share of these countries in present total OPEC production; the former is 75% (Al-Chalabi, 1989).

7. Williamson uses the phrase 'forms of protection' instead of instruments.
8. The relevant arguments are discussed extensively in the literature concerning the proposals of the CEPG. Articles in favour of these proposals are Godley and May (1977), Cripps and Godley (1978), Cripps (1978), Fetherstone and Godley (1978), and Godley (1982). Articles opposing them are Blinder (1978), Hall (1978), and Sauernheimer (1983).
9. Such a subsidy implies that the ratio between the market price of electricity from wind and the market price of electricity from conventional plants is more in line with the ratio between the relevant social prices. However, if one wants the ratio between the market prices to reflect the ratio between the social prices, one could also tax electricity from conventional power plants more heavily. In this place this possibility cannot be evaluated, because in this study no attention has been paid to the question what the market price of electricity should be in absolute terms. However, with regard to the argument in the main text the level of the absolute prices is not important; what counts is that the substituton of electricity from wind for electricity generated in a different way (taken by itself) should not increase the market price of electricity.

CHAPTER 9

Summary and conclusions

This study has dealt with two problems. The first – a methodological one – is how to analyse and evaluate projects in situations of unemployment from a social point of view. The second problem is the question which projects and portfolios of projects have positive effects in such situations.

The treatment of the first problem started with a discussion of the existing methods of project appraisal in situations of unemployment. A distinction has been made between methods based on welfare theory, and methods without a welfare-theoretical foundation. Another distinction is that between dual and primal methods. A dual method is based on the calculation of the social profitability of projects by means of shadow prices for inputs and outputs. These shadow prices reflect the contribution of using inputs or producing outputs to the objective function of the decision-maker. A primal method is a method by which the effects of each project on variables as employment, consumption, and the government deficit are first estimated, and subsequently evaluated.

Dual methods based on welfare theory have been discussed first. These methods have two problems. First, they are generally based on models that are unrealistic. This problem is particularly serious with regard to the methods devised for developed countries. It is less serious with regard to the Little–Mirrlees method, which has been applied to projects in less developed countries.

The second problem can be explained as follows: suppose that, at micro-level, individual small projects are analysed with a model that pays no attention to changes in the price level or in the interest rate. At first sight this may seem justifiable, because a small project cannot be expected to affect the price level or the interest rate. Suppose that the analysis at micro-level shows that there are many individual small projects that have positive effects. This seems to imply that the government should invest in a large portfolio of projects. However, suppose that the effects of macroeconomic policies are analysed with a macroeconomic model that gives a reasonable estimate of the actual effects. Suppose that according to this model the portfolio of projects mentioned above has negative macroeconomic effects, which is related to increases in inflation and in the interest rate. This implies there is no consistency between the analysis at micro-level and at macro-level. In relation to this, the analysis of individual projects described above is not justifiable. None of the dual methods based on welfare theory pays attention to this problem. Therefore, these methods are not satisfactory, especially not if they are applied in countries in which factors such as inflation and changes in the rate of interest are important.

Primal methods based on welfare theory use models similar to those on which the dual methods mentioned above are based. In relation to this, a similar criticism applies.

The only dual method without welfare-theoretical foundation is that of Malinvaud *et al.* (1983). In this method the shadow prices for various inputs and outputs are calculated by means of an econometric macro-model. The method is not satisfactory because it neglects the fact that in reality payments are based on market prices, not on shadow prices.

There is a number of primal methods without welfare-theoretical foundation. One of these is the 'effects method' of project evaluation. Essentially, it consists of two steps. First, the first-round spending effects of the project and of the expenditures replaced by the project are estimated by means of an input–output model. Second, these effects are evaluated on the basis of criteria related to the objectives of macroeconomic policy. Thus, the method aims at consistency between project appraisal and macroeconomic policy. Nevertheless, the problem of consistency has not been solved adequately, which is related to the fact that a number of factors which are important at the macro-level, such as inflation, are not taken into account by input–output models.

Another primal method that is not based on welfare theory concerns the use of an econometric macro-model. Two simulations are made with this model. One simulation concerns the economic development with project(s), the other one the economic development without project(s). The effects of the project(s) are calculated as the difference between the outcomes of these simulations. With regard to the application of this method to large projects, or to portfolios of projects, there are two problems. First, it is difficult to check whether the outcomes of the simulations contain errors. Second, little attention has been paid to the evaluation of the effects. As far as I know the method has not been applied to small projects. The reasons for this have not been discussed thoroughly in the literature; apparently, it is taken for granted that it is not sensible to use econometric macro-models for the analysis of small projects.

In view of the deficiencies of the existing methods, an improved method for the appraisal of both small and large government projects (and projects stimulated by the government) has been developed. This method consists of three steps. First, the macroeconomic effects of certain 'standard changes' are calculated by means of an econometric macro-model. Second, the macroeconomic effects of the project are calculated by combining the results of the first step with information about certain parameters of the econometric macro-model, project-specific characteristics, and specific input–output effects. Third, the effects are evaluated on the basis of neo-Paretian welfare theory. The following variables are taken into account: consumption during the period analysed with the econometric macro-model, (un)employment during this period, and the government debt, net foreign assets and the stock of capital goods at the end of this period. The question how to determine the relative importance of these variables on the basis of neo-Paretian welfare theory has been discussed.

With regard to large projects, or portfolios of projects, the method has two advantages compared to the conventional method of using an econometric macro-model for the analysis of projects. First, it is relatively easy to check whether the outcomes of the simulations contain errors, which is related to the fact that the econometric macro-model is only used to calculate the effects of certain standard changes, while in the conventional method this model is used to calculate the effects of a unique project. Second, it pays attention to the evaluation of the effects.

At first sight, the application of the method to small projects involves serious problems. This can be explained as follows. The method is based on the principle that the macroeconomic 'effects' of a small change should be set proportional to the macroeconomic effects of a similar large change. This principle implies that a possible result is that a small project has, for instance, an 'effect' on the rate of interest of 0.00015%, which causes a decrease in investment with 98,000 guilders. However, in reality the rate of interest cannot change with 0.00015%. Speaking more generally, in an economic system the whole may be different from the sum of the parts, so that at first sight the principle of proportionality does not seem to be justifiable. Moreover, even if this problem did not exist, there would still be another problem: the macroeconomic effects of a small change cannot be estimated without a relatively high uncertainty. This is partly related to the law of large numbers.

Despite these problems the application of the method to small projects can be justified. The justification is essentially as follows: first, the government is not interested in the effects of a small project taken in isolation, but in the contribution of a small project to the effects of the portfolio of projects to which it belongs. Second, the 'effects' of a project as calculated by means of the method can be regarded as the expected value of the contribution of the project to the effects of the portfolio. Third, it has to be admitted that the actual value of this contribution may deviate to a considerable extent from its expected value. This holds good for each project. Fourth, however, many of the resulting errors are cancelled out at the portfolio level. Fifth, insofar as errors are cancelled out at the portfolio level, they can be neglected by the decision-maker. In relation to this, from the point of view of a decision-maker the errors related to the calculations are less serious than they appear to be at first sight.

Because the method is based on the use of an econometric macro-model, the appraisal of small projects is consistent with macroeconomic analysis. Another advantage is that the method is efficient when a large number of small projects has to be evaluated: once the effects of a certain number of standard changes have been calculated, the effects of any number of projects can be calculated without ever using the econometric macro-model again.

The primal method discussed above can be converted into a dual method. As an illustration, shadow prices for three different inputs have been calculated with the help of the Freia model of the Dutch Central Planning Bureau. This approach could further increase the efficiency of project appraisal: once shadow prices for various inputs and outputs have been calculated, they can be used for the evaluation of different projects.

The second problem discussed in this study is the question which projects and portfolios of projects have positive macroeconomic effects. To begin with, the effects of certain portfolios of projects in certain situations of unemployment have been studied in a qualitative manner. Most attention has been paid to portfolios consisting of projects that lead to savings on fuels and other raw materials. It has been argued that, (even) if the effects on the environment are neglected, these portfolios of projects have positive effects for countries facing a situation of unemployment such as the one faced by many western countries since the end of the seventies. These positive effects even occur when the projects are not wholly profitable from the private point of view. As far as countries importing raw materials are concerned, the main reason is the following: the expenditures on these projects, which by and large have an average import coefficient, replace expenditures on raw materials with an import coefficient of almost one. Thus, expenditures on domestic goods increase at the cost of imports. As far as countries exporting raw materials are concerned, the positive effects are related to the increase in the exports of raw materials made possible by the savings on the domestic use of these materials. Speaking more generally, the main cause of the positive effects is that unemployed labour is substitued for scarce raw materials.

The larger the country, the more positive the effects (per unit of investment), because of two reasons. First, the effects of increases in spendings are relatively more positive when the country is larger. This point has been illustrated by a hypothetical oil-saving project, which is implemented in the Netherlands. The project has been analysed by means of two simple models, one relating to the Netherlands and the other to the EU. Regarding the effects for the Netherlands, the following holds good. Suppose that the oil price is such that the project needs a subsidy of 29% to be profitable from the private point of view. In that case the project will not lead to a change in the government debt despite the provision of subsidy, while the effects on other variables will be positive or (for one variable) neutral. If a higher subsidy is needed, the government debt will increase however. When one analyses the effects of the project for the EU, the conclusions are more positive. For instance, when the oil price is such that the project needs a subsidy of 50% to be profitable from the private point of view, the project will not lead to a change in the total debt of the governments of the EU countries taken together.

The second reason why the effects are relatively more positive when the country is larger only concerns countries which are net importers of the raw materials saved. If a large country realizes a substantial reduction in its imports of raw materials, this will lead to reductions in the prices of raw materials, and therefore to a decrease in the import costs of this country. The resulting benefits have been analysed for the case of oil on the basis of empirical estimates for the elasticities of demand and supply of oil. Although there are big differences of opinion regarding the values of these elasticities, it is not unlikely that for the EU the benefits due to a reduction in the oil price is in the order of 20% of the value of the savings on oil.

In addition to the qualitative analysis, attention has been paid to some econometric studies on the macroeconomic effects for the Netherlands of portfolios of projects which lead to savings on fuels and other raw materials. The study of Driehuis *et al.*

(1983) seems to contradict the qualitative analysis given above. However, in contrast with the argument given by Driehuis *et al.*, I have argued that the results of Driehuis' study support the proposition that in situations of unemployment the policy has positive effects. The study of the CPB (1989) also seems to contradict the qualitative analysis given above. The CPB concludes that a policy of saving on fuels and other raw materials has negative effects on a number of variables in the long run. However, it has been argued that this conclusion would probably have been reversed if the CPB had not made two serious mistakes.

The method of project appraisal developed in this study has been applied to a 660 MW Dutch wind energy project. This application has been based on the Freia model. The wind energy project produces between 1 and 2% of total Dutch electricity production. It consists of a number of wind farms dispersed over the country. The investments are made by the public utility companies, with financial support from the government. The main part of the benefits consists of savings on the use of fuels in conventional power plants. Besides, there are savings on investments in these power plants.

One result is the following. If there is unemployment, and if fuel prices are such that the investments in wind farms need to be subsidized with 17% in order to make them profitable for the utility companies, then providing subsidies will not change the government debt on balance. At the same time there will be positive effects on net foreign assets, the stock of capital goods, consumption and employment. If a higher subsidy is needed, there will be an increase in the government debt. Taken by itself this leads to the following conclusion: if subsidizing is the most suitable instrument to promote wind energy, and if any action leading to an increase in the government debt is out of the question, it will be justifiable to subsidize wind energy with 17% in a situation of unemployment, without setting a limit to the total budget for subsidies. If the government also takes the other variables mentioned above into account, higher subsidies can be granted.

Some comments have to be made here. First, there are considerable uncertainties related to the calculations with an econometric macro-model. In this context it is a relevant point that the Freia model is a model that leads to relatively negative conclusions for wind energy in comparison with models used in other countries (including countries smaller than the Netherlands). This is related to the fact that in the Freia model capital market effects are very important. From this point of view it is not impossible that the conclusions given above are too pessimistic.

Second, the calculations with the Freia model concern a period in the past. The analysed wind energy project however concerns investments made in the future. Therefore, it is not sure that the calculated macroeconomic effects are a fair representation of the actual effects of the wind energy project (which will occur in the future). This will only be the case if the characteristics of the economy do not change in a fundamental way in the future (and if the Freia model gives a fair description of the situation in the past). In this context the situation on the labour market is of paramount importance. If in the future there exists full employment instead of unemployment, the project will have less positive macroeconomic effects than indicated above.

It is possible that in the future (more) wind farms will be subsidized by the EU instead of by the Netherlands, so that they should be evaluated from a European point of view. It has been argued that such an evaluation would lead to (even) more optimistic conclusions regarding the amount of subsidy that is justifiable on the basis of the macroeconomic effects. Higher subsidies are of course also justifiable if one takes account of environmental effects, which are neglected in the Freia model.

A limitation of this study is that no attention has been paid to the question which instrument is most suitable to promote savings on raw materials. For instance, the possibility of levying higher taxes on fuels has not been considered. It can also be noted that a policy of saving on raw materials might be supplementary to other policies. For example, a good policy might be to stimulate projects which lead to savings on fuels and other raw materials, and to reduce other government expenditures at the same time, or to improve the functioning of the labour market at the same time. This point, however, has not been analysed.

Given what has been said above, an interesting hypothesis presents itself: a subsidy of 50% or more on projects which lead to savings on raw materials does not lead to an increase in the total debt of the governments of the EU countries taken together. If this hypothesis is accepted, this could, for example, imply that ecologically sustainable methods of agriculture, in which the use of inputs with high import coefficients is relatively low, should be supported on a large scale.

In one of the last chapters the effects of a policy of saving on fuels and other raw materials on countries other than the countries pursuing this policy have been analysed. This has led to the following conclusions: first, other countries will benefit from this policy because it reduces transboundary pollution. Second, although the policy is an import-substitution policy, it may lead to an increase in world trade and global levels of employment and income (or, if the policy is implemented on a small scale, the expected value of the contribution of the policy to world levels of trade, employment and income may be positive). However, the effects vary between portfolios of projects. For example, if, since the end of the seventies, the western countries had invested more in oil-saving projects, this would have led to a rise in the world levels of trade, income and employment, and it would also have reduced the debt problem. The effects of projects which lead to savings on raw materials other than oil have not been studied, but it is not *a priori* impossible that they are less positive.

Finally, attention has been paid to the debate about the domestic consequences of import substitution. The common means to promote import substitution, such as tariffs and quotas, all aim to increase demand for domestic goods, which is supposed to lead to an increase in employment and production. The main disadvantage of these methods is that they lead to distortions and limitations on competition at micro-level. Because of this their overall effects may be negative. The promotion of import substitution via project selection also leads to an increase in demand for domestic goods. However, this form of import substitution, which is partly based on an analysis at the micro-level, need not lead to distortions and limitations on competition at the micro-level. Therefore, a policy of import substitution based on project selection is superior to a policy of import substitution based on common means.

In retrospect, the most important implication of this study concerns the formulation of environmental policies. There are two types of environmental policy. The first one concerns the abatement of pollution without reducing the use of raw materials. In this context one can think of measures such as water purification and flue gas desulpherization. If the effects of this policy on the environment are neglected, and if it is pursued by one country in isolation, its overall effects are not positive; although in the short run it may lead to an increase in demand, production and employment, its long-run effects on all kinds of variables are negative (e.g. CPB, 1989). The second type of environmental policy consists of measures to save on fuels and other raw materials. Many economists have the following point of view: if the effects of this policy on the environment are neglected, and if it is pursued by one country in isolation, its overall effects are not positive; there may be some positive short-run effects, but in the long run the effects are negative (e.g. CPB, 1989). In relation to this, but mainly due to the lack of integration of pollution abatement and energy policy, the Dutch government spends more money on the first type of policy than on the second.

In this study it has been argued that the second type of policy will have positive consequences for the economy both in the short and in the long run, even if the effects on the environment are neglected, and even if the policy is pursued by one country in isolation. This implies that more importance should be attached to the second type of policy in proportion to the first. This could lead to a policy mix such that a far-reaching environmental policy will have positive macroeconomic effects.

As indicated at the beginning of this study, Keynes already recognized the importance of distinguishing between different types of government expenditure. In this study this insight has been applied to some specific types of government expenditure. It has been concluded that a policy of stimulating expenditures which lead to savings on raw materials is a special kind of Keynesian policy, which has the advantages of stimulating expenditures, but which has no disadvantages with regard to the balance on current account and the government deficit.

References

Al-Chalabi, F.J. 1989. *OPEC at the crossroads*. Oxford, Pergamon Press.

Arrow, K.J. and R.C. Lind. 1970. Uncertainty and the evaluation of public investment decisions. *American Economic Review*, 60 (June), 364–378.

Balassa, B. 1976. The 'effects method' of project evaluation. *Oxford Bulletin of Economics and Statistics*, 38 (4) (Nov.), 219–231.

Balassa, B. 1977. The 'effects method' of project evaluation once again. *Oxford Bulletin of Economics and Statistics*, 39 (4) (Nov.), 345–353.

Blinder, A.S. 1978. What's 'New' and What's 'Keynesian' in the 'New Cambridge' Keynesianism?, In: Brunner, K. and Meltzer, A.H. (eds), *Public Policies in Open Economies*. Carnegie-Rochester Conference Series on Public Policy, vol. 9 (supplement to Journal of Monetary Economics), Amsterdam, North-Holland, pp. 67–86.

Boadway, R.W. 1974. The welfare foundations of cost – benefit analysis. *Economic Journal*, 35, 939–962.

Bovenberg, A.L., Mulder, R.J., Oudshoorn, C. and Van Sinderen, J. 1991. Instrumenten vooor het energiebesparingsbeleid. *Economisch-Statistische Berichten*, Mei, 540–545.

Chan-Lee, J.H., and Kato, H. 1984. A comparisation of simulation properties of national econometric models. OECD *Economic Studies*, 2 (Spring), 109–150.

Chervel, M. 1977. A reply to Bela Balassa. *Oxford Bulletin of Economics and Statistics*, 39 (4) (Nov.), 333–345.

Chervel, M. 1984. Premières applications de la méthode des effets en France. *Etudes pour le développement*, 3 (juin), 3–13.

CPB (Centraal Plan Bureau). 1983. Freia, een macro-economisch model voor de middellange termijn. *CPB Monografie no.* 25, Den Haag, Centraal Planbureau.

CPB (Centraal Plan Bureau). 1983a. Macro-economische effecten van de aanleg van het Markerwaard-gebied. Notitie voor Rijkswaterstaat, Den Haag, Centraal Planbureau.

CPB (Centraal Plan Bureau). 1989. Economische gevolgen van een drietal scenario's voor milieubeleid in Nederland tot 2010. *Werkdocument no. 29*, Den Haag, Centraal Planbureau.

CPB (Centraal Plan Bureau). 1990. De macro-economische gevolgen van energiebesparing op de lange termijn. *Werkdocument no. 37*, Den Haag, Centraal Planbureau.

Cripps, F. 1978. Causes of growth and recession in world trade. *Economic Policy Review*, 4 (March), 37–43, Cambridge, Department of Applied Economics.

Cripps, F. and Godley, W. 1978. Controls of imports as a means to full employment and the expansion of world trade; the UK's case. *Cambridge Journal of Economics*, 2, 327–334.

De Haan, J. 1989. *Public debt: Pestiferious of propitious? On the economic consequences of the creation and existence of government debt*. Groningen, Faculteit der Economische Wetenschappen (dissertation).

Den Butter, F.A.G. 1985. Freia and Kompas, The Central Planning Bureau's new generation of macro-economic policy models: A review article. *De Economist*, 1, 43–63.

Drèze, J., and Stern, N. 1987. The theory of cost-benefit analysis. In: Auerbach, A.J. and Feldstein, M.

(eds), *Handbook of Public Economics*, Vol II, Amsterdam, North-Holland.
Driehuis, W. 1982. Zes scenario's voor economische politiek. *Maandschrift Economie*, (Dec.), 485–496.
Driehuis, W., Van Ierland, E.C. and Van den Noord, P.J. 1983. *Economie, energie en milieu in Nederland. 1980–2000*. Amsterdam, Stichting voor Economisch Onderzoek der Universiteit van Amsterdam.
Durufle, G. 1984. Evaluation des projets charbonniers: méthode des effets et modèles macro-économiques. *Etudes pour le développement*, 3 (juin), 29–41.
Fetherstone, M.J. and Godley, W.A.H. 1978. 'New Cambridge' macroeconomics and global monetarism: some issues in the conduct of U.K. economic policy. In: Brunner, K. and Meltzer, A.H. (eds.), *Public Policies in Open Economies*, Carnegie-Rochester Conference Series on Public Policy, vol. 9 (supplement to *Journal of Monetary Economics*), Amsterdam, North-Holland, pp. 33–66.
Fourgeaud, C., Lenclud, B. and Picard, P. 1986. Shadow prices and public policies in a disequilibrium model of an open economy. *European Economic Review*, 30, 991–1012.
Friedrich, R. and Vos, A. 1989. Die sozialen Kosten der Elektrizitätserzeugung. *Energiewirtschaftliche Tagesfragen*, 39 (10), 640–649.
Godley, W. 1982. Protéger le marché intérieur, seul moyen d'atteindre le plein emploi: quelques remarques sur la théorie macro-économique de l'échange international. In: Bourguinat, H. (ed.), *Internationalization et autonomie de décision*, Paris, Economica.
Godley, W. and May, R.M. 1977. The macroeconomic implications of devaluation and import restriction. *Economic Policy Review*, March, 32–42, Cambridge, Department of Applied Economics.
Hall, R.E. 1978. A comment on the Fetherstone and Godley and Posner Papers. In: Brunner, K. and Meltzer, A.H. (eds), *Public Policies in Open Economies*. Carnegie-Rochester Conference Series on Public Policy, vol. 9 (supplement to *Journal of Monetary Economics*), Amsterdam, North-Holland, pp. 87–90.
Hohmeyer, O. 1988. *Social Costs of Energy Consumption*. Berlin, Springer-Verlag.
Jackman, R., Mulvey, C. and Trevithick, J. 1981. *The Economics of Inflation*. Oxford, Martin Robertson.
Jeuring, A.J., and Tijsma, S. 1982. Windenergie en Economie. Groningen, *Wetenschapswinkel voor Economie* EV4.
Johansson, P.O. 1982. Cost-benefit rules in general disequilibrium. *Journal of Public Economics*, 18, 121–137.
Johansson, P.O. and Löfgren, K.G. 1989. Disequilibrium cost-benefit rules: an exposition and extension. In: Folmer, H. and Van Ierland, E. (eds), *Valuation Methods and Policy Making in Environmental Economics*, Amsterdam, Elsevier, pp. 161–186.
Keynes, J.M. 1936 (1973). *The General Theory of Employment, Interest and Money*. London, MacMillan.
Klaassen, G., Kee, P., Nentjes, A., Hafkamp, W. and Olsthoorn, A.A. 1987. *The Macroeconomic Impacts of the EC Large Combustion Plants Directive Proposal*. Amsterdam, Institute for Environmental Studies.
Kregel, J.A. 1987. Rational spirits and the post Keynesian macrotheory of microeconomics. *De Economist*, 135 (4), 520–33.
Laidner, D.E. 1975. The end of 'demand management': how to reduce unemployment in the 1970s. London, *The Institute of Economic Affairs, Occasional Paper*, no. 44.
Lal, D. 1974. *Methods of Project Analysis, A Review*. Baltimore, John Hopkins University Press.
Lesourne, J. 1975. *Cost-benefit analysis and economic theory*. Amsterdam, North-Holland.
Lipsey, R.G. 1960. The relation between unemployment and the rate of change of money wage rates in the United Kingdom, 1862–1957: A further analysis. *Economica*, 27 (Feb.), 1–31.
Little, I.M.D. and Mirrlees, J.A. 1974. *Project Appraisal and Planning for Developing Countries*. London, Heinemann.
LMO (Landelijk Milieu Overleg). 1985. *Werk maken van zure regen*. Utrecht, Landelijk Milieu Overleg.
Maddala, G.S. 1977. *Econometrics*. Singapore, McGraw-Hill.
Mäler, K.G. 1990. International environmental problems. *Oxford Review of Economic Policy*, 6 (1), 80–107.
Marchand, M., Mintz, J. and Pestieau, P. 1984. Shadow pricing of labour and capital in an economy with unemployed labour. *European Economic Review*, 25, 239–252.
Marchand, M., Mintz, J. and Pestieau, P. 1985. Public production and shadow pricing in a model of disequilibrium in labour and capital markets. *Journal of Economic Theory*, 36, 237–256.

Malinvaud, E. (1985). *The Theory of Unemployment Reconsidered.* Oxford, Basil Blackwell.

Malinvaud, E., Guesnerie, R., Goudard, D., Walliser, B., a.o. (Groupe Travail 'Calcul Economique'). 1983. *Calcul Economique et Résorption des Déséquilibres.* Paris, La Documentation Francaise.

Middeldorp, J. 1987. Over de grootte van de rentecoëfficiënten in een monetair model: een eerste aanzet to simultaan schatten. *CPB Onderzoeksmemorandum*, no. 32., Den Haag, Centraal Planbureau.

Mishan, E.J. 1981. *Cost-Benefit Analysis.* London, George Allen and Unwin.

Moulignat, J.H. 1984. Le charbon de Ladrecht -Une problématique de sélection des projets. *Etudes pour le développement*, 3 (juin), 13–25.

NEI. 1983. Een verkenning van de macro-economische effecten van de aanleg van het Markerwaard-gebied. Rotterdam, Nederlands Economisch Instituut.

Nentjes, A. 1988. An economic model of transfrontier pollution abatement. In: Tanzi, V. (ed.), *Public Finance, Trade, and Development, Proceedings of the 44th Congress on the International Institute of Public Finance*, Instanbul, pp. 243–261.

Nentjes, A. 1989. Macroeconomic cost benefit analysis of environmental programmes. In: Folmer, H. and Van Ierland, E. (eds), *Valuation Methods and Policy Making in Environmental Economics*, Amsterdam, Elsevier, pp. 187–216.

Nentjes, A. and Zuidema, T. 1987. A determination of the opportunity costs of government projects: a neo-classical versus a Keynesian approach. *Public Finance*, 1, 119–136.

Pearce, D.W. and Nash, C.A. 1981. *The Social Appraisal of Projects. A Text in Cost-Benefit Analysis.* London, Macmillan.

Prou, C. and Chervel, M. 1970. *Etablissement des programmes en économie sous-développée, tome 3, l'étude des grappes de projets.* Paris, Dunod.

Samuelson, P.A. and Vickrey, W. 1964. Discussion, *American Economic Review Proceedings*, 59 (May), 88–96.

Sauernheimer, K. 1983. Die aussenwirtschaftlichen Implikationen des 'New Cambridge Approach'. *Konjunkturpolitik*, 29, H. 6, 348–366.

Stoffers, M.J. 1985. Een eerste aanzet tot een wereldolieprijsmodel, en enkele exercities. Den Haag, Centraal Planbureau, *Occasional Papers*, no. 35.

Sugden, R. and Williams, A. 1978. *The Principles of Practical Cost-Benefit Analysis.* Oxford, Oxford University Press.

Thibault, J.L. 1984. Pour une application élargie de méthode des effets: l'exemple d'un produit innovant. *Etudes pour le développement*, 3 (juin), 41–51.

UNIDO. 1972. *Guidelines for Project Evaluation.* New York, United Nations.

Van Bergeijk, P.A.G. 1987. OPEC-inkomsten onder druk. *Economisch-Statistische Berichten*, Sept., 816–819.

Van de Klundert, T. and Peer, H. 1983. *Energie: een economisch perspectief.* Leiden, Stenfert Kroese.

Van den Beld, C.A. and van Middelhoek, A.J. 1971. Evaluation of seaport projects. Den Haag, Centraal Planbureau, *Occasional Papers* no. 3/1971.

Van den Berg, P.J.C.M., Gelauff, G.M.M. and Okker, V.R. 1988. The Freia-Kompas model for the Netherlands. *Economic Modelling*, July, 170–236.

Van den Bosch, F.A.J. and Veerman, C.P. 1984. Macro-economische consequenties van een kustuit-breiding tussen Hoek van Holland en Scheveningen: een eerste aanzet. *Economisch-Statistische Berichten*, Sept., 818–823.

Van der Burg, T. 1982. Milieu-beleid: een bijdrage tot de oplossing van de macro-economische problemen. Groningen, *Wetenschapswinkel voor Economie EV4.*

Van der Burg, T. 1984. De bepaling van de kosten en baten van concurrerende projecten in de energie- en grondstoffensfeer. Theorie en voorstellen tot empirisch onderzoek. *Memorandum nr. 151 van het Instituut voor Economisch Onderzoek*, R.U. Groningen.

Van der Burg, T. 1989. De macro-economische effecten van windmolens voor de electriciteitsvoor-ziening. Groningen, Economische Faculteit, mimeo.

Van der Burg, T. 1991. *Project Appraisal and Macroeconomic Policy.* Dissertation, University of Groningen, The Netherlands.

Van der Vlies, J. 1985. Macro-economische effecten van de Olympische Spelen in Nederland. *Economisch-Statistische Berichten*, juli, 684–687.

Van Ees, H. and Garretsen, H. 1990. The right answers to the wrong question? An assessment of the microfoundations debate. *De Economist*, 138 (2), 123–145.

Van Wijk, A.J.M. 1990. *Wind Energy and Electricity Production*. Utrecht, Vakgroep Natuurwetenschap en Samenleving van de R.U. Utrecht.

Weintraub, R.E. 1979. *Micro-Foundations, The Compatibility of Microeconomics and Macroeconomics*. Cambridge, Cambridge University Press.

Williamson, J. 1983. *The Open Economy and the World Economy*. New York, Basic Books, Inc., Publishers.

WECD (World Commission on Environment and Development). 1987. *Our Common Future*, Oxford, Oxford University Press.

Zuidema, T. 1982. *Een onderzoek naar de alternatieve kosten van overheidsprojecten: theorie en empirie*. Groningen, Faculteit der Economische Wetenschappen (dissertation).

Index

MIX
Papier aus verantwortungsvollen Quellen
Paper from responsible sources
FSC® C105338

If you have any concerns about our products,
you can contact us on
ProductSafety@springernature.com

In case Publisher is established outside the EU,
the EU authorized representative is:
Springer Nature Customer Service Center GmbH
Europaplatz 3, 69115 Heidelberg, Germany

Printed by Libri Plureos GmbH
in Hamburg, Germany